FEELING CANADIAN

Film and Media Studies Series

Film studies is the critical exploration of cinematic texts as art and entertainment, as well as the industries that produce them and the audiences that consume them. Although a medium barely one hundred years old, film is already transformed through the emergence of new media forms. Media studies is an interdisciplinary field that considers the nature and effects of mass media upon individuals and society and analyzes media content and representations. Despite changing modes of consumption—especially the proliferation of individuated viewing technologies—film has retained its cultural dominance into the 21st century, and it is this transformative moment that the WLU Press Film and Media Studies series addresses.

Our Film and Media Studies series includes topics such as identity, gender, sexuality, class, race, visuality, space, music, new media, aesthetics, genre, youth culture, popular culture, consumer culture, regional/national cinemas, film policy, film theory, and film history.

Wilfrid Laurier University Press invites submissions. For further information, please contact the Series editors, all of whom are in the Department of English and Film Studies at Wilfrid Laurier University:

Dr. Philippa Gates, Email: pgates@wlu.ca
Dr. Russell Kilbourn, Email: rkilbourn@wlu.ca
Dr. Ute Lischke, Email: ulischke@wlu.ca

75 University Avenue West
Waterloo, ON N2L 3C5
Canada
Phone: 519-884-0710
Fax: 519-884-8307

FEELING CANADIAN
TELEVISION, NATIONALISM, AND AFFECT

MARUSYA BOCIURKIW

Wilfrid Laurier University Press
WLU

This book has been published with the help of a grant from the Canadian Federation for the Humanities of Social Sciences, through the Aid to Scholarly Publications Programme, using funds provided by the Social Science and Humanities Research Council of Canada. Wilfrid Laurier University Press acknowledge the financial support of the Government of Canada through its Canada Book Fund for its publishing activities.

Library and Archives Canada Cataloguing in Publication

Bociurkiw, Marusya, [date]
    Feeling Canadian : television, nationalism, and affect / Marusya Bociurkiw.

(Film and media studies series)
Includes bibliographical references.
Also issued in electronic format.
ISBN 978-1-55458-268-6

    1. Television broadcasting—Social aspects—Canada. 2. Television broadcasting—Canada—Psychological aspects. 3. Television and politics—Canada. 4. National character-istics, Canadian. I. Title. II. Series: Film and media studies series

PN1992.3.C3B63 2011   302.23'450971   C2010-907874-8

Electronic formats.
ISBN 978-1-55458-308-9 (PDF); ISBN 1-978-55458-354-6 (EPUB)

    1. Television broadcasting—Social aspects—Canada. 2. Television broadcasting—Canada—Psychological aspects. 3. Television and politics—Canada. 4. National character-istics, Canadian. I. Title. II. Series: Film and media studies series (Online)

PN1992.3.C3B63 2011b   302.23'450971   C2010-907875-6

© 2011 Wilfrid Laurier University Press

Waterloo, Ontario, Canada
www.wlupress.wlu.ca

Cover design by Blakeley Words+Pictures. Cover images: beaver: Wikimedia; Canadian flag: Blakeley; moose: myfreewallpapers.net; ski boots: Blakeley; Peace Tower: Blakeley; hockey puck: Jussi Santaniemi/iStockphoto; tracks in snow: Blakeley; TV set: Grafissimo/iStockphoto; Mount Robson: Wikimedia; Mountie: Wikimedia; Canada goose: mwellis/Fotolia; plaid shirt: Jitalia17/iStockphoto. Text design by Catharine Bonas-Taylor.

This book is printed on FSC recycled paper and is certified Ecologo. It is made from 100% post-consumer fibre, processed chlorine free, and manufactured using biogas energy.

Printed in Canada

CONTENTS

ACKNOWLEDGEMENTS

It took a village to complete this book over several years; as there are a great many people to thank, the reader will excuse both my excesses and my omissions.

I offer huge thanks to friends, colleagues, and family who provided vast quantities of encouragement, populist and scholarly feedback, technical support, taped TV programs, as well as shelter during research trips in the early stages of writing: Lydia Bociurkiw, Vera Bociurkiw, Billie Carroll, Joanna Clarke, Anh Hua, Bobbi Kozinuk, Haida Paul, Larissa Petrillo, Deanna Reder, Terri Roberton, Jacky Sawatzky, and Kim Stewart. I especially thank Penny Goldsmith for careful editorial reading of the first and final drafts.

This book began life as a Ph.D. thesis. I am grateful for a doctoral fellowship from the Social Sciences and Humanities Research Council of Canada. Appreciation is also due to my Ph.D. supervisory committee for the breadth of their scholarly input: Sneja Gunew (supervisor), Zoë Druick, Helen Hok-Sze Leung, and Sunera Thobani. Gratitude also to Ann Kaplan and Elspeth Probyn, whose lectures, insights, and encouragement inspired certain crucial aspects of this book.

My research was immensely aided by Arthur Schwartzel, head of the CBC News Archives in Toronto, by the staff of the National Archives of Canada in Ottawa, and by a writing retreat at Gibralter Point on Toronto Island. A tip o' the hat to Libby Davies and Kim Elliott for facilitating my time on Gambier Island, where I was able to complete final revisions. Thanks also to Gloria Massé, who made Gambier feel like home.

Thanks are due also to the organizers of conferences and symposia I attended, where I was able to workshop certain chapters: Sneja Gunew, co-ordinator of the Transculturalisms seminars at the University of British Columbia, 2001–2; Ayse Lahur Kirtunç, organizer of the Seventh International Cultural Studies Symposium in Izmir, Turkey, May 2002; and Dorota Glowacka, organizer of the sessions on genocide and trauma during the CSAA meetings at the National Congress of the Humanities and Social Sciences in Halifax, May 2003. I am also grateful to those who published extracts of this work and whose detailed commentary enriched the final product: Davin Heckman, former editor of the online journal *Reconstruction: Studies in Contemporary Culture*; and Zoë Druick, co-editor of *Programming Reality: Perspectives on English-Canadian Television*. I gratefully acknowledge as well editorial comment provided by the anonymous readers who helped shape the final draft.

I could not have completed revisions of this book without the detective skills of a tiny band of research assistants: Aaron Hancox, Dana Iliescu, and Lee Parpart. I am indebted not only for the mountains of books and articles they surveyed but also for savvy insights and stimulating conversation. My students at Simon Fraser University and more recently at Ryerson University provided lively sites of irreverent debate, enquiry, and affect that fed this book in subliminal ways. A publications grant from the Faculty of Art and Design at Ryerson University helped smooth the way, as did colleagues in the School of Radio and Television Arts. Other friends and colleagues, by example, encouragement, or the sharing of food and ideas, helped me to find an equilibrium between affect, writing, teaching, research, and life itself: John Bailey, Jen Chambers, Jim Drobnick, Greg Elmer, Jennifer Fisher, Karleen Pendleton-Jimenez, Chandra Siddan, Claire Sykes, Charles Zamaria, and the excellent writers' group Write or Die. My deep appreciation also to literary consultant Sally Keefe-Cohen for her help with the business side of writing and publishing. Finally, thanks to the staff at Wilfrid Laurier University Press for their hard work and commitment to this project.

INTRODUCTION

IT WAS 1999. Nunavut was the newest Canadian territory. Former TV host Adrienne Clarkson had been appointed Canada's first Chinese-born Governor General. Over 50,000 protesters converged on Seattle to protest the effects of globalization. And Molson, responding to the dampening effects of free trade, developed a new TV ad for its "Canadian" line of beer (Wagman).

Molson dubbed this ad "The Rant." In it, Joe Canadian stood on a stage before an unseen audience and delivered an emotional tirade in which he politely but proudly distinguished Canada from the US with a litany of everyday Canadian artifacts and practices: "I believe in peacekeeping, not policing; diversity, not assimilation; and that the beaver is a truly proud and noble animal. A toque is a hat, a chesterfield is a couch, and it is pronounced 'zed' not 'zee.' 'Zed!'"

Behind Joe Canadian, a rear-screen projection showed flickering images of dogsleds, beavers, and, of course, beer. The pounding music score rose in volume as Joe's voice became more emotive and the audience began to cheer.

"The Rant" became a viral hit, spawning countless fan sites and consumer spinoffs, and becoming popularly referenced on Canada Day and at hockey games. Molson received such overwhelming response to the ad that they set up a special website where people could post their own rants (Bodroghkozy 110). A second edition of the Joe Canadian ad, "Anthem," aired in 2001, repeated this performative speech act but sutured it to space:

I know this place is where I am.
No other place is better than
No matter where I go I am
Proud to be Canadian.

Sung by a choir of untrained voices, the song was heard over a sequence of images beginning with dramatic re-enactment of the Last Spike (the hammering of the final spike into the cross-Canada Canadian Pacific Railway in 1885). Various iconic Canadian moments or places were shown in the ad—troops going off in a train to World War II; Canada's victory over Russia in the 1972 hockey series, shot off a TV screen; kids in Newfoundland. In the penultimate shot, Joe Canadian stood drunkenly in front of a microphone singing the song's final words—"I am Canadian"—while behind him on a green screen was a wide shot of the October 1995 "No" rally in Montreal, in which thousands of pro-sovereigntist Canadians demonstrated against Quebec separation in a rally funded by the federal government. The giant Canadian flag hoisted by the demonstraters was centred in the ad's frame. The final shot, so brief as to be almost subliminal, depicted a beer bottle top with the words "I AM" superimposed over a maple leaf.

In both ads, consumerism, television, and affect work together to produce a sense of mastery over national space—not to mention the desire for a cold beer.[1]

Television is a marker of an affective Canadian national space, one that promises an idea of "home." Home is a site of affect—of embodied feeling, of longing, of pride, and perhaps even of shame. Like the train to which it is often compared, Canadian television travels through national space, connecting Canadians to one another, creating contact zones.[2] These zones can be seen as sites where people, bodies, social spaces, and culture intersect.

National broadcasters commonly imagine national space as unified, perhaps in a way that is similar to the way tourists do as they look out the windows of a train. But Ira Wagman, in writing about the Molson ads, states: "What is significant about these advertisements is the way in which 'nation' and the threats typically associated with its survival, becomes the rhetorical surrogate for 'competition' and the threats typically associated with the company's survival" (78–79). Joe Canadian's rant demonstrates the ways in which, in the late twentieth century, Canada is a *contested* space (contested by the apparitional others of US dominance, First Nations claims, Quebec separatism, and "foreign" immigration). This serves only to underline the necessity of understanding affective modes, produced through consumerism.

In this book I examine the ways in which affect operates in relation to these factors, producing national practices framed by a television screen. Affect theory emerges from a nexus of disciplines: psychology, neurobiology, philosophy, deconstructionist and post-structuralist thought. It is an avowedly interdisciplinary theory: a crossing of disciplines, a breaking of binaries, and a movement into ontological and epistemological possibilities.

Affect theory is the examination of intensities of *feeling* rather than of emotion. As I watch Joe Canadian's rant, even for the second, or fifth, or fifteenth time, I get chills down my spine. This feeling is irrational, given my ardent critiques of nationalism; it has happened before I've had a chance to understand it. It is the body, then, and not the mind, that first registers affect, marking it as pre-discursive and pre-emotional (Grusin).

[handwritten margin note: affective response different (and more immediate) than the rational one]

Teresa Brennan describes affect as a process of movement from the sensory to the cognitive, rather than a binary between the two (120). In this way, affect displays itself on and through the body—by way of gestures, expressions, sounds—and these displays are always in relation to what other people are doing with their bodies. As Gay Hawkins points out, echoing Peter Brooks, affect theory is not so much about having individual feelings or drives as it is about acknowledging the ways in which we feel in and with the world (Hawkins par. 5–6). It may be that my pre-discursive affects (about which I later feel some shame) indicate my interest in belonging to the community of nation even as I disavow nationalism itself. And it may well be that the ad affectively interpellates ambivalent citizens just like me.

Affect theory has only recently appeared on the radar of cultural and media studies. Departing from the somewhat more individualized notion of the drive within psychoanalysis, affect theory can help us to think through what people are doing and feeling in relation to national television. Affect is exclusive neither to text nor to audience, but occurs in the contact of each to the other. Affect, then, as something fairly common in television content (especially in the genres of the commercial, the soap opera, and reality TV), produces a sense of audiences being touched or moved, which can cause viewers to connect, in empathy, in fear, in pleasure, or disgust, with other bodies. Massumi, for example, discusses how media images have multiple affective flows. Rather than seeing cinema and television as mimetic devices that produce certain effects—i.e., TV ads are sexist and they produce sexist behaviour—affect theory allows us to see cinematic and televisual images in a more open-ended way. Massumi provides the example of TV images of Ronald Reagan: his shaky voice and folksy expressions didn't so much send a message as lull the viewer into complacency ("The Autonomy of Affect").

Thus, affect theory helps us to think about television in terms of what passes between television and bodies and then other bodies, and transforms those bodies in their multiple association. This focus on the relational can attempt to illuminate how one person's affect impacts another's and how affects change and transform each other. As such, affect theory expands upon the notion of one-way flow (from screen to audience) that characterizes some of the earlier Canadian television studies canon.

Television, Discipline, and the Nation

This book also analyzes how television operates as an organized system of knowledge that is in turn marked by the nation, by means of the filaments of history, politics, technology, and economy. As such, it contains apparati of discipline within it, whether the discipline of highly gendered broadcast schedules and flow or the discipline of festive viewing in which mandatory viewing and collective affect occur.

Affect here intersects with nationalism, marking affect as one of the ways in which discipline and governmentality can emerge. In *The Archaeology of Knowledge*, Michel Foucault examines the relationship between discourse and discipline. He posits three criteria for the forming of discourse: surfaces of emergence, authorities of delimitation, and grids of specification (45–47). As an example, he uses the discourse of psychopathology from the nineteenth century onward and notes that a multiplicity of new objects, or agreed-upon symptoms, of psychopathology appear at this time. In effect, he observes that discourse is unitary but that its objects change constantly. He argues that it is important to observe the process of discourse formation in order to undercut and question the obviousness of certain discursive statements and their institutional power.

The dispersion of psychopathological objects in Foucault's model of archaeology of knowledge is not unlike the dispersion of Canadian nationalism's objects, emerging at vastly different and often contradictory sites: a beer commercial, a sporting event, an elder statesman's funeral, same-sex marriage. These sites make discourse, in Foucault's words, "manifest, nameable, and describable" (46). Foucault argues that only by examining the process of discourse formation do we denaturalize its workings. In so doing, we can identify Canadian television as a crucial surface of emergence for nationalism since the mid-1990s.[3]

Within this commercial medium, US dominance, Quebec separatism, and the immigrant are highlighted as nationalism's objects. Certain institutions, working together—the law, the corporation—delimit these objects, lending them authority through what I call *technologies* of affect: speech-acts, music, image-editing. The "rules" of nationalist discourse prescribe certain ways of talking about these topics and exclude others. For example, Canada must be spoken of as a peaceful, tolerant nation, generally excluding mention of slavery, internment camps, and so on. At different times, different objects are more or less important. Since 9/11, for example, immigration has become an object of knowledge within the discourse of Canadian nationalism. Before 9/11, American dominance was a primary force in the construction of nationalist discourse. Joe Canadian's declarative statement, then, "I am Canadian," is a very rich one, embodying in a literal sense the rules of nationalist discourse at a particular moment in Canadian popular culture.

As Flaherty and Manning suggest, "it may be in *popular culture* that Canadian sovereignty finds its most meaningful and potent expression" (xii; italics mine). Although perhaps less interested in sovereignty, I would concur with the importance of looking to popular culture as a surface of emergence for discursive national sites of official memory and forgetting as well as for ethical spaces of resistance and reparation. A seemingly trivial pop cultural product—a beer ad—becomes both a metaphor for nationalism *and* its very content. Whether it's a hockey fan bearing a sign saying "I Am Canadian," a fan weeping at the sight of a celebrity, or a *Canadian Idol* contestant jumping for joy at being chosen to "go to Toronto," popular culture is a decidedly affective and nationalist realm.

Increasingly, these affective moments are experienced within and across media. We may have strong affective attachments to particular television programs and characters or hosts, but we may also have an affective relationship with our flat-screen TVs, our smartphones, iPads, and laptops (Grusin). In other words, both the content and the technology evoke intensities of feeling, making affect theory an ever more necessary tool in cultural studies' approach to contemporary media.

I have chosen to focus on Canadian television as a *primary* surface of emergence for Canadian nationalist feeling. Morley points out that it is television, perhaps more than any other medium, that enters into domestic space, "linking the national public into the private lives of its citizens, through the creation of both sacred and quotidian moments of national communion" (106). And it is television, I argue, even in an era of multiple and ambient screens, that is most interested in the maintenance of home as an affective, passionately *emotive* place. This affective home place stands in for the nation; it is here, in this domestic space seemingly apart from governmentality, that affective televisual moments attempt to manage threats to the imagined community of nation.

Television is heavily invested in the construction of national identity. British television theorist Chris Barker cites such examples as the South African Broadcasting Corporation (whose slogan, post-apartheid, was "We Are One"), and the Latin American *tele-novela*, or soap opera. He insists that television plays a crucial role in constructing national identity "through the circulation of national symbols and myths together with the creation of feelings of solidarity and simultaneous identity" (66). Caughie asserts that television theory has focused on gender to the exclusion of nation, ignoring the fact that the act of television viewing is specifically located within national and local social sites and histories. Within the context of television studies' current preoccupation with the global, he argues for "the embarrassingly persistent category of the nation" (47). Tinic argues that nationalist affects on Canadian television are produced not by literal nationalist artifacts but rather by means of a process of "'symbolic distancing, whereby people engaging with foreign media programs get "glimpses' of life elsewhere" (21). These foreign images, argues Tinic, can serve to reinforce an appreciation of the local (22).

[handwritten margin note: we appreciate home via images of away]

Besides linking the local and the global, national television is inextricably linked to other technologies and to social sites. As part of the larger text of television, I also examine its *flow* (or what McLuhan might have called extensions) between television and body, between program and commercial, between TV, telephone, cellphone, and Internet, and between television and the spaces of home, workplace, and street.

Canadian Television Theory and Its Affects

The canon of Canadian television theory, compact though it is, has historically concerned itself with technology and policy, generally leaving discussions of content to popular sources—with some notable exceptions. Since useful and comprehensive overviews of both Canadian communications policy and Canadian television theory have appeared elsewhere (Beaty and Sullivan; Druick and Kotsopolous), I review just a few key texts, whose slightly varying discourses constitute an interesting affective narrative of the nation. E. Valentine Daniel, in discussing the affective tendencies of the nation-state, mentions a "hope [that] is drenched in nostalgia, the imagined glory that once was" (309–10). This "glory that once was" is generally seen as the years in which Prime Minister Pierre Trudeau was in power, 1968–1984.[4]

One of the earliest books to deal exclusively with Canadian television, and one of very few to address content, is Mary Jane Miller's book, *Turn Up the Contrast* (1987). It touted itself as "the first book to explore the content of Canadian television drama" (front-cover blurb). Written from a nationalist and somewhat modernist perspective, the book proudly proclaimed its avoidance of what it called "the jargon of communications and semiotics" (front- and back-cover blurbs). It constitutes an opinionated and rather chatty catalogue of such Canadian dramas as *Wojeck, King of Kensington,* and *The Beachcombers,* using content analysis and reflection theory to develop a notion of a non-transparent Canadian narrative with a single interpretation. "We are ambivalent about authority and authority figures and yet we acquiesce to them," writes Miller in her conclusion. "We are almost proud of the absence in our national and provincial life of grand gestures, yet our cameras are in love with our infinitely varied landscape" (378). Echoing feminist "images of women" theory of the mid-1970s, these statements concern themselves with images of Canada rather than the social meanings of those images, treating Canadian as a homogenous category and assuming a unifying nationalist effect on audiences. On the cusp of the multiple-channel cable universe, Miller warned her readers, somewhat ominously, of "the satellites of other countries [that] can now easily displace our own pictures, interpretations, visions about the shape of our landscape with broadcasts made elsewhere" (378). One can assume, given the rules of nationalist discourse, that the imminent, readily available smorgasbord of American programming, from CNN to Spike TV, was Miller's primary object of concern. Still, it's interesting to note the figure of the foreigner lurking in the background, a discordant note that only appeals to the nation-state can harmonize.

Culture, Communication, and National Identity: The Case of Canadian Television (1990), by British scholar Richard Collins, is generally seen as the ur- ~~original~~ text of Canadian television. It set the tone for a succession of books on Canadian broadcast policy written from a political economy perspective. Moving from the Broadcast Act of 1968 to the late 1980s, the book's major contribution is its decoupling of politics and culture: national broadcast policies, argued Collins, achieve little in terms of nation-building. While conceding that "old-style nationalism" was still in force in Canada (23), decoupling, he argued, was "the new international norm" (4).

Collins noted a contradiction that was to puzzle a generation of Canadian media theorists to come: despite their high level of consumption of American television—relatively unchanged a decade later (Cochrane)—Canadians maintain a high level of nationalist sentiment. "Nations," wrote Collins, "can survive in robust health, even when their media are … American" (18). Conversely, he argued, transparently nationalist Canadian television dramas alienated audiences weaned on American cultural products. As an example he

Canadian's don't feel less Canadian for watching US media.

offered the most popular Canadian drama of 1984, *Nightheat,* which had no identifiable Canadian elements (12). Collins seemed enamoured of a Trudeau-esque vision of Canada as a model for the internationalizing world, a civic-minded mosaic of multiple identities unencumbered by regulation. Canadians, he argued, while lacking a shared symbolic culture, have an anthropological culture (government, institutions, health care, welfare plans, relative absence of racism, peace, order, etc.) (35). In that sense, Collins, while critical of national broadcast policies, adhered to the rules of nationalist discourse, which at that time were moving toward neo-liberalism. The moral disorders of regulation, as Collins saw them, were to be healed and soothed by an organic nationalist sentiment. Daniel writes, "the nation-state is aestheticized by the national-ization of its past, which is projected onto the future—by which act the pres-ent is appeased" (310). That future—a more globalized and privatized world—demanded comfort from a localized affect of pride, nostalgia, and hope. Unexamined but certainly significant for this book's purposes is the interdependence of the American other and Canadian nationalism—Ameri-can dominance as a primary force not only in the construction of nationalist discourse but in nationalist sentiment itself.

Also in 1990, Paul Rutherford's *When Television Was Young: Primetime Canada 1952–1967* was published, examining the so-called golden age of Canadian television. Nostalgia and longing here are more aesthetically than nationalistically motivated. Rutherford agued that these pre-colour and pre-cable years were more innovative and experimental: "a brief era of experi-mentation ... [in an] innovative art-form that was soon snuffed out (or was it perverted?) by the dominion of commerce" (5). Rutherford addressed post-war Canadian culture and argued that that era of government, influenced by cultural intelligentsia, imposed a "highbrow"—as he called it—approach to tel-evision broadcast policy (Collins had noted a similar propensity in both Canada and Quebec). According to Rutherford, this "highbrow" approach to programming ignored the fact that most viewers preferred American televi-sion. More importantly, Rutherford argued for the "commonality of the expe-rience" (482) of CBC programming in that era, which he saw as a virtue of public broadcasting. His comments anticipated contemporary analyses of the digital era: "Increasingly people could watch, as individuals rather than in a family setting, programs that suited their own tastes and moods ... it did mean that the mass sharing of the same messages once a part of the prime-time experience no longer applied" (482).

As Beaty and Sullivan point out, the twinned forces of digital technology and globalization helped to push analyses of Canadian television into more

adventurous territory, with collections and monographs that begin to destabilize Canadian identity and infer a more globalized, if not entirely critical, way
of looking at the nation. Serra Tinic's *On Location: Canada's Television Industry in a Global Market* (2005) uses the Vancouver film industry as a window
onto issues of globalization and television in Canada. Here, she laments the lack
of regional voices in a climate dominated by runaway (US) productions. She
places some of the blame on the CBC, which, she argues, moved from a focus
on national unity to national identity. The unity mandate, she feels, was more
supportive of regional programming; national identity politics, which she says
originated with the Quebec separation debate, has produced a more central-
ized, Toronto-centric vision of TV programming. Tinic argues for a national programming policy that would recognize Canada as made up of local communities.
She claims that "nation-states do not emanate monolithic, unified identities ...
Canada epitomizes the challenges of connecting cultural identity to the physical space of the nation-state within the symbolic realm of broadcast media production" (viii). In that sense, she is arguing for the nation as multiple site of
identity, a post-national imaginary not unlike that of Arjun Appadurai's.

In a smiliar vein, *Canadian Television Programming Made for the United
States Market* (2007) by American librarian Marsha Ann Tate examines the high
number of television programs produced in Canada for the American market, arguing that Canadian television's increasing presence in the export market works to dilute nationalist sentiment in the content of said programs.
Robert Wright's essay collection, *Virtual Sovereignty: Nationalism, Culture,
and the Canadian Question* (2004), deploys ambivalence as a framework for
Canadian nationalism, which he sees as an imagined unitary affect that seems
built on nostalgia for the "Canada of my youth, a Canada of social-democra-
tic consensus ... a Canada that cared deeply for young people and understood
them to be central to the project of nation-building" (17). Wright identifies
consumerism as a key element of citizenship and notes that in Canada this consumption encompasses not only commercial products but, interestingly, government programs as well (121). However, as Ryan Edwardson points out in
his book *Canadian Content: Culture and the Quest for Nationhood* (2008),
agencies such as the Canada Council were often more interested in funding
national unity by way of the arts than in funding artists themselves (221).

Interestingly, none of these authors (Miller is the exception) see the pre-
dominance of American programming on Canadian TV screens as a threat to
a real or imagined sense of the nation. The US remains a productive other, high-
lighting Canada's attributes. Quebec frequently appears as a secondary other,
either as an ominous threat to unity or as an admirable example of passionate

regionalism. Programming that blatantly promotes the nation as site of unity is frowned upon by the authors. More conducive to nationalist sentiment is what Druick and Kotsopolous, in their edited collection on Canadian television, *Programming Reality* (2008), have dubbed "banal nationalism": implicit, rather than explicit, national narratives "found in hockey programming, current affairs, news parodies, and even in talent shows" (8). As Spitulnik has pointed out in her reception study of uses of radio in Zambia, it does not necessarily matter whether audiences are watching or listening to these programs closely or even regularly (152). Audiences make use of their *presence*, in the background, in their daily schedule or in the general fabric of superficial cultural attributes: the opening bars of The National, hummed ironically; the ability to imitate a character in *Trailer Park Boys*; or the traces of a beer commercial, embedded in a joke, a gesture, or a banner at a hockey game. John Ellis has described these sorts of seemingly trivial cultural signifiers as "instances of national identity at its most everyday and intimate" (112).

I contend that it is the examination of these everyday affective practices, as seen on and off TV, many of them related to consumerism, that is especially relevant to the study of nationalism and television in Canada.

From Traumatic Point to Traumatic Point: Uses of Trauma and Affect Theory

While a comprehensive theoretical overview of Canadian television is yet to be written, my own timeframe in this project is fairly narrow: roughly 1995 to 2002. Like Tinic, I argue that the 1995 Quebec referendum on sovereignty was a turning point in Canadian nationalist representations on television. Indeed, as Druick and Kotsopoulos point out, the years immediately after 1995 saw a rise in both policies and funding meant to increase what the Canadian Film Fund described as "visibly Canadian elements," while the CBC secretly used government sponsorship funds to produce its *Heritage Minutes* series (3). However, I examine this moment through the lens of content (in relation to audience and site of reception) rather than state or broadcast policy, and illustrate how, through affective modes of consumerism (television, advertising, national products), Canada began narrating itself as a unified, albeit multicultural, nation in an unprecedented manner. While others (Collins, Mary Jane Miller) have argued that the Trudeau era was the most clearly nationalist in terms of both government television policy as well as content, I feel that it is the particular consumptive mode of national address that marks the post-1995 period as a unique chapter.

I begin by outlining certain methodologies to do with theories of nation and affect (chapters 1 and 2). My chronological starting point is the televised lead-up to and documentation of the Quebec referendum of October 1995 (chapter 3), followed by the launch of two very different but similarly nationalist TV series—*Loving Spoonfuls* (chapter 4) and *Canada: A People's History* (chapter 5)—and an examination of other historical moments and particular programs: the state funeral of Prime Minister Pierre Trudeau (chapter 5) and, finally, Canadian television coverage of the period from September 11, 2001, to the Salt Lake City Olympics in February 2002 (chapter 7).

Rather than divide my objects of analysis into genre or content area, I move from traumatic point to traumatic point—moments in televised Canadian history that ruptured, and then tried to resolve, the imagined community of nation—and to the idea of a national self and national others. These moments include the ways in which contemporary television serials, while different from a news documentary's sense of liveness, maintain a sense of immediacy in relation to national or world events.[5] I argue that witnessing world events (or serialized re-enactments thereof) in the intimate context of the home, and television's co-presence in that experience, can produce anxious affects resulting in the need to work things through (Ellis). Indeed, Ellis's work points to a need for a wide-ranging interdisciplinary and a trans-genre approach to understanding traumatic affects in relation to television. He writes: "Television's explicit and flexible generic organization allows it to spread as wide as possible, and to provide many emotional points of contact with the idea and lifestyles, problems and opportunities, that it is working through" (126). Thus, I ask the reader to imagine not a linear narrative of expanding or diminishing nationalist affect but rather a constellation of traumatic contact zones: the near-death of the nation, the death of of an elder statesman, the deaths of thousands in New York City.

I begin with the English-language television coverage of the 1995 Quebec referendum debate. This coverage provides an emotive narrative arc that, I argue, constituted a super-text (Browne). This super-text was to endure for several years and, I believe, served to introduce a new discourse of belonging and national identification on Canadian television. As the No (federalist) side won and Quebec lost its bid for sovereignty, Canada lost its other. "Canada is still here tonight—but just barely," announced CBC news anchor Peter Mansbridge immediately after the referendum vote (*The National*, October 30, 1995). *Other* othered bodies then had to be invoked.

I argue, finally, that the Olympic Winter Games at Salt Lake City, held only five months after September 11, were a particular moment of unity and false closure in which hybridity disappeared against images of triumphant nation-hood. Much like the Joe Canadian phenomenon, this unity was inscribed and delimited in part by way of a corporate logo: the Roots-designed (and -logoed) uniforms of the Canadian Olympic team.

— remember the disappointment/ alarm when Roots lost that contract?

Official Omissions

Forgetting and denial are crucial to notions of belonging. Thus, I examine certain absent histories in Canadian television programming, like that of the First Nations, Ukrainian Canadians, Muslim Canadians, and other so-called ethnic groups, and the ways in which multiculturalism was harnessed as a discursive and representational regime to contain the trauma of these omissions. Rinaldo Walcott writes about the exclusions inherent within official representations of Canada, noting that it is not the omission but the *denial* of these omissions that remains to be fully theorized (7). The question is then not so much a matter of listing the omissions but, rather, asking why they exist. National meanings are produced through a complex interplay of absence and inclusion. What are the effects of power that result from certain questions not being asked? I argue that these gaps or fissures in knowledge within the narratives of nations are actually presences with their own epistemic regimes.

In *Discipline and Punish*, Foucault examines power/knowledge in relation to the prison: the body of the prisoner becomes an object of knowledge, and one of many vehicles of institutional power. Power, in his terms, does not flow from a single source but rather is a system of relations. Similarly, I do not examine any single source of power, such as a particular broadcasting network, a particular producer, a body of criticism, or a particular instance of state regulation. Rather, I am interested in scattered, multiple sites of power and the ways in which television programs support, or act as conduits between and across these sites, with affect.

Certain notions of Canadian nationalism, heard frequently on Canadian television—that we are better than the US, that we are a peacekeeping nation, that we value ethnic and racial diversity—have gained the status of truth, making nationalist sentiment an acceptable practice. Affect—intense feeling at sports events, state funerals, national crises, and the like—is a social practice that supports these "truths," and television helps to relay these affects, in turn affecting other bodies. Foucault argues that this "will to truth" is a powerful system of exclusion.

But power, in Foucault's lexicon, is also productive; it produces institutions, which in turn produce power. Power can even produce ethics. To paraphrase Foucault, racialized representations are not simply about "negative mechanisms"; the network of television's discursive practices is also linked to positive effects, as well as to pleasure ("The Will to Knowledge"). Progress, like history, is never linear, and certainly not on TV. Eva Mackey describes such contradictory representations, from First Nations stereotypes to defiant expressions of self-determination, as being constitutive of Canada's "heritage of tolerance." Mackey traces this project back to eighteenth-century treaties that allowed for Aboriginal self-government and recognized Quebec's distinct society. She identifies these as management strategies to deploy Québécois against Indian and to make Canada distinct from the US (23).

The Québécois, the immigrant, and the Indian also function as figures of desire. In chapter 5, by means of an analysis of the representation of the other within the Canadian cooking show genre, I examine ethnic cooking shows such as *Loving Spoonfuls* (W Network) in the context of Canadian multicultural policy. Here I focus on multiculturalism as a disciplinary practice produced within the discursive field of Canadian nationalism. *Loving Spoonfuls* provides a compelling example of multiculturalism's affective modes. Ahmed notes, "eating with aliens, or even eating one (up) might enable us to transcend the limits and frailties of an all-too-human form" (*Strange Encounters*, 2). In this case, this form is the nation: its limits are the US and Quebec and the trauma of boundary loss.

Theory, Memoir, and Methodology: Contingent Relations

To utilize trauma theory and affect theory is also, at times, to remember or even re-experience certain traumatic emotions or experiences from one's own personal or cultural history.

During the course of this project, the bombing of the World Trade Center in New York City occurred. Like so many others, I found that I could not write about the traumatic aftermath of 9/11 without musing upon my own losses: some recent deaths in my own family. The "real" of my own affect broke the skin of my theoretical work and moved it into a wholly different territory. Grief fragmented me, deprived me of narrative. Personal experience and theory overlapped in peculiar ways. My writing became more aligned with Deleuze and Guattari's post-structuralist fantasy of what a book can and cannot do. In their terms, a book is a multiplicity, a text with multiple roots that will not submit to a single identity (*A Thousand Plateaus* 3–4).

I developed more respect for theory, which had played an important role in my own process of grieving. Similarly, Jane Gallop writes about having begun her project of writing about anecdotal theory—theory grounded in "the subjectivity of the theorizing subject" (14)—and then being interrupted by a significant episode in her personal life. She writes, "although I can't say that I like it, I can see that it is precisely this ability to interrupt and divert a project conceived in theory which makes incident a force to be reckoned with" (15). The form of this book acknowledges the contingent relationship between analysis and memory, and thus between theory and memoir.

Feminist theory's early work in the area of memory (Lionnet; Nancy K. Miller; Nussbaum; Smith and Watson) has attempted to legitimize the use of memoir, anecdote, and autobiography as a particular epistemology: a way of knowing and memorializing history. The autobiographical becomes a way to move along the different surfaces of the self: inside and outside, theoretical and social, and, more importantly, the ways in which these surfaces overlap, bleed into one another, inform one another, and then *become* something else. This flux, this instability at the heart of identity, may help to make theory more accountable to the site of the social subject, less certain of itself: in Gallop's words, "to make theorizing more aware of its moment, more responsible to its erotics, and at the same time if paradoxically, both more literary and more real" (11).

"Writing itself becomes a matter of becoming," write Deleuze and Guattari; "in this way, the reader is drawn into the implicit and hitherto unimagined community which the text anticipates through its matter of expression" (*Anti-Oedipus* 22). As I write about the televised Trudeau funeral of 2000, I find myself writing against a limit—that of the unimagined community of the immigrant in Canada; a world of postwar trauma, middle-class aspiration and hope, multicultural festivals in sports arenas, the quiet, deadly xenophobia of suburban high schools and shopping malls, the bitterness and gratitude of my immigrant elders toward their new "home." Deleuze and Guattari see limits as sets of possibilities; there is not an end or a limit toward which lives move; rather, lives and bodies strive internally to maximize possibilities. An ethnic childhood diverges into "lines of becoming." Its very proscriptions can produce new ways of thinking and writing about the nation. Memoir as embodied history; theory that ruptures the general or universal and becomes specific—skin, body, flesh and blood.

As a child of immigrants growing up in a tight-knit émigré community, most of what I ate at home (perogies, garlic sausage) or did on the weekend (learning Ukrainian geography and history, visiting the graveyard) was certainly incomprehensible—and probably laughable—to my schoolmates. Thankfully, we were allowed unlimited access to TV in my family, and it was, perhaps, my deep familiarity with Canadian and American prime-time programming that provided me with enough Anglo-Canadian cultural capital to get by. From

The Friendly Giant to the opening refrains of the national news, Canadian television evokes a world of nostalgic sensations for its citizens that puts into
proximity otherwise distant sites of knowledge.

Television Theory: Privileging Content, Defining Text

Television theory has traditionally defined itself along a limited number of
theoretical binaries: sociology versus cultural studies, American versus British,
Frankfurt School versus Birmingham School, text versus audience, quantita-
tive versus qualitative, ritualistic versus ideological. I use a *transdisciplinary*
approach, deploying a wide range of textual and critical strategies to inter-
pret, criticize, and deconstruct cultural artifacts. This approach brings media
analysis into a contemporary global context, where pop-cultural forms are
re-territorialized into investment opportunity and, concomitantly, national
identity. The struggle to reclaim public culture must then necessarily include,
as Giroux argues, the theoretical work of analyzing how seemingly innocent
pop-cultural products engage the ideology of nation using a *variety* of intertextual strategies (*From Mouse to Mermaid*). There are, however, certain sources
or strategies I rely upon more frequently than others: television content and
its related texts and technologies (fandom, criticism, Internet, cellphone, print
media, radio), audience, and sites of reception. I pay less attention to industry and policy, given, as I mentioned earlier, the already strong contribution
of Canadian media scholarship in these areas.

In *Understanding Media*, Marshall McLuhan elaborates upon his infamous
phrase "the medium is the message." It is the form rather than the content of
any particular medium, he claims, that defines the scale and pace of human
activity. He writes, "the 'content' of any medium blinds us to the characteristics of the medium" (9). This book, however, *privileges* this much-maligned
content. More specifically, I examine television's speech acts, its generic repetitions and compulsive returns.

Although audience research and spectatorship theory have been crucial to
certain branches of communications theory, there now seems to be a crisis of
audience in cultural studies. Ethical/political questions surrounding ethnographic research, the complex interpellative strategies of mass media within
global capitalism, and fragmentation of audience communities have necessi-
tated, to my mind, a considered return to the text. To this end, I look at television programs, print media reviews, and related Internet sites in addition to
theoretical texts. The audience enters into discussion in a limited way through
chat groups on the Internet and through anecdote and memoir.

more justification

What then of the active audience and its alleged ability to resist television's web of corporate and national signifiers? Stuart Hall was instrumental in conceptualizing a multiply situated reader for whom viewing is an active process embedded within social relations. Depending on their social location, readers find different ways of negotiating the televisual text ("Encoding/Decoding"). Negotiation can produce a pleasurable reading; such a reading can be seen as resisting what Fiske calls "the structure of domination" (19). He provides a useful critique of Hall's encoding/decoding theory, introducing complexities that Hall at the time overlooked: that readers do not so neatly divide themselves into three roughly equal teams (preferred, negotiated, oppositional) but rather engage in "structures of preference in the text that seek to prefer some meanings and close others off" (65). This set of ideas—that neither mass culture nor mass audiences are monolithic, that pleasure, and even power, can be found within commodified cultural products—was a reaction to the influence of the Frankfurt School and its condemnation of mass media as a product of industrial forces buttressing capitalist ideology. At the same time, the idea that power and pleasure are not mutually exclusive echoes Foucault's dictum that "we must cease once and for all to describe the effects of power in negative terms" (*Discipline and Punish* 194).

Certainly, resistance can be overstated, as when Meaghan Morris famously writes, "I get the feeling that somewhere in some English publisher's vault there is a master disk from which thousands of versions of the same article about pleasure, resistance, and the politics of consumption are being run off under different names with minor variations" (29). John Caughie is also critical of an inordinate focus on audience, describing it as a kind of displacement: "The privileged objects of much of television studies—the audience, the institutions, the market—are effective ways of displacing the theoretical problems of values, politics, and texts onto empirically testable bodies ... the question of television's textuality—untestable, uncertain, repressed—will keep returning" (55).

The truth, as usual, lies somewhere in between. This book is aligned with what Douglas Kellner has dubbed a "multiperspectival" approach to cultural studies, in which one can make use of a range of textual and critical strategies to analyze cultural artifacts. Intriguingly, Kellner advocates in favour of both the Frankfurt School *and* the cultural studies approach, arguing that, "certain tendencies of the Frankfurt School can correct some of the limitations of cultural studies.... Cultural studies has over-emphasized reception and textual analysis while under-emphasizing the production of culture and its political economy" (41).

This work's alignment with a multiperspectival approach is certainly not to propose a return to a hypodermic notion of audiences as cultural dopes. However, I have come to the conclusion that a more text-based approach can illuminate how genres such as comedy and melodrama regulate, without wholly eliminating, the possibilities of diegetic transgression and audience resistance.

Textuality with regard to television is of course different from textuality in literature and film. Film theory and literary theory are traditionally more reliant on linguistic analysis; television theory, while it may draw from those modes, also overlaps with analyses of political economy, with cultural studies (itself an interdisciplinary field), and with philosophy. The more intimate space of the home as site of reception also places television in a different textual category. In part because of its commercial imperative, television is always intertextual and always interactive, in the sense of allowing for multiple readings and even, through fandom, intervention. Here one might concur with McLuhan, who described television as a "cool" medium because, carrying less detail than a "hot" medium such as print, it allows for more participation (22). In a more insistent way than literature or film, television has always acknowledged this interactivity (by way of the domestic site of reception) into the structure and flow of its texts. Finally, the economic (advertiser-funded) nature of North American television means that its texts are also more determinedly sutured into a commodity-oriented framework, and have embedded within them a flow of attention and distraction, unity and fragmentation. A television program, then, can never be seen as a discrete unit but rather as one of a series of texts whose unity is designed to attract an audience for the longest period of time possible (Allen).

Specific to television, I have found Nick Browne's notion of the "super-text" useful. Distinct from the mega-text, which is the sum of what appears on television—its history, logic, and organization—the super-text is "a text that extends beyond the parameters of a single program and includes advertising, the sequencing of programs and the serial character of television programming" (qtd. in Bailey 46). But I hope *not* to isolate television or even technology from other sites of discourse. Television's convergence with other forms of broadcast and digital transmission—the Internet, the cellphone, the DVD player, the DVR, the radio—must be acknowledged in terms of how these other forms resituate the viewer within the home. John Corner, following Raymond Williams, discusses this convergence as productive of "a kind of domesticated individualism set within a complex of abstract, public systems ... radically increasing the privatization of television" (17–18). At the same time, 9/11 provided a vivid and unprecedented example of the blurring of boundaries between the private site of the home (which is where most people first saw the collapse of the Twin Towers) and the public realm (the street, the workplace), where private grief and fear became publicly shared and passed on. The connections that linked these spaces were, more often than not, digital; the Internet and the cellphone became technical apparati that connected rather than isolated people and allowed for an interactivity and perhaps even a cultural competency that television was unable to facilitate at that time.

One could argue then that 9/11 constituted a super-text, one that lasted intermittently for a year and will presumably continue to do so for some time. From the actual coverage on the day, to fundraising ads by the American Red Cross, to special dramatic episodes of *West Wing* and *Third Watch*, to talk shows featuring victims' families and newscasts of the war on terrorism, 9/11 and its aftermath constitute one of the most compelling examples of intertextuality in the history of television.

But there is also a kind of super-text that extends beyond the TV frame, which Bailey describes as:

> the simultaneous articulation of a set of highly ideological figures across a variety of discursive formations, centered in some sense in the diegetic content of television programming but permeating discourses seemingly far removed from the mere fictional content of dramatic programming.... this second (super) text ... might be conceived as vertical in the sense that it slices across a set of varying media and discursive fields. (46)

We might, for example, see Olympics coverage as a super-text, centred on television programming but operating as a highly ideological text across the fields of consumption, activism, human rights, and tourism ("We'll be landing very close to the 2010 Olympic skating oval in Richmond," the pilot intoned helpfully as our plane approached Vancouver). Browne claims, "television presents and sustains consumption as an answer to the problems of everyday life" (72). In this case, the Olympics are literally and symbolically an answer to the trauma of recession, inner-city poverty, and national malaise.

This approach, then, goes beyond form and genre and begins to consider televisual diegesis *and* discourse: the play of power relations that overflow into the social site of the audience. It is a way to account for ideology and to address some of the limitations of British cultural studies' notions of cultural competence, in which an almost unlimited agency has, at times, been attributed to the active audience.

In this sense, then, I write about Canadian television from 1995 to 2002 as a *set* of super-texts, a kind of super-genre distinct from (though certainly not unconnected from) both American and British television. This super-genre is distinct by virtue of its "national" characteristics, however constructed, and its convergence with local spaces, global forces, and cultural communities, including my own. A blockbuster historical drama series back to back with patriotic ads for a Canadian beer. The funeral of a queer-acting Canadian statesman juxtaposed with Cuban socialism and my own queer youth.[6] Lines of connection, lines of flight. Perhaps it is at this nexus of global economic interests that regulate the flow of bodies, the infantile desire for the dark, originary continent of the other, and the power of interpellation, that the Canadian imaginary is produced, flickering at the rate of sixty different light patterns per second on a TV screen.

ONE

AFFECT THEORY
Becoming Nation

I WRITE ABOUT THE NATION from where I live: from my living room, with its Panasonic flat-screen TV next to bookshelves with their weight of theory; from the narrative of my so-called "ethnic" identity and its necessarily othered relationship to Canadian identity. My own critique of roots, and of the terms of power embedded within the nation, intersects with desire: for roots, for citizenship, for power, for home. In this way, I too become national.[1]

Affect theory, with its emphasis on change and relationality, is a useful tool with which to discern how people become part of a nation. I argue that television's role in this is neither one of simple mimicry nor of cause and effect but rather that nationalism emerges out of a complex series of relationships: of the body to disciplinary power, of television to the body, of pleasure to television, of citizenship to pleasure, of citizenship to shame. None of these pairs of terms exists as a stable entity but rather circulates, exchanges meanings, and forms new combinations and relationships, in a sense fragmenting notions of nationalist sentiment. Rather than engaging in traditional audience analysis, then, I am interested in the affects that proceed from the text. I wish to examine the television text in relation to bodies, and those bodies, in turn, in multiple relation to one another.

Uses of affect theory in the humanities originated from a critique of the monolithic, culturally undifferentiated spectator or reader. Sedgwick and Frank, in reviving the work of postwar psychologist Silvan Tomkins, have done much to create a critical space for affect in theory. Tomkins, an American psychologist-philosopher, is the author of *Affect, Imagery, Consciousness*, first published in 1962. He is credited with the discovery of the mechanisms responsible for human emotion. His affect theory outlined the relation between thought, feeling, and motivation. He defined nine basic brain mechanisms: interest–excitement, enjoyment–joy, surprise–startle, fear–terror, distress–anguish, anger–rage, disgust, and shame–humiliation.

Affect theory allows for different viewer responses to infect and transform one another, as well as for the potential for new subjectivities to emerge from this process. While both cine-psychoanalytic theory and media effects theory presume a more or less direct connection between text and spectator, affect theory opens up this paradigm, acknowledging viewers' unpredictable responses, unsutured from the text. In her research into online responses of female soap-opera viewers for example, Warhol noticed that the intensities that viewers experienced were not the same as those represented on TV (116). She observed that while a soap-opera couple might be distraught due to an argument, a viewer might be jubilant to see that one character is being shot down by another, or what she called "responses that parallel the episodes' structures of affect without mirroring them" (118). In this sense, affect operates as a conduit between media and body and then between bodies.

Many affect theorists take pains to distinguish the field from psychoanalytic theory. Sedgwick, citing Tompkins, elaborates some distinctions:

> "It is enjoyable to enjoy. It is exciting to be excited. It is terrorizing to be terrorized and angering to be angered. Affect is self-validating with or without any further referent" (3: 404). It is these specifications that make affect theory such a useful site for resistance to the teleological presumptions of the many sorts historically embedded in the disciplines of psychology. (*Touching Feeling* 99–100)

Standard dictionary definitions of affect vary widely, but all seem to maintain its distinctness from the unconscious, as for example "the conscious subjective aspect of an emotion" (*Merriam-Webster's Collegiate Dictionary*, 11th ed.). At the same time, affect is also seen as unusual, "a state of feeling opposed to the normal" (*Oxford English Dictionary* 210). Affect is visceral, embodied, and seemingly pre-discursive. These distinctions also connote a subject-in-process, as opposed to the more normative and fixed structure of the drive. Its clinical definition, "feeling or emotion, manifested by facial expression or body language" (http://www.thefreedictionary.com), reminds us that affect locates itself in the body—a frown, or the downturned eyes of shame. Its definition as a verb provides clues as to its contagious aspects: "To attack or infect, as a disease" (*Concise Oxford English Dictionary* 22).

In other words, affect is the body's way of translating the personal and the social by responding to them as stimuli. The tenor of voice or the intensity of facial expression, as seen on a screen, creates an intensity in the body, and this intensity, impersonal and non-linguistic, can easily communicate itself to other bodies. Affect, then, is entirely relational: one affected body encounters another affected body, and something occurs out of that (Deleuze and *Guattari, A Thousand Plateaus*).[2]

Contact Zones: The Fluidities, Contagions, and Becomings of Affect

Affects are becomings.
—Gilles Deleuze and Félix Guattari, *A Thousand Plateaus*, 256

Silvan Tompkins was the first to argue that affect is contagious: someone observing an affected person may well start to experience the same, or parallel, intensities. Anna Gibbs invokes the useful image of sparks setting fire: "affect leaps from one body to another, invoking tenderness, inciting shame, igniting rage, exciting fear" ("Contagious Feelings" par. 1).

There are several ways that affect can be seen as either changeable in relation to other affects or affected bodies. Sara Ahmed argues, "If emotions are shaped by contact with objects, rather than being caused by objects, then emotions are not simply 'in' the subject or the object" (*The Cultural Politics of Emotion* 6). We might think, for example, of the ways in which grief concerning the death of Trudeau was passed on through multiple contacts with television rather than caused *by* television. This contact often occurred in the presence of other bodies, at the site of the television showroom or the sports bar, in a non-linear circuit of contact.

Elspeth Probyn describes contact zones in practical, concrete terms: "The contact zone seems like an abstract idea, but it is continually reenacted in everyday life: bedrooms can be contact zones, as can streets, libraries, shops and pubs, classrooms and workplaces. They are the spaces where different people come together—where, for various reasons, they are forced together" (*Blush* 112–13). Contact zones can be sites of oppressive surveillance, such as a border checkpoint, or they can be sites of pleasure, such as sex. They produce, or make visible, embodiment: the colour of skin, the perversions, pleasures, or traumas that a body has experienced (Probyn, *Blush* 112–13). Contact zones can easily be full of shame, or excitement, or unhappiness or all of the above. Standing in a crowded elevator at my university, I am surrounded by people of varying status: students, a lab assistant, a senior faculty member. I feel a mild sense of shame, though I can't, at that moment, explain why. Later, I reflect upon my consensual presence in this hierarchy, which is a place both of privilege and of oppression. In the elevator, the different embodied and unequal aspects of my being come into sharp and unsettling focus: female, white, middle-aged, middle-class, queer. Affect is, according to Deleuze, "whatever comes into being when something is affected or affects something else" (qtd. in Bourassa 65). Affected by the uncomfortable proximity of bodies in a small space, awareness of my place in a complex social structure comes into being.

Deleuze and Guattari are particularly interested in this sort of embodied relationality. They write, "We know nothing about a body until we know what it can do, in other words, what its affects are, how they can or cannot enter into composition with other affects, with the affects of another body, either to destroy that body or to be destroyed by it, either to exchange actions and passions with it or to join with it in composing a more powerful body" (*A Thousand Plateaus* 257). They apply ethology, originally the study of animal behavior, to philosophy. In ethology, organisms under study are never separable from their relations to the world. Ethology is interested in intersections, in spaces between. In the spirit of endless possibility, Deleuze and Guattari counsel the reader on how to become a dog: "This will involve not imitating a dog, nor an analogy of relations. I must succeed in endowing the parts of my body with relations of speed and slowness that will make it become a dog.... For I cannot become dog without the dog itself becoming something else" (*A Thousand Plateaus* 258).

In these terms, becoming is flux. It refers to the post-structuralist, destabilized subject; the self in process, a self that has not submitted to regulation. Becoming is an alternative to being; becoming is always relational. As Rosi Braidotti writes, "the space of becoming is therefore a space of affinity and symbiosis between adjacent particles" (115). Languages of representation, like those on television—and, therefore, the self produced through language—are constantly in a state of becoming, as they change and develop over time. Braidotti maintains that this process is liberatory: "the affective as a force capable of freeing us from hegemonic habits of thinking" (14). Affect, then, speaks to an ethical idea of collective belonging—the interconnectedness of body, culture, and emotion; the ways in which this assemblage moves across and transforms surfaces of skin and identity. This impulse toward embodied theory also, I argue, parallels affect theory's engagement in connections between bodies, and in an idea of a self, and perhaps even a nation, in process.

As in any field, there are contradictory positions on affect. While Grossberg, for example sees affect as a site of new conservatism (*We Gotta Get Out of This Place*), Deleuze and Guattari see affect as transformational (*A Thousand Plateaus*). For all of them, however, affect's transformative power occurs only in the relation between affects, or between bodies. Affect creates an intensity of thought that allows bodies to cross borders and make virtual connections. Braidotti, for example, mentions the aftermath of Diana's death as just such an affective moment, in that so many of Diana's mourners were queers and people of colour, embedded more firmly than ever into British identity (*Nomadic Subjects*).

It is certainly true that the relationship between two or more affected bodies can both exacerbate and challenge institutional power. Certain collective, mythical notions of Canadian nationalism—that we are better than the US, that we are a peacekeeping nation, that we value ethnic and racial diversity—have gained the status of truth, making nationalist sentiment an acceptable practice. Affect—intensity at sports events, state funerals, national crises, and the like—can be a social practice that supports these "truths," and television helps to relay these feelings, in turn affecting other bodies. Foucault argues that this "will to truth" is a powerful system of exclusion ("The Will to Knowledge").

Trauma and Affect: Theoretical Overlaps

The original (Greek) meaning of the word "trauma"—wound—speaks to an embodied rupture of skin; in early usage, trauma was understood as a wound inflicted on the body, not the mind (Cvetkovich). Ann Cvetkovich has pointed out how resonant and visceral is the body in Freud's descriptions of trauma as an excitation from the outside that breaks through a physical shield (53).

Affect theory, interested as it is in intensity and the body, overlaps with trauma theory. Like affect, trauma is often seen as prediscursive, beyond articulation (Kaplan). Both trauma and affect theory produce ethical possibilities, actions, and passions that can join with other bodies. Both are anti-memory, in the sense of memory as repetition, a compulsive response to trauma. For Deleuze and Guattari, memory represents a desire for a lost origin. If interested in memory at all, Deleuzian thought invokes short-term memory, a kind of collective, historical memory, which I see as not unlike the ethical "working through" of recent trauma theory (*A Thousand Plateaus*).

Trauma theory's interest in remembering about the nation that which has not been remembered represents an ethical turn in deconstructionist theory.[3] For Derrida, hauntology takes the place of memory: spectral presences that will return to the future, destabilizing ontologies, rather than stay in the past. Hauntology is in opposition to the archive, which is a site of "memorization, of repetition, of reproduction, of reimpression … which incites forgetfulness, amnesia, the annihilation of memory … the archive takes place at the place of originary and structural breakdown of the said memory" (*Archive Fever* 11). This turn to ethical remembering can also be heard in LaCapra's notion of the intellectual as opposed to the scholar: "The intellectual goes beyond an area of professional expertise to address problems that are of broader social and cultural interest, and in that sense he or she does not simply mind their own business" (*Writing History* 218). Trauma, then, produces connections between politics, ethics, and feeling. This is because trauma moves theory into the site of the social, which can create fissures, or instabilities, within theory and provides further rationale for the use of autobiography, memoir, and anecdote.

Eve Sedgwick, in her critique of what she calls "paranoid theory," is one of those who takes theory to task:

> It is possible that the very productive critical habits embodied in what Paul Ricoeur memorably called the "hermeneutics of suspicion"—widespread critical habits indeed, perhaps by now nearly synonymous with criticism itself—may have had an unintentional side-effect: they may have made it less rather than more possible to unpack the local, contingent relations between any given piece of knowledge and its narrative/epistemological entailments for the seeker, knower, or teller. (*Touching Feeling* 124)

"Paranoia knows some things well and others poorly," she says (130). While allowing for paranoid theory's agency, she argues that paranoia's alertness to danger, its resistance to surprise, its very tautology, may prevent positive affect and hinder ethical strategies. Trauma theory, affect theory, and memoir, then, in their commitment to speaking from and to the intersections of distant and proximate, global and local, become a way to intervene in theoretical modes that may have outlived their critical and ethical efficacy.

Parallel to Sedgwick's formulation is Arthur Kroker's notion of the "ethical lag," which addresses not theory but technology. He argues that "outmoded" public and private moralities have not kept pace with technological change and the effects of technology on bodies, minds, and communities:

Just like the "jet lag" in which the psychological consequences of life in the mainstream of technology are experienced only after the event is finished, "ethics lag" means that we are blindsided on the real effects of technology until it is too late.… Technology without a sustaining and coherent ethical purpose, and ethics, public and private, without a language by which to rethink technology. (127)

There was, for example, an ethical lag on 9/11, but one that was, I would argue, productive. Bodies were falling from towers; the screen was a horizon in excess of what we could fully know. What was one to feel, or do, as the television conveyed live satellite feed from New York on September 11, 2001? Compassion, anger, despair, grief, and even love emerged through a digital storm of emails to and from colleagues in New York and around the world and emotive phone calls to and from friends and fellow activists. As I further analyze in chapter 7, 9/11 was a moment when, in the collision of ethics and technology, affect was dissociated from object; a moment where, to paraphrase Deleuze, we did not know what a body could do ("Ethology" 627).

In these moments of trauma, affect marks the pre-discursive moment, that gap of time before anything makes sense, before the taxonomic categories of emotion are set in place. One cries before one knows what one is crying about. One is ashamed before understanding why.

Emotion versus Affect: Locating an Interdisciplinary Methodology

Affect is not, according to Deleuze and Guattari, a sentiment or personal feeling. Rather, it is "an encounter between the affected body and a second, affected body" (*A Thousand Plateaus* xvi). Eric Shouse clarifies this distinction: "Feelings are personal and biographical, emotions are social, and affects are prepersonal" (Shouse par. 2).

Brian Massumi further underlines the differences between emotion and affect: "Affect is most often used loosely as a synonym for emotion. But one of the clearest lessons of this first story is that emotion and affect—if affect is intensity—follow different logics and pertain to different orders." Emotions, he says, are subjective and personal: "qualified intensity" (221). Affect on the other hand is "unqualified … not ownable or recognizable" (222). Massumi makes the point that one of the things that distinguishes affect from emotion is the former's relation to ethics and to the body. He argues that psychoanalytic theory assumes too great a distance from the screen; that we are, in fact, ineluctably drawn into the film image—and that we must account for that—

by means of affect. Probyn is more equivocal, simply identifying the different functions described by drives and affect: "if the drives operate in a 'stop/start' way, the affects are more 'and/and/and'" (*Blush* 21). Sianne Ngai argues that emotion is subjective, a first-person position, while affect is more objective, something that is to be observed. She points out, following Lawrence Grossberg, that affect does not have narrative structure, and neither is it directly reactive (25).

Interestingly, Sara Ahmed shies away from making firm distinctions between bodily sensation, emotion, and thought. But her consistent focus on the body as being shaped by emotions—for example, "she made an impression," "he's a soft touch"—places her, for the purposes of this project, more firmly within cultural studies' affective turn (*Cultural Politics of Emotion* 2). Emotion, she argues, is part of a psychological notion of interiority and individuality. Building on Durkheim's notion of interiority, she proposes the model of social emotion, in which intensities of feeling—say, in a crowd of people grieving the death of an elder statesman—do not come solely from within individual bodies in the crowd but rather move between the surfaces and the insides of bodies. Thus she parts ways with the notion of contagion, which she feels posits a concept of feeling as individual property and makes often mistaken assumptions about a particular shared feeling. It is intensity, rather than a single specific feeling, Ahmed argues, that happens in crowds (*Cultural Politics of Emotion*). Thus the crowd gathered to mark the statesman's death may have diverse feelings of grief, pleasure, and so on, circulating as intensity that is both movement and stability. "What moves us," she writes, "what makes us feel, is also that which holds us in place, gives us a dwelling place" (*Cultural Politics of Emotion* 11).

Perhaps a distinction between emotion and affect can be mapped upon the subtle differences between autobiography and memoir. If emotion is singular and individual, then the same can be said of autobiography, which Nussbaum has described as "a technology of the middle-class self" (xi). Memoir, on the other hand, with its intersections with history, culture, and identity, occurs more vividly as a system of affects, of interlocking sites of passion and intensity. Jane Gallop's comments on the use of the personal, or what she calls "anecdote," as a legitimate theoretical practice are significant here. She locates anecdotal theory firmly within a deconstructionist tradition: "Although deconstruction was often held to be in opposition to the sort of personal discourse favoured by seventies feminism, by the nineties it became possible to recognize a deconstructionist personal and speak a personalized deconstruction" (5). To Gallop, anecdotal theory is productively and explicitly affective: "romantic, unreasonable, perverse and queer" (7). She argues that, in a Derridean fashion, it concerns itself with the marginal, the exorbitant, and cites Derrida's justification of Of *Grammatology*: "We are preparing to privilege, in a manner that some will not fail to judge exorbitant, certain texts" (7). As I argued earlier, memoir, operating as it does *ex orbit*, outside of theory's "metaphysical closure" (Gallop 8), can have the potential to cut through theory's density and highlight its contradictions, like wine that both unifies and simplifies the flavours of a complex sauce. Gallop writes: "'Anecdote' and 'theory' carry diametrically opposed connotations: humor vs. serious, short vs. grand, trivial vs. overarching, specific vs. general. Anecdotal theory would cut through these oppositions in order to produce theory with a better sense of humor, theorizing which honors the uncanny detail of lived experience" (2).

If deconstruction involves decentring the text, then memoir's function in this book can be seen as deconstructionist in that it decentres theory. The anxieties generated therein (my own, those of the academic readers of this text) follow from this destabilizing moment, that of inverting the binaries of reason and madness, truth and falsehood, theory and memoir, emotion and affect.

Affect theory, then, like the strategic use of memoir, is concerned with the interconnectedness of body, culture, and feeling; the ways in which this assemblage moves across and transforms surfaces of skin, of identity, of nation. Affect theory is positioned by Deleuze and Guattari as a way to move out of drive theory. In this formulation, affect theory is in process rather than the more fixed site of emotion. It notes *positions* of feeling and intensity rather than types.

While being careful to attend to these differences, I occasionally use the word "emotion" to describe more individualized self-expression. I would argue that the different terms mark disciplinary boundaries. Affect theory derives from deconstruction, cultural studies, and post-structuralism, while emotionology is more aligned with the social sciences. Since this is an interdisciplinary project, I draw from both fields while privileging affect theory.

Affect and Media

Only recently have affect theory and media studies begun to intersect. As the fixed site of cinematic viewing gives way to mobile technologies or the Internet download, affect theory is a useful theoretical tool to grasp the body's relation to technological convergence and the restless, fluid movement between technologies. In that sense, Metz's all-perceiving cinematic spectator, fixed in place by the cinematic process in a "pure act of perception," may hardly exist anymore (48, 49).

Television's interface with the digital realm encourages us to think about bodies and affects, as television emerges from the singular site of the home into the accelerated contact zone of the crowd—what Anna McCarthy has dubbed "ambient television" (1). As I have argued elsewhere, the field of television studies has been placed in a crisis of meaning in recent years due to the convergence of broadcast and digital technologies (Bociurkiw 538). While standard media relentlessly forecast the demise of broadcast television, it would seem that television—whether the ritualized viewing of nightly news or the attenuated real-time narrative of *Amercian Idol*—is still central to the home and to peoples' lives. It is important, however, to take note of the different ways in which people are watching television—more often alone, as they watch shows online, or alone in a crowd, as they watch television in waiting rooms, bars, or airports.

Using the photos from Abu Ghraib as a case study, Richard Grusin argues that the availability and instantanousness of digital technologies produces what he calls "mediality." Following Foucault, he defines mediality as the ways in which digital technologies themselves create affective contact zones that merge with disciplinary zones and practices. This aligning of media with what he calls "techniques of power" (par. 8) is not a new one: there are echoes here of the Frankfurt School's intractable notions of mass deception and of a Chomskyist formulation of bewildered herds. More interesting for the purposes of this book are the gestures that Grusin has us notice: the "taking, uploading, and distributing" of digital photos, TV shows, YouTube clips (par. 9). Indeed, the very ways in which we hold, gaze at, and depend upon our mobile devices create new opportunities for thinking about relations between media, affect, and the body. Because we recognize the Abu Ghraib photos as being congruent with our own "everyday media practices," argues Grusin, our precognitive affects of shock or disgust precede the content of the photographs and may have much to do with our own imbrication in these consumer technologies (par. 11). And whether it's us or the soldiers who pass these sorts of images on, the act of doing so is an attempt to distribute these affects and to allay trauma (par. 16).

Sianne Ngai's *Ugly Feelings* (2005) attempts to analyze such negative feeling—or what she describes as "affective gaps and illegibilities, dysphoric feelings" (1)—in literature, television, film, and theory. She looks specifically at envy, anxiety, paranoia, irritation, a racialized affect she calls "animatedness," and her made-up word "stuplimity"—a combination of shock and boredom. These negative affects, she argues, mark states of helplessness and passivity, a situation she feels to be deeply political, "the psychic fuel on which capitalist society runs" (2–3). Her intent is to uncover the ways in which artistic works, including film and television, might bring about amoral and non-cathartic affects, providing new ways of reading texts. The ambiguity of these ugly feelings, their lack of object or narrative logic, makes them much more like affects than emotions. Stuplimity in particular might be useful to understand the complex ways in which audiences attended to the long televisual narrative that was 9/11, followed by the invasions of Afghanistan and Iraq. Indeed, it makes me think of a waitress I overheard the night that the US entered Iraq. Handing over the menus to a couple, she said cheerfully, "Takin' a break from the shock and awe, are ya?"

Anna Gibbs is one of very few theorists who analyze affect in relation to television. Television amplifies affect by means of its technologies of sound and image (loudness, music track, close-ups of faces) as well as by the very fact of broadcast and global reach ("Contagious Feelings" 1). Intriguingly, she begins one of her articles by inferring connections between television and spiritualism; in particular, television's seeming ability to address a viewer directly, amplified by contemporary viewing conditions in which audiences increasingly watch television alone ("In Thrall" 1). These sites of reception create feelings of intimacy and safety on a very singular level, which Gibbs likens to the Freudian notion of cathexis, affective engagement with a single object. This cathectic state, she further argues, is not unlike being hypnotized, engaging "a human capacity for dissociation" ("In Thrall" 2). Televisual flow exacerbates this dissociative state. Thus 9/11 may have brought people into a temporary trancelike state in which audiences may have ended up believing their own enactments of hyper-nationalism ("In Thrall" 3). Or, as she puts it, citing sound artist Paul de Marinis: "the way bodies and affects are coded within the melodies of speech so that 'as our leaders talk [we hear] not the words but the music, we sing ourselves into a sleep of understanding'" ("Fictocriticism, Affect, Mimesis" par. 20].

In their ethnographic studies of working-class female television audiences in Britain, Helen Wood and Lisa Taylor map affect as a form of gendered emotional labour. In a study of reality-TV audiences, they note the ways in which affects can change from empathy to judgment within the duration of a half-hour show. These judgmental feelings seemed to occur when the characters' lives became uncomfortably similar to their own: "a moral framework in which female audiences are impelled to locate themselves as well as others, revealing the current pressures and politics of class and gender as they are firmly ensconced within modes of neoliberal citizenship" (148). These studies provide useful empirical data on the ways in which television, even in its most banal forms, can enact governmentality by means of affect.

Melissa Gregg has written a comprehensive overview of the uses of affect theory in cultural studies, some of which are media-related. She notes that cultural studies has begun to question "habitual judgements and value-laden frameworks" (5), opening the way for an affective turn in the field, which may in turn help to blur the distinction between political theory and practice. In particular, she cites Laleen Jayamanne's exhortation to read films in terms of how they make one feel rather than by way of narrative address or theoretical analysis. Film-studies theory is taken to task here, for foreclosing appreciation of the sentiment and sensibility of a film. Like Massumi, Gregg makes a case for "affective writing" within theory, the refusal of a detached analysis (18). She turns to television through John Hartley, citing his notion of television as furthering empathy among vastly diverse audiences, thus playing an important democratic role.

E. Ann Kaplan provides a useful account of the intersections of media, affect, and modes of belonging during 9/11, and particularly its contagious and transformative modes:

> The events [of 9/11] radically altered my relationship to New York, to the United States qua nation and produced a new personal identity.... One finds the complex interconnections between individual and cultural trauma—such that, indeed, where the "self" begins and cultural reactions end may seem impossible to determine. One can also find the single hopeful thread of a catastrophe, namely the perhaps short-lived but real creation of new public-sphere communities as specific crises are "translated" from group to group. (2)

But affect can also, at such moments, operate as a vector of power. Grossberg writes about affect as a hegemonic force. He argues that within popular culture affect often stands in for content, becoming an expressive force for right-wing politics (259). As an example, we might think of the arrest in Toronto, in June 2006, of seventeen Muslim men and youth. It was an exciting and, for some, frightening moment, if we were to believe the radio call-in shows and TV interviews. A group of "home-grown" (alleged) terrorists were alleged to have procured an enormous amount of common garden fertilizer in order to (allegedly) bomb Canadian targets. It's a moment that may not, initially, have deployed specific commitments or beliefs but foregrounded "the need to believe in belief, to make a commitment to commitment"—and, perhaps, to emote about emotions (Grossberg 271).

Affect calls forth cognition: passionate sites of feeling are evoked that then produce certain ideas and attitudes. As anger and fear over the so-called terrorist threat built in momentum, I kept the radio on so I could hear any alternative views should they be aired. I stopped listening to the content of what people were saying and instead tracked the emotional timbre of their voices, which invariably spanned just a few predictable affects: hurt and fear resulting in anger. Affect really is contagious: I too felt anger, but my anger had a different object: government and media. Affect is not always, then, related to content; it gives us something to think about alongside content. The maudlin, even tragic tone of reportage marks a moment we see as festive or memorable—this affect-laden moment then connecting us with other people, with our own pasts, or with national history. These vectors of feeling can produce feelings of pleasure and unpleasure, belonging and unbelonging—a paradox of bodies that long to, but cannot fully, inhabit the nation.

Foucault in his introduction to Deleuze and Guattari's *Anti-Oedipus* writes: "Develop action, thought and desires by proliferation, juxtaposition and disjunction, and not by subdivision and pyramidal hierarchization.... Prefer what is positive and multiple difference over uniformity, flows over unities, mobile arrangements over systems" (xiii). This book, moving back and forth as it does between historical moments and televisual genres, attempts to rearrange traumatic moments in recent Canadian history into a system of multiple affective practices. Canadian television is the normative site where these multiplicities in Canadian nationalist affect are organized.

TWO

THE TELEVISUAL ARCHIVE AND THE NATION

No MATTER how you hope to proceed, there is always the archive.

You must obtain permission; it takes time to do this. You will be regarded with mild suspicion or perhaps bemusement. Your body will pass, a metallic shadow, through various security devices; you will enter a sterile, windowless room. You are going home as you do this, though you do not know it yet. An *unheimlich* home. You are returning to the place you thought you had left, where you have dwelt so uneasily: the space of the nation.

You have spent days, even years, in this archive. You have spent your entire life there. It is an archive of memories, fantasies and spectral presences; a site of regulation, but also of desire.

A newscaster in a skinny tie grimly announces a hostage-taking in Montreal, October 1970; Pierre Trudeau in cinematic medium-closeup shrugs, mutters, "Just watch me." Switch channels and decades, through a semiotic chain: Fidel Castro watches patiently as Justin Trudeau delivers a eulogy to his father, October 2000. Look away for a moment, and they're gone. A flurry of white dresses fills the screen. It is August 1957. "Friends and neighbours, how are ya? It's a real pleasure to have ya with us tonight," drawls *Country Hoedown* host Gordie Tapp. Live from a hay-bale-strewn set in downtown Toronto, fiddler King Ganam winks roguishly at the camera. You can hear American folk music sung by Canadian country singers: the Haynes Sisters with their identical dresses and thick harmonies; a very young, tall Tommy Hunter earnestly singing "Teenage Love Is a Losing Game." East Europeans sneak in by virtue of their fiddle-playing and passing-as-white skin: Eddie Gerky from Woodstock, Ontario, with Coke-bottle glasses, cowboy shirt, and cowlick, wins the fiddle-playing challenge. Lorraine Foreman sings the melodious words of a square-dance caller: "Ladies in the lead, that's Injun style [she puts her hand up, miming a feather behind her head], and swing that gal behind you."

You are at the archive; you have finally gained entry. Nostalgia fills the air. You feel a kind of pride as these ghostly images flicker in front of you. You know that the other side of this pride is shame. For archives, as Ahmed has pointed out, are also affective contact zones (*The Cultural Politics of Emotion* 2004).

As part of my research for this book, I watched these programs and others at CBC's enormous panoptical headquarters in Toronto and at the pala-tial National Library and Archives, set on the banks of Ottawa's Rideau River, metres from Parliament Hill. The placement of these programs in an archive marks them as public documents, and yet it is here that the nation assumes discursive control. For Foucault, the archive is synonymous with the rules of discourse: "it is that which differentiates discourses in their multiple existence and specifies them in their own duration" (*The Archaeology of Knowledge* 129). The rules of the archive, he claims, govern how we speak.

In this book, I examine archival and contemporary footage from a vari-ety of Canadian networks: CBC, CTV, W, Knowledge Network, and Vision TV. Most of the programs I examine, however, are from CBC. There are two reasons for this. First, the CBC, as a state-subsidized and heavily regulated corporation, offers a discursive site rich with nationalist speech-acts and i-dentity claims. Although other Canadian broadcasters may be subsidized and may engage in nationalist practices, CBC has taken the lead in attempts at nation-building. Druick and Kotsopolous note the many ways in which CBC has done so. They point out, for example, that in the 1980s CBC instituted a plan to "Canadianize" its programming as a way to differentiate itself from other Canadian broadcasters. They write: "By providing services and pro-gramming that the private Canadian broadcasters did not, the argument went, the CBC would make itself relevant to Canadians as a public broadcaster con-necting the regions, reflecting the nation, and serving its citizens" (Druick and Kotsopolous 3). By 2003 CBC was advertising itself as "Canada's Own"; more recently its slogan has been "Canada Lives Here." Public perceptions of the CBC seem to bear out this notion. "CBC was a cultural church," writes media critic Wayne Skene. "It was a place to go to feel more Canadian, to learn more about being Canadian, to contribute our little bit to national purpose" (4).

Second, the CBC archive is unique in that it offers selective scholarly access to its well-organized holdings. However, I make no claim to a scholarly analysis of the CBC *as broadcaster*. My object of theory is neither institutions nor apparati but practices as they intersect with power. Thus, I have found it more useful to gesture toward the role of archives and archival documents in the production of national discourse.

In *Archive Fever*, Derrida draws upon the etymological roots of "archive." Archive originates from the Greek word *arkheon*, which initially meant house or domicile, an esteemed site of power: "It is thus in this domiciliation, this house of arrest, that archives take place. The dwelling, this place where they dwell permanently, marks this institutional passage from the private to the public, which does not always mean from the secret to the nonsecret.... They inhabit this uncommon place, this place of election where law and singularity intersect in privilege" (2–3).

The meanings of public and private resonated in my mind as I spent time at the CBC. It had taken me many months to gain entry to an archive that is heavily advertised on the CBC website. Although you can view clips of selected archival footage on the Internet, unlimited access is usually provided only to those who pay considerable amounts for archival footage. Thus, footage produced using public funds is made available almost exclusively through private (corporate) money. My relatively free access (I had to pay only for my own airfare and expenses) was contingent upon the goodwill of the archives coordinator, a fastidious, overworked, and essentially good-hearted man who nonetheless made it his business to obtain every program I asked for *himself*, thereby, perhaps, keeping a close eye on my research. In a sense, Derrida's progression "from the private to the public" was inverted (2). In a rather disturbing way, public documents had become privatized. Derrida cautions that any public document can remain secret, and I would conjecture that the CBC's secretiveness about its documents contributes to the significant lack of critical scholarly writing *about* the CBC.[1] In this way, the CBC's archival footage has acquired meaning not just as a document of history but as *history itself*. In 2002, for example, the CBC celebrated its fiftieth anniversary, in part with a series of one-hour programs, hosted by TV personality Rick Mercer, that packaged archival footage into decades. Much in keeping with the CBC Archives' website slogan, "Relive our history through CBC Radio and Television," this footage was presented as a snapshot of Canadian history *itself*, heavily mediated by the nostalgic patriotism of Mercer and his "streeter" interviews. In a Foucauldian sense, these documents are monumentalized; history becomes archaeologized, interested only in the description, rather than the analysis, of the document/monument (*Archaeology of Knowledge* 7).

My project became one of de-monumentalizing these documents and of finding a place for affect and bodies. As I watched this procession of flickering images, I tried to imagine the living rooms and rec rooms in which these representations first revealed themselves, and the pride, nostalgia, grief, anger, and fear they may have evoked. Bodies connecting to machine, affects transforming other affects.

Television, with its proximity—its placement in the intimate, emotive space of the home—has always been well suited to both the portrayal and the contagious spread of collective affect. This chapter attempts an overview of the ways in which an idea of the nation is produced, and television's role in this discursive construction.

While Canadian cultural studies is renowned for its analysis of the technological apparati of the nation, there exists very little critical writing about the nationalist *textual* practices of Canadian television.[2] The reader will note, then, that this is a book concerned with Canadian television that does not lean heavily on the canon of Canadian media theory—Innis, McLuhan, Kroker, et al. In a sense, these figures appear cameo-like, transitional characters in a different story. Canadian media theory, with its modernist concern for technology and the material products thereof, in the context of the nation-state, constitutes a useful point of departure for questions regarding practices of nation. These questions demand, I would argue, a methodology oriented toward questions of discourse and power, which is also informed by feminist and queer epistemologies.

As I disseminate this methodology in the following pages, I hope to maintain a dialogue between the nationalist canon and my own "postnational" (Appadurai 167) and interdisciplinary approach.[3]

Affect and the Nation

Affect (or, in Ernest Gellner's terms, "sentiment") seems to be crucial to mobilizing a nation to patriotism, to war, and to unity. Gellner writes: "Nationalism is primarily a political principle which holds that the political and the national unit should be congruent.... Nationalist sentiment is the feeling of anger aroused by the violation of the principle, or the feeling of satisfaction aroused by its fulfillment. A nationalist movement is one activated by a sentiment of this kind" (52).

This idea of the *constructedness* of the modern nation (Anderson, Gellner, McClintock, Renan) prioritizes culture and the everyday symbols and practices of citizenship in the nation, which would include sites of affect. Here, nationalism *becomes* nation (Eley and Suny). Chris Barker, however, makes a distinction between the nation-state as a political apparatus concerned with the administration of space or territory and, following Anderson, nationalism as the *imaginary* identification with that space: "The nation-state as a political apparatus and symbolic form has a temporal dimension in that political structures endure and change, while the symbolic and discursive dimensions of national identity often narrate and create the idea of origins, continuity and tradition" (64–65). In a similar vein, Kaja Silverman writes that a material relation to the nation-state (citizenship rights, health care, geographical relation) is invested in an imaginary relation, or what I would call nationalism. This relation is, she argues, underpinned by affect: it is a *hope*, or a nostalgia, rather than a reality (22). Going further, Ghassan Hage argues that nationalism is the imagining of an ideal nation, and that that imaginary assumes mastery of national space. In effect, he equates nationalist practices with racism: "practices which assume, first, an image of a national space; secondly, an image of the nationalist himself or herself as master of this national space, and, thirdly, an image of the ethnic/racial 'other' as a mere object within this space" (*White Nation* 28). As such, he argues that the everyday practices of nation include such commonsense affects as anxiety about walking through your neighborhood at night or joy over your country's win of an Olympic medal.

In a Canadian context, the examination of sentiment and affect in relation to television is a relatively recent and, I would say, somewhat tentative endeavour. David Hogarth, in an analysis of dramatization and dramatic re-enactment in the early years of Canadian television, talks about the producers' attempts to make the nation "an object of audio-visual pleasure" (17). He writes that such dramatizations were meant to inspire "new types of affective citizenship" (21). In a similar vein, Aspa Kotsopolous, in examining historical miniseries on Canadian TV such as *Trudeau* (2002) and *Shattered City: The Halifax Explosion* (2003), infers that citizenship is produced at both a rational and an affective level, "in stories that make the performance of citizenship possible through the invitation of empathy, investment, enthusiasm, and commitment" (164).

Other (non-Canadian) scholars (Brooks, Carton, Stearns) have noted the relationship between sentiment and national identity, and the state's role in managing emotion to create nationalism. Using the founding of the American nation as a case study, Evan Carton traces the ways in which the notion of what he calls "natural self-expression" arose out of an eighteenth-century condition of "ontological instability." This instability gave rise to what Carton describes as "the massive and multifaceted effort of 18th Century writers and thinkers to anchor the self in the ostensible immediacy and inalienability of feeling" (24). The nation, in a sense, had to function as an affective space where family and marketplace could not—a compensation for the "loosening of the Puritan bond" (Carton n41). Carton argues that the American nation is founded not only on national but emotional self-determination.

Similarly, both Brooks and Stearns have discussed self-expression as a marker of a new individualism, post-Enlightenment. In his study of the history of emotions, Stearns discusses the notion of emotional management that emerged in the postwar era. He notes that "control over fear and anger protected a sense of individuality and also served to lubricate group relations" (190). Kaja Silverman has noted the ways in which alarm over post-traumatic stress disorder among soldiers returning from WW II was reproduced in melodrama films such as *The Best Years of Our Lives* and *It's a Wonderful Life* that individualized the trauma as crises of masculinity within heterosexual relationships.

The gendering of national sentiment is, as Ann McClintock has pointed out, insufficiently theorized within canonical theories of the nation (*Imperial Leather*). Television coverage of the Quebec referendum provided ample opportunity to observe this gendering, as when the female pronoun was used repeatedly in reference to Quebec or the language of heterosexual romance was used to conceptualize the relationship between English and French Canada.

The intersection of sentiment, nationalism, and gendered embodiment provides representational space for familial metaphors. McClintock describes this as "an indispensable metaphoric figure by which national difference could be shaped into a single historical genesis narrative" (357). In this construct, national time becomes familial time, with indigenous peoples constructed as infantile against the parental figures of nationalizing colonists (358).

The televisual representation of queer or queered bodies, politics, and historical moments are posited, in this book as well as by other theorists (Dyer, Silverman, Wray), as an ethical practice with the potential to destabilize nationalism. I intend "queer" to mean a progressive politics or ethical practice rather than an umbrella term of identification. In this sense, queer becomes a challenge to the normal, a practice rather than a stable position. If queer *is* a questioning of normative behaviours and practices, then nationalism as a way of belonging is altered by direct queer interventions into the everyday structures of nationalism, especially its most gendered and heterosexualized practices. Butler argues that that normalcy is a continual production, sutured through repetition, and that queer bodies can make this production happen differently (*Gender Trouble*). Queer or queered representations, therefore, have the potential to make visible the normalizing structures of nationalism—but perhaps not the possibility to dismantle it. For it must also be said that "queer" and "nation" are two very unequal terms, and, that, generally, queer becomes subsumed by the nation.[4]

The Role of Media

Benedict Anderson famously wrote that print capitalism was one of the primary ways of drawing individuals, or small communities of individuals, into the imaginary community of nation (43–44). In a useful critical take on Anderson's *Imagined Communities*, Prasenjit Duara implies a kind of essentialism in Anderson's grand narrative of nation: "Nationalism is rarely the nationalism of the nation but rather represents the site where very different views of the nation contest and negotiate with each other" (152). He argues that Anderson's emphasis on print ignores the significance of oral cultural practices. Such a critique opens up space for expanding the notion of print capitalism into other media: radio, television, the Internet, or what Arjun Appadurai describes as "electronic capitalism." Appadurai writes: "Part of what the mass media make possible, because of the conditions of collective reading, criticism and pleasure, is what I have elsewhere called a 'community of sentiment'" (8). He argues that these communities are often transnational in their flow and sometimes even "postnational," "creating the possibility of convergences in translocal social action that would otherwise be hard to imagine" (8).

Anderson's notion of national time is similarly applicable to theories of simultaneity with regard to television. Television, as a time-based medium with daily, weekly, and yearly programming schedules, is particularly suited to the creation of national time, providing an awareness of people across a geographical space witnessing an event together through television. The faraway is made proximate, but this shift does not necessarily mean that we care more for this faraway world. Instead, the faraway is associated with anxiety, trouble, and disaster, and television works to reinforce the distance (and "our" proximity within the nation) even as it brings the faraway into the home. In Canadian television history, the chronological narrative of the nation unfolds in costume drama like *Dateline* (CBC, 1955–56), which dramatized episodes based on the Battle of the Plains of Abraham and the Riel Rebellion, and the more recent *Canada: A People's History* (CBC, 2001–2), in which gaps in historical accuracy are sutured together with the affective technology of music, voice-over, and special effects. The use of the generic conventions of drama and melodrama—posing, in the latter case, as documentary—allows for the prioritization of sentiment and nostalgia.

In the Canadian context, the nation is negotiated at the level of everyday practices—from canoeing to beer-drinking—which work to naturalize the workings of state power and are crucial to the production of a cohesive national identity. Passions that may no longer properly attend the basic practices of patriotism—veneration of the national totems such as flags, monuments, and heads of state—are overlaid onto consumption and the enjoyment of national *pastimes* (Keohane). Just as Dana Frank has determined that buying nationally produced commodities can be an expression of citizenship (qtd. in Wagman 78), so too does the consumption of Canadian television shows and advertising, no matter how lacking in sophistication, help the viewer construct themselves as citizens. Indeed, that very lack of sophistication (the CTV sitcom *Corner Gas* is a vivid recent example), echoing other consumer items such as maple syrup and Molson's beer, is yet another national commodity.

Wagman makes the point that the Molson's "I Am Canadian" ad series appeared at a time when Canadian dominance of its domestic beer market was being challenged by the US through new global trade agreements (GATT, WTO). These trade challenges succeeded, allowing American beer companies greater access to Canadian markets. An ersatz nationalism became the means by which Molson defended its corporate might. I would add that these ads are also significant as being part of an increase in patriotic meaning, post-1995.[5] Audiences made use of a consumer item (Molson's beer) to create their own defensive, emotive forms of nationalism.

Duara makes an interesting distinction between *feeling* and *meaning* with regard to the nation. He notes that there are moments when everyone is drawn into the affective economy of nationhood, especially in relational situations. But Duara claims that there are *degrees* to the intensity and endurance of this feeling (165). The strength of Canadian *feeling* derives from a network of discursive and symbolic meanings that can often lead to national *meaning*, or what I would call patriotism. That these everyday practices are often truth-claims for white Anglo-Saxon identity provide further weight to the argument that nationalist practices lead to racism. Put another way, everyday national practices are inseparable from the linguistic narrativizing mechanisms of racialized national discourse.

Television is the ultimate commercial vehicle, bringing audiences to advertisers. Ellis notes that television is deeply connected to changes in practices of consumption, in part due to its primary location in the home, a major market for twentieth-century consumer-capitalism (42). Television has always familiarized audiences with lifestyles more affluent than their own. Historically, television was the crucial consumer item that, as Ellis argues, "encouraged purchase of all the others. And it drove the will to work to acquire these items" (42).

Television is instrumental in the everyday narrativizing of the nation. So much so that in recent national struggles, satellite communication, television stations are the first to be targeted by invading armies. The insertion of the colonizer's programming into national channels signals their victory even more than the raising of a new flag. The 2003 invasion of Iraq by the US followed this trajectory, from the bombing of the Arab Al-Jazeera network to the subsequent installation of the Washington-based Arabic-language Radio Sawa[6] and the anticipation of a parallel television channel, the Middle-East Television Network. Although audiences may prove resistant to these practices, media coverage itself encourages the notion of media as formative to nation-building. Accompanying a *Globe and Mail* feature article was a half-page photo montage of the famous image of soldiers at Iwo Jima raising the American flag. Replacing the flag, however, is a satellite dish (August 2, 2003, R1).

The Affective Economy of the TV Nation

As Silverstone points out, television is a way for families to access certain emotions (*Television and Everyday Life*). Television's polysemy provides representation of carefully controlled excessive affect (soaps, state funerals, national catastrophes, state weddings, and funerals) *and* of a complete lack of affect. Stearns notes that early television supported ideas of emotional control in the workplace at a time when postwar trauma was at its height. It also provided images of docility and service, crucial to the postwar economy: "by the 1950s television … helped to translate the ever-smiling models of service success into daily viewing" (219). By the 1980s the bland faces of newscasters and the made-for-TV smiles of politicians, even in the face of protests or catastrophes, marked contemporary standards for emotional control.

Television commercials became a primary site of affect, filling in the lack in regular programming. Since the postwar era, emotional control has been balanced by the encouragement of passion for consumer items and what Stearns calls the expression of "great joy over often modest accomplishments" (288): The kids have no cavities! The shampoo is fantastic! The laundry is whiter than white! Representations of leisure activities on TV—sports, or the extreme activities of contemporary reality-TV shows—provide expressions and symbols of joy that may be mimicked in daily life.

Television's need to produce national sentiments and emotions can be seen as a defensive reaction to demands of globalization of industry (Hall, "Culture, Community, Nation"). Canadian media are, in fact, leaders in mergers and convergence, and Canada has one of the world's most consolidated media networks.[7] At time of writing, a handful of corporations own most of the country's television networks and most of its major and minor newspapers. The federal government began promoting convergence in 1996, which signalled, according to Winseck, "a greater tolerance of ownership concentration and a new hierarchy of values that privileged the expansion of information and media markets over concerns about freedom of expression" (796–98). Indeed, as Winseck points out, freedom of speech with regard to this unprecedented convergence has never been studied by the CRTC, Canada's main broadcasting regulator.

Convergence always produces a loss of the local: layoffs in local centres and centralization of editorial control.[8] Some Canadian media scholars have noted that the transnationalist forces of globalization—while working to break down national distinction, also somehow manage to *reinforce* nationalism (Collins, Tinic). We might, for example, think back to the Molson Canadian advertising campaign and the ways in which its determinedly localized strategy existed alongside pressure to become transnational. Stuart Hall has noted that efforts to restore these lost national characteristics have set the stage for the return of nationalism as a major historical force ("Culture, Community, Nation"). Nationalism then becomes a way to maintain a fantasy of bounded national space to which one maintains a strong affective tie.

Longing, Belonging, and Shame

A nation is a soul, a spiritual principle [composed of two elements]. One is the possession in common of a rich legacy of memories, the other is present-day consent, the desire to live together, the will to perpetuate, the value of the heritage that one has received in undivided form.
—Renan, qtd. in Wagman 76 (italics mine)

From the time of Renan's late-nineteenth-century meditation on the nation to the present day, scholars have reflected on reasons for the desire to be part of the nation. In her exploration of modes of belonging, *Outside Belonging*, Probyn explores geographical sites in relation to their sexualized, nationalized, classed, and gendered desires. She sees belonging as a highly affective state that is always relational and always performative: "I want to figure the desire that individuals have to belong, a tenacious and fragile desire that is, I think, increasingly performed in the knowledge of the impossibility of ever really and truly belonging, along with the fear that the stability of belonging and the sanctity of belonging are forever past" (8).

It is often immigrants who are seen as performing that longing for citizenship of the nation. Television coverage of every Canada Day I can remember includes celebratory footage of immigrants acquiring citizenship and singing the national anthem. "Their" longing for "our" nation provides evidence of "our" tolerance and moral superiority. However, this footage is always a representation with strict discursive limits. As calls for deportation of undesirable others increase in the post-9/11 era, non-immigrants express their longing for the nation *through* the abjection of these alien bodies (Hage, *White Nation*).

In *The Dark Side of the Nation*, Himani Bannerji has done much to take apart the imagined Canadian nation and expose what she calls its "dark side." "What," she asks, "are the terms and conditions of our 'belonging' to this state of a nation?" (91). She too equates nationalism with racism, arguing that national characteristics are rooted in a whiteness with moral qualities of "masculinity, possessive individualism and an ideology of capital and market" (107). She notes certain affects that accrue to Canadian nationalism—an anxiety about Aboriginals and the hate and aggression of "official nationalism" and the love and sacrifice of "popular nationalism." Bannerji contends that the Canadian state is founded in the former, and that popular nationalism, if it exists, "contains legal/coercive strategies and the means of containment and suppression of all 'others'" (106). Visual regimes play a crucial role here. The specularity of the visible minority encodes skin as "some sort of social zone or prison" (*Returning the Gaze* 149). The repetitive display of new Canadians on Canada Day reinscribes them within a specular system of tutelage in which immigrants performatively become the well-behaved children of a parental state.

I do not recall that my refugee father ever once expressed a desire to belong to Canada. The walls of our home were covered with images of Cossacks, beribboned maidens, and villages set amid the green steppes of Ukraine. To be nationalist in our émigré community meant to be in support of an independent Ukraine. But my father's fierce diasporic nationalism, forged in trauma and grief, sutured him into a notion of a multicultural Canada. As one of those elite "ethnics" who pushed the government into the development of official multiculturalism, my father always desired inclusion rather than belonging. A subtle difference, really, but one that allowed for the maintaining of an outsider identity. My father knew well "the impossibility of ever really and truly belonging" (Probyn, *Outside Belongings* 8). Becoming national was an assemblage, connected to, and transformative of, other positions and affects: the trauma of war, the sentimentality of Ukrainian folk songs sung while shaving, framed degrees and academic gowns. And also, the ethnic shame that these accomplishments could never quite erase.

Silvan Tomkins, as interpreted by Sedgwick and Frank, describes shame as perhaps the most important of affects—the affect most constitutive of sense of self (*Shame and Its Sisters*). Shame, with its lowered head, its constriction of the body, directs attention back to the body as bearer of affect. It also flags interest, a connection to other bodies, engagement in the world (Probyn, *Blush*).

How then, is shame belonging's other? Thomas Scheff writes, "The urge to belong, and the intense emotions of shame and pride associated with it, may be the most powerful forces in the human world" (277). Probyn makes the point that sport, which is tied to shame, emerged at the same time that ideas about the homosexual and the nation were being formed ("Sporting Bodies"). Sport, as I argue in chapter 6, plays a large role in consolidating the nation. As such, writes Probyn, sporting bodies bring to mind "the visceral dynamics of pride, shame and bodily affect in ways that have been notably missing within much feminist and cultural analysis" ("Sporting Bodies" 14). Like Sedgwick, Probyn sees shame as productive: "a force that refigures the connections between bodies, subjectivities, politics and what, for want of a simpler phrase, I'll call the ethics of existence" ("Sporting Bodies" 24).

As at state funerals and national disasters, the 2002 Olympic Winter Games at Salt Lake City, Utah, were situated on a shame–pride axis. Pat Quinn, the Canadian hockey team's head coach, said in a TV interview at the games, "emotion is our biggest enemy and our biggest friend"—emotion was something that could mobilize the nation but also, perhaps, interrupt the masculinity necessary to win and, therefore, shame the nation. Emotions, as Sara Ahmed argues, are not merely internalized drives but operate on and across surfaces, asserting national boundaries and becoming invested in power (*The Cultural Politics of Emotion*). In that sense, then, shame works hard to produce the boundaries of the nation and the longing to belong.

Following Tomkins, Sedgwick and Frank write about the relationship between shame and interest: "the pulsations of cathexis around shame … are what either enable or disenable so basic a function as the ability to be interested in the world" (114). Shame, then, is an attitude of, in part, reading—"reading maps, magazines, novels" (114), as Sedgwick and Frank put it—but also, one might assume, reading TV. Indeed, as a scholar of television I constantly encounter the degree of shame (especially among academics) that is attached to television-watching and that often coexists with a detailed knowledge of its doings. Sedgwick and Frank maintain that shame, in its productivity, coexists with pleasure:

Without positive affect there can be no shame: only a scene that offers you enjoyment or engages your interest can make you blush. Similarly, only something you thought might delight or satisfy can disgust. Both these affects produce bodily knowledges: disgust as when spitting out bad-tasting food, recognizes the difference between inside and outside the body and what should and should not be let in. (116)

Sedgwick writes about how, after 9/11, she, along with other New Yorkers, kept looking, reflexively, for the Twin Towers: "But of course the towers were always still gone. Turning away, shame was what I would feel" (*Touching Feeling* 35). This was, for her (following Tomkins), the shame of the *unheimlich*, of looking at something that was meant to be familiar but had gone strange: "I was ashamed for the estranged and denuded skyline; such feelings interlined, of course, the pride, solidarity and grief that also bound me to the city" (36).

Perhaps there was also shame in the *entertainment* that 9/11 provided. Sitting in front of the television for three solid days, I felt pleasure at something that should not have been pleasurable. I was enjoying the excessive, paranoid moment: televisual images and conspiracy theories that overlapped with one another. An inside and an outside to what, in activist circles, we used to call "the dominant culture" that seemed to have merged. The bombing of the Pentagon! Rumours of attempts to bomb the White House! How many activists secretly admitted their fantasies of just such destruction, and how many felt a sudden, transient shame?

Gibbs advocates a need to "think with shame": it may signal an object that requires our interest and attention ("Mixed Feelings" 229). Similarly, Sedgwick is critical of strategies that try to undo shame (examples: memory work in Germany, pride movements), arguing that shame is constitutive; it is associative, connected to zones of the body, behaviours, identities, other affects. She writes, "The forms taken by shame are not distinct 'toxic' parts of a group or individual identity that can be excised; they are instead integral to and residual in the process by which identity itself is formed" (*Touching Feeling* 63).

Also worthy of analysis are the connections between shame, guilt, humiliation, and embarrassment. Here, trauma and affect theory converge once again, at the site of the nation. Nathanson writes that shame is an umbrella term for a multitude of emotions ranging from embarrassment to mortification (19). However, he differentiates between shame and guilt, in a distinction that parallels LaCapra's notion of acting out versus working through:

Whereas shame is about the quality of our person or self, guilt is the painful emotion triggered when we become aware that we have acted in a way to bring harm to another person or to violate some important code. Guilt is about action and laws. Whenever we feel guilty, we can pay for the damage inflicted. The confessional system is a system of release from guilt, for it allows us to do penance.... No such easy system exists to facilitate our return from shame. (19)

This distinction points to notions of reparation, a notion Sedgwick asserts is missing from post-structuralist theory. Canadian television programs like *Canada: A People's History* reveal a steadfast lack of acknowledgement, let alone atonement, for racist acts. Bannerji scathingly demands: "What discursive magic can vanish a continuously proliferating process of domination and thus of marginalization and oppression?" (*The Dark Side of the Nation* 106). Does the *lack* of acknowledgement and punishment of wrongdoing, then, lead to shame? And is this shame (potentially a site of transformation) also one of repetition, of representations that return again and again to trauma without the ability to move forward into present-time? Shame is then constitutive of the nation; shameful affects obscure the shameful past.

These days, embarrassment often stands in for shame. Embarrassment, which emerged in the post-Victorian era, allowed emotion to be replaced by reason, embarrassment being the affect that controlled potentially debilitating emotions such as shame and guilt (Stearns). Embarrassment would seem to be one of the defining emotions of Canada's foreign policy, legitimizing increases in defence funding.[9] "Canada's Chrétien has proved to be a national embarrassment," wrote Bob MacDonald in the *Toronto Sun* (September 26, 2001). Comparing Bush's and Chrétien's responses to 9/11, MacDonald found Chrétien to be lacking in moral authority or military initiative, and declared him to be pandering to the "ethnic vote." Here, ethnicity produces embarrassment, which signals a need for power and regulation, at the borders of otherness. In the Canadian context, embarrassment can be seen as a way for Canadian identity to bypass any actual working through of shameful actions, and also marks its subordination and relationality to the US.

As we have seen, this combination of pleasurable and painful affects works to produce national sentiment. Berlant hyperbolizes this notion of sentiment and describes its particularly American version as "national sentimentality, a rhetoric of promise that a nation can be built across fields of social difference through channels of affective identification and empathy" (309). In other words, the suffering of others less fortunate than ourselves can also be part of our feeling for the nation.

In the run-up to the 2010 Olympic Winter Games in Vancouver, grainy images and abject sounds from Vancouver's Downtown Eastside, Canada's poorest neighbourhood, proliferate on television and radio. It is as though this community, whose trials have existed for decades, has only now become attached to national feeling and therefore to meaning. The burgeoning national sentiment of a Canadian Olympics, with its images of youth and health, seems to require a darker contrast, a sign of tolerance for suffering.

Pleasure

See Jane walk. See Mother cook. See Spot run. Grade one was for me an unsettling mix of familiar Catholic ritual and exotic Anglo-Canadian custom. Such a crowded, hybrid universe: the national anthem, portraits of Queen Elizabeth and Pope Paul, the Act of Contrition, Jesus on a cross. But the grade-one reader resolved all contradictions. With its drawings of white English people living in an amazingly ordered and cohesive universe, it both comforted and dazzled. It was my job not only to *look* at Jane, Mother, and Spot but to see them, to let them enter and fill my visual field. As Bannerji writes, "Invisibility ... depends on the state's view of [some] as normal.... They are true Canadians" (*Returning the Gaze* 148). This was a visual economy that promised its readers a kind of transparency through its spectacular pleasures, and a mode of belonging.

Pleasure, as Raymond Williams reminds us, is constitutive of belonging to the nation. Williams writes about the childhood "pleasure" of learning, and a sense of friendship and community attached to the song of a monarch or a flag: "The powerful feelings of wanting to belong to a society are then in a majority of cases bonded to these large definitions" (*The Year 2000* 182).

As I mentioned earlier, affect can be harnessed in the service of ideology. Grossberg argues that optimism can sometimes stand in for conservative politics: "The new conservatism does not replace a lost source of optimism but rather speaks directly to a desire for optimism.... The new conservative alliance does not need to deploy specific commitments or beliefs, but it has to foreground the need to believe in belief, to make a commitment to commitment" (271).

In a post-9/11 CTV News report entitled "The Optimism of Canadians," a national television network took upon itself the task of characterizing the affect of an entire nation. It was, in the anchor's words, "a snapshot of how people are feeling about themselves and their futures in the wake of September 11th." According to CTV, a poll revealed that, despite rising unemployment and a sluggish economy, Canadians were experiencing "the highest level of optimism in two decades." After interviewing "ordinary Canadians" at a drive-through Chicken Burger outlet in Bedford, Nova Scotia, the report ended with a call to unity: "collectively, Canadians will be able to overcome the challenges posed by this new world" (CTV News, November 8, 2001).

It is no accident that these optimistic Canadians are situated at a site of consumption and of nostalgia: an old-fashioned burger joint. Keohane writes about the political economy of pleasure. In his view, the Canadian nation is defined by "national enjoyment," in which nationalism becomes consumption and nation becomes commodity. The famous ambiguity of Canadian identity is, he writes, "a void around which enjoyment is structured and organized" (32).[10]

> The enjoyment of a historical identity—that is, the innumerable social practices, languages, signs, codes that animate a particular identity—is constantly under threat of being stolen away by the necessary coexistence of otherness, because the Other's enjoyment, or rather, the infinitude of the difference apparent in the Other's enjoyment, an infinitude that appears as the Other's excess enjoyment, exposes the arbitrariness and contingency … of the enjoyment of the One. (23)

Several theorists (Duara, Hall, McClintock) have touched upon just such a relational nature of national identification. Hall writes: "[The English] have to know who they are not in order to know who they are…. There is no identity that is not without the dialogic relationship to the Other" ("Culture, Community, Nation" 345). Similarly, Duara writes: "As a relationship among constituents, the national 'self' is defined at any point in time by the Other…. The national self contains various smaller 'Others'—historical Others that have effected an often uneasy reconciliation among themselves, and potential Others that are beginning to form their differences. And it is these potential Others that are most deserving of our attention" (163). Several scholars (Collins, Mackey, Manning) have described Canadian identity as relational, heavily dependent on its difference from the US and Quebec. Aniko Bodroghkozy follows that trajectory: "The [I Am Canadian] ads were so pleasurable because of the effective ways in which they mined that lode of contrasting [US–Canadian] stereotypes but also the parodic ways in which the stereotyped Canuck ends up on top" (117). Keohane argues a Canadian identity that is relational to the immigrant. The immigrants' "excessive" enjoyment of their own customs shows up the lack of Canadian identity: "The 'successful' immigrant and the 'lazy' immigrant are rendered equivalent in the racist discourse, as both are marked by some obscene excess enjoyment…. But it is this very excess, pertaining to the Other's enjoyment, that constitutes the object field of desire. The same qualities that we hate in the Other are those qualities that we envy, that we desire" (24).

Pain

The traumatic moment becomes encoded in an abnormal form of memory.
—Judith Herman, *Trauma and Recovery* 36

In recent trauma theory, national memory is constituted at the site of forgetting. Painful affect—grief, sorrow, a sense of loss—becomes that which defines national memory, as when Cathy Caruth asks, "What does it mean, precisely, for history to be the history of a trauma?" (15). For how else to explain the ways in which a nation has not fully narrativized its past?

According to Kaja Silverman, following Jacques Rancierre, trauma produces a certain kind of history, which she calls "the dominant fiction" (47). Moving away from an individualistic clinical model that dominates much of trauma theory, Silverman theorizes the symbolic order and ideology: "When a modified Althusserian paradigm is brought into intimate connection with psychoanalysis and anthropology, it provides the basis for elaborating the relation between a society's mode of production and its symbolic order" (41). The dominant fiction helps form not only a subject's identity but also a nation's reality.

Pain is an embodied term, implying surfaces, skin, sensation. A wound is a contact zone, visible and evocative, circulating in the public domain (Ahmed, *The Cultural Politics of Emotion*). Traumatic narratives can materialize the nation, but official national narratives strive to represent a nation without pain by means of healing gestures such as official apologies (Sawchuk). As I note in chapter 4, even those who suffered internment and near-death at the hands of a racist nation-state are recuperated back into a healing narrative. Renan too asserts that it is suffering, more than joy, that unites the nation: "Where national memories are concerned, griefs are of more value than triumphs, for they impose duties, and require a common effort" (53). But he argues that a nation's trauma obscures memory. "The essence of a nation," writes Renan, "is that all individuals have many things in common and also that they have forgotten many things" (45). He cites forgetting as crucial to nation-formation. The nation is then reconstituted in historical error.

• • •

You have been in the CBC archives for weeks. Somehow, summer has dissolved into autumn, and wind whips your face as you leave the building each evening. You are chilled, but not by the weather. You have been watching the news, years and years of Peter Mansbridge, Alison Smith, Hana Gartner. You even watch the ellipses, the unedited spaces between: the way that Alison always licks her finger and fixes a strand of her hair before going to air; Peter's nervous half-smile as he straightens his tie. You feel some affection for them, parental figures, objects of infantile desire.

Ahmed writes, "Some forms of [archival] contact are presented and authorized through writing ... while other forms of contact will be missing, will be erased, even though they may leave their trace" (*The Cultural Politics of Emotion* 14). The presences and absences shape each other. And so, more than anything you feel chilled: by the absences, the spaces of forgetting, the long historical silences.

Can national television ever be otherwise? According to Caruth, listening, or bearing witness, is a crucial component to the healing or integration of the wound: "the story of the way in which one's own trauma is tied up with the trauma of another, the way in which the trauma may lead, therefore, to the encounter with another, through the very possibility and surprise of listening to another's wound" (8).

Certainly, Canadian television is not monolithic, nor is it impervious to resistant readings. At certain points in this book I suggest that even the televisual act of representation has the possibility of being such a witnessing. Certain moments, be they comedic ruptures of *This Hour Has 22 Minutes* or the uncanny historical flashbacks in *North of 60*, provide a site for audiences to listen to a voice "it cannot fully know" (Caruth 9). Resistance and reparation are also machinic entities, which occur both within and outside of, but always in contact with, the media text.

But as we shall see in the following chapter, at certain moments of national trauma the nation reconstitutes itself through an affective racialized discourse. This discourse flows through television programming and between television and audience, deploying fantasies of belonging and registers of shame, pleasure, and pain.

Following Foucault, it is the discourse, rather than the surfaces of emergence themselves, that might provide the answer to my overarching question: Why did Canadian nationalism increasingly become an object of Canadian television in the mid-1990s? How did this era differ from other hyper-nationalist eras, such as for example the Trudeau years? What is affect's role in this resurgence of nationalism? Canada's media-ted relation to the 1996 sovereignty debate, and in particular the CBC's use of dramatic seriality, may provide some clues.

THREE

WHOSE CHILD AM I?
The Quebec Referendum and Languages of Affect and the Body

You cut the umbilical cord of a baby, it's a kind of separation, but one that brings new life.
—Quebec sovereigntist, interviewed on *The National*, October 23, 1995

It's like taking apart a piece of your heart—it's a piece of my country. I don't want to see it hurt.
—Canadian nationalist, interviewed on *The National*, October 27, 1995

Separation will be painless.
—Jacques Parizeau, *The National*, September 26, 1995

AS EARLY AS THE 1960S, McLuhan claimed that the electronic age would lead to the separation of Quebec. He argued that technology "would permit Quebec to leave the Canadian union in a way quite inconceivable under the regime of railways. The railways require a uniform political and economic space. On the other hand, airplane and radio permit the utmost discontinuity and diversity in spatial organization" (33).

McLuhan also, as I mentioned earlier, argued that electronic media have a more intimate connection with the body than print media and are in some ways extensions of our bodies. He described television as "the most recent and spectacular electric extension of our central nervous system" (317). Although Quebec never did quite separate, the televisual coverage of the 1995 referendum and the technologies, bodily metaphors, and affective practices that attended it bore out many of these earlier claims.

On October 30, 1995, residents of Quebec went to the polls for the second time (the first referendum was in 1980) to decide whether their province should separate from Canada to become a sovereign country.[1] In the run-up to this event, Canadian national media made a concerted effort to uphold a very particular narrative of an undivided nation—a narrative saturated with the feminine codes of melodrama. My examination of two years of CBC news programming about the referendum (news coverage, news documentaries, and special programs) reveals a recurring language of affect, punctuated with words and phrases such as "vulnerability," "tragedy," "anger," "hurt," "pain," and "healing." Generally, it is not just people who are described as having these feelings but the country itself, the nation become corporeal. I argue in this chapter that CBC news coverage of the referendum debate constituted an affective super-text that, with its narrative of heterosexual romance, operated in a fashion reminiscent of the emotion-laden dramatic serial,[2] making use of many of the codes of melodrama.

If, as Foucault contends, all systems of discipline and punishment are tied up in a "political economy of the body," one might also extend this to the narrative of rebellion and consequence that was the referendum debate: "It is always the body that is at issue—the body and its forces, their utility and docility, their distribution and submission" (Discipline and Punish 25). Indeed, it was at the moment of this so-called Unity Rally, five days before the referendum, that English Canada reasserted its colonial fantasy of managing a docile province of Quebec through the language of the body. Here too Quebec separatism emerged as a crucial object of Canadian nationalist discourse.

The narrative of the Quebec referendum relied heavily on the paradigm of a body in both psychic and physical pain. A variety of bodily metaphors— from birth to death by cancer—were discursively utilized, but it was the troubled heterosexual couple that became the overriding metaphor of Quebec's relationship to Canada. In relation to Quebec separatism Kim Sawchuk writes, "The language of pain ... not only humanized the [national] body, but it gave it an age, a gender, and a life in a traditional heterosexual family structure" (Sawchuk 98). Melodrama, then, as constitutive of a set of psychic determinations which take shape around the family (Nowell-Smith) was the ideal genre for this particular family drama.

My study of the Quebec referendum differs from that of Sawchuk and others by utilizing affect theory. The notion of affect as relational is particularly useful in analyzing moments of simultaneity like the televised reportage of the Quebec referendum. But affect theory also functions as a kind of corrective to theories of melodrama, moving beyond the primary text to extend consideration to audiences, bodies, and communities. Departing from psychoanalytic theory's more fixed notion of spectator as sutured by text, affect theory allows for different viewer responses to infect and transform one another, as well as for the potential for new subjectivities to emerge from this process.

News as Drama

News reportage has often been described as a dramatic, and even melodramatic, form. Derrida, for example, writes that news media become a kind of drama, with politicians playing characters: "mere silhouettes, if not marionettes, on the stage of televisual rhetoric. They were thought to be actors of politics, they now often risk, as everyone knows, being no more than TV actors" (*Spectres of Marx* 80).

If the news, in this formulation, becomes a national drama, its structure and placement evokes the television serial. Nick Browne argues that the serial is television's "paradigmatic form." He writes that it "orders and regulates television programming—from daily news and talk shows through the typical weekly sequencing of prime-time entertainment programs" (72–73). Historically, the serial was a way of doing away with sponsor-financed drama anthologies like CBC's *General Motors Presents* (1954–61). These were replaced with the more profitable system of selling advertising spots, which also gave networks more institutional and creative autonomy (Browne 73). Browne's point is that the text of the serial is a result of negotiation between advertiser, network, and audience.[3] CBC news is not, I argue, immune to these tropes, negotiating as it does between the axes of commercial interest and national identity. Writes Browne, "it is one of the traditional commitments of network programming to try and secure a loyal flow of audience attention through the prime-time hours, warding off potential defections through strategies of continuity" (77). Like any other genre of television, news programming is never a discrete unit. It exists, rather, as one of a series of texts whose unity is designed to attract an audience for the longest period of time possible. In other words, news coverage is also commodified by means of a serial structure—even, I would argue, under the aegis of a public network. The serial mode, then, demands that television be studied as an ongoing narrative that comprises many smaller open-ended units (Dumm).

The serial nature of CBC's coverage of the Quebec referendum served to narrativize national sentiment in the form of the romance genre, in a heavily coded language of embodied affect. As I noted earlier, romanticism is constitutive of nationalism.[4] Peter Brooks points out that romanticism and melodrama were, historically, closely linked, both evidence of a post-Enlightenment rise in the notion of individualism. This genre helped to reformulate the sacred in highly personal terms with simplified characters occupying moral binaries.

Melodrama, which emerged from early-nineteenth-century French theatre, has been theorized as a genre that, with its dualistic forces of good and evil, could stand in for the sacred in the modern age (Brooks, Gripsrud). Brooks has pointed out that melodrama was (and perhaps remains) more than a literary or theatrical genre: it was a way of being in the world, or what he called "the central fact of the modern sensibility" (21). Melodrama has been recuperated by feminist theory as a way to theorize the relationship between gender and genre (Walters). The soap opera, then, with its waves of emotion and affective responses of its audiences (Warhol), becomes another way to think about melodrama as a cultural force that makes central the feminized themes of family, excess, romance, and hysteria, and that also produces nodes of community and collective affect among its audiences.

In the case of the Quebec referendum, I argue that affect became a way of organizing bodies and minds at an extremely unstable moment in Canadian history. Thus, national sentiment, embodied on English television in a kind of melodramatic battle between the good of federation and the evil of separation (the good of Chrétien, the evil of Parizeau), then became narratively mobilized as a means of managing Quebec on behalf of English Canada.

Early Days

The coverage of the referendum debate began in earnest in February 1995, nine months before the actual referendum itself, echoing another bodily process, pregnancy. The gestation of the televisual debate began with the equilibrium (and whiteness) of Carnavale in Quebec City. Over footage of snow and dancing ice skaters, a voice-over said that the rumblings of the upcoming debate seemed at this point "somewhat faint" (*Sunday Report,* February 1995). Interviews with the usual suspects—doughnut-shop denizens, seniors, and the inhabitants of Main Street, Quebec—confirmed that while people's identification with or against sovereignty is "from the heart … it's still too early to get excited" (*CBC News,* February 5, 1995). Certainly this was a narrative arc in the making. This foreshadowing of a rising tide of emotion is characteristic of melodramatic narratives. As Warhol has pointed out in her study of soap opera, such narratives allow for a limited range of emotional affect to rise and fall in a regular pattern, resulting in an open-ended seriality that "keeps the pattern of affect constantly moving" (117).

The referendum discourse in Quebec triggered a parallel nationalist discourse in Canadian news media that was to change the tone and syntax of representations of Canadian nationalism for the decade to come. On February 5, the anniversary of the current Canadian flag, a special episode of *The National* showed images of flag-waving children, a flag cake, and the designer of the flag—conveniently, a Québécois by birth—pointedly intercut with sovereigntist billboards in Montreal. "Ironically," said host Pamela Wallin (with no sense of irony at all), "the Canadian flag has emerged as the principal symbol of the campaign to keep Quebec in the country." Paul Henderson, who famously scored the winning goal in the 1972 Canada–Russia hockey series, was moved to say: "We need to become flag-wavers. I think it would bring us together" (*The Magazine*, February 15, 1995). As many scholars have noted, a relationship exists between sentiment and national identity, and the state's role in managing emotion to evoke patriotism.

Questions of race and gender produced disequilibrium within this narrative early on, providing regular crises true to melodramatic form. Eva Mackey, following on the heels of British race theory, has pointed out that the Canadian national project differs from that of Britain by disguising racism not as homogenous (read: white) nationalism but as multicultural nationalism. The Quebec referendum debate, however, leaned heavily on what British intellectuals have dubbed the "new racism," in which national culture and its enactments of patriotism are *implicitly* white. Keohane has described the project of Quebec separatism as being similar to that of right-wing racist projects like the Reform Party and the Heritage Front: "These projects seek to solve the problem of the diversity and multiplicity of Canadian identities by categorically identifying and demarcating a singular centre and systematically excluding elements that do not fit that category" (7).

In a foreshadowing of the race scandal that was to become the downfall of the Parti Québécois, Lucien Bouchard, the Quebec premier and leader of the referendum campaign, appeared on CBC and said, "Do you think it makes sense to have so few children in Quebec? We are one of the white races that has the fewest children" (*CBC Special Report*, October 17, 1995). Astonishingly, the CBC completely ignored the racial implications of this remark, allowing critiques of sexism, but not racism, to surface. Bouchard was later shown on television reconciling with a feminist leader of the Yes (sovereigntist) campaign. As often happens when race relations are at issue on Canadian television, it was women (and "women's issues") that became the bearers of discourse regarding inequality, obscuring the race issue yet again.[5]

Race came up again on CBC television, if briefly, when the Cree of Quebec held their own referendum, one week before the Quebec referendum. The Cree vote resulted in an overwhelming No victory. This story was buried in larger stories about the economic uncertainties of Quebec separation, making literal Prasenjit Duara's notion of the "hidden other" that works productively to destabilize the nation at the same time that its otherness is crucial to the *relational* identity of nationalism ("Historicizing National Identity" 164). Hiddenness and unspeakability are also characteristic of the melodramatic mode. If, in melodrama, taboos are broken at all, the information comes too late and cannot, like the Cree referendum or Parizeau's revealing post-referendum utterances, be made use of (Cvetkovich).

Seriality, Soaps and Melodrama

The titles of the CBC "special reports," magazine shows, and mini-documentaries, as well as the music and lead-ins that went with them, evoked notions of seriality, soap-opera-style. Indeed, television theorist Glen Creeber's description of seriality could well describe CBC's referendum coverage: "Like the soap opera, the series reoccurs regularly throughout the schedule, weaving in and out of the domestic space…. Simply in terms of hours alone the series can produce a breadth of vision, a narrative scope and can capture the audience's involvement in a way equaled by few contemporary media" (441).

If the etymology of melodrama is the Latin melos (music) and "drama," a genre in which music marks moments of excessive affect (Nowell-Smith), then the violin strains accompanying the introductory programs about the referendum, overlaid with sound bytes of different political actors in the debate (intercut with a Parliament Hill Peace Tower splitting in two) presented the emotional terms of the family romance that was about to unfold. Peter Brooks develops the relation of music and narrative further: "The emotional drama needs the desemanticized language of music, its evocation of the 'ineffable,' its tones and registers … called upon to invest plot with some of the inexorability and necessity that in pre-modern literature derived from the substratum of myth" (14). Melodramatic music, so characteristic of the soap opera, signals passion, pleasure in excess, and the operatic registers of emotional expressivity. Within the soap's narrative structure, it is the family that provides the raison d'être of such musically accompanied affect.

In Freudian terms, the "family romance" is an imaginary scenario played out by a child regarding her paternity, in which she asks, "Whose child am I?" (Freud, "Mourning and Melancholia"). Questions of paternity are prevalent in the plots of Western melodrama and especially within soap opera. These questions set the stage for the enactment of bourgeois familial concerns: property ownership, inheritance, lineage, and crises of masculinity. Within melodrama, the family is a kind of fortress constantly besieged by infidelity, alcoholism, and other social ills. Separation—of husband from wife, child from father—is the great evil of melodrama, the wellspring of all tragedy, and the antithesis of community and family, which is always melodrama's unfulfilled desire. Women, usually charged with the responsibility of holding the fortress together, were later to become a predominant theme in the referendum's own family romance.

Federalist politicians repeatedly used the spectre of family dissolution as an emotive hook. In an eleventh-hour address to the nation, Prime Minister Jean Chrétien was pictured in his office between two sets of photos: that of his wife on the left and a grouping of family snapshots on the right. In the middle, visually holding the two ends of the family together, was Chrétien himself. Leaning forward slightly, and speaking in a low, intimate voice, he asked: "Do you really think that you and your family will have a quality of life and a better future in a separate Quebec?" In the same news program, New Brunswick premier Frank McKenna was reported as saying, "It's a time for all Canadians … to show their affection for their brothers and sisters in Quebec" (*The National*, October 25, 1995). Subsequent television coverage echoed this trope, as when CBC reporter Hana Gartner blurted out on referendum night, "Clearly, we are a dysfunctional family."

A poll conducted by the CBC in the spring of 1995 presented a 60–40 split between those who opposed and those who supported Quebec's separation. Subsequent polls revealed that women of Quebec formed the largest number of undecided voters. Suddenly, the province of Quebec had a gender: female. This only served to underline Quebec's feminization as a vulnerable and possibly expendable member of the federation. As CBC's Mark Kelley reported: "The province is ready to decide—but *she* can't. *She's* not alone. Ten per cent of Quebec women—twice that of men—can't decide either" (*The National Special Report*, CBC, September 16, 1995; italics mine). The gendered corporeality of the campaign had begun in earnest.

Gendered and Racialized Corporeality

Eight months into CBC coverage of the referendum debate, anxiety was at its height—to be expected, presumably, in the month preceding birth. This produced a kind of uncanniness: news coverage began to mimic actual plays and

TV shows; love stories and romantic tragedies were narrated again and again. In Freudian terms, this uncanniness meant that these familiar genres and tropes framed a narrative that was frighteningly foreboding. A special report on the female vote was titled *The Women*, as though it were a play. In it, the first of many anglo–franco romances was featured in a round table of women voters hosted by Hana Gartner. One woman said, "I fell in love with a Quebecer and then with Quebec." Another, a francophone married to an anglophone, declared her intention to vote No (*The Women*).[6]

Not long after this feature, Gartner introduced an even more pointedly narrativized news documentary called *All in the Family*, an intertextual reference to the 1970s TV sitcom of the same name, about a bigoted blue-collar worker, Archie Bunker, and his dysfunctional family. The CBC documentary, about a biracial (white and South Asian) family on different sides of the debate, began with Gartner's voice-over: "All in the family: the father's voting Yes, the mother's voting No, and the daughter has to make up her mind. The story of one woman caught between the two solitudes at home."[7] *All in the Family* repeatedly expressed anxieties concerning miscegenation through the marriage of Archie's blond daughter Gloria to Polish-American Mike, whom Archie referred to as "Polak" and "meathead." Similarly, the CBC TV documentary serial evoked not the two solitudes of French and English but of French and allophone—as well as fears, expressed earlier by Bouchard, about the declining numbers of white Quebecers.

Francine Pelletier, a well-known journalist, hosted the three-episode program. With her mention of the long-running Québécois TV series *La Famille Plouffe*, she made yet another intertextual reference to television seriality. In the clip that followed, M. Plouffe was shown as saying, "I'm beginning to get tired of Canada." Running from 1954 to 1959, that hugely popular (in Quebec) program attempted to bridge the English–French cultural divide by spawning an English-language version, *The Plouffe Family*. As Ira Levin writes, the spinoff "provided "English-speaking audiences with a French-Canadian family they could care about, in a limited sort of way" (136).[8]

In the CBC documentary, Monsieur Gauthier, a sovereigntist, stands in for Plouffe *père*, while, according to Pelletier, "Mama Gauthier is a new Canadian and just as fervent a federalist." Cut to Madame Gauthier, who says, "When I see all the problems all over the world I think Canada is the best country in the world" (2002).[9] Archie to Mme Gauthier's Edith, M Gauthier says (in French), "We want complete control of our economy, of our culture.... We want to be sovereign master in our own home" (*All in the Family*).

The Gauthier's daughter, twenty-four-year-old mixed-race Natasha, is, like Gloria Bunker, caught in between: between races and thus between nations. She is, as Pelletier reports with pointedly affective language, "neither in love with Canada nor with a sovereign Quebec." Pelletier painfully extends the narrative of heterosexual romance, turning the Gauthier couple into a convenient, if racially and emotively over-determined, metaphor for Quebec:

> PELLETIER (TO MME GAUTHIER): But you're not about to divorce, are you?
> MME GAUTHIER: No, we've been married twenty-six years.
> PELLETIER: You'll still be sleeping with your husband after the referendum.
> GAUTHIER: Yes!

Natasha, the daughter, seems confident, hip, politicized. Her strong sense of herself as a Québécoise represents both excess and lack. As a woman of colour she lacks the ability to reproduce the white race in Quebec; as a self-determined allophone Québécoise she exceeds the sovereigntist expectations of allophones in Quebec.

While people of colour and immigrants were presented on English-language television as tangential to the referendum's outcome (sitcoms to the referendum's drama), their significance was enormous, both in terms of votes and in the ways in which Quebec politicans' fear of otherness became vocalized. In the final weeks of the referendum debate, racism was to become visible in Quebec as never before—in Duara's terms, productively destabilizing the sovereigntist agenda ("Historicizing National Identity").

"Quebec on t'aime": The Final Week

A kind of hysteria pervaded the last week of the referendum. The word "danger" was used repeatedly by reporters and anchors, the danger of economic consequences being paramount. Descriptions of panic and hysteria also figured in news reports. And the language of romance, presented as an affective solution to this political and economic crisis, was only to increase in the days leading up to the referendum.

In an extended CBC newscast on September 27, 1995, the word "emotion" was used a dozen times in one hour, and an improbable lexicon of intimate words such as "hurt," "desperation," and "love" came up repeatedly. CBC reporter Paul Adams introduced a story about a No rally in Montreal with the following words: "For many of the thousands who came here from outside Quebec it was an emotional journey" (*The National*, September 27, 1995). Cut to a middle-aged white woman attending the rally, flanked by federalists of all ages. The woman says, for all the world like a spurned lover, "It's like taking a part a piece of your heart—it's a piece of my country. I don't want to see it hurt." Cut to an enormous Canadian flag floating on a sea of people chanting "Canada! Canada! (in French, no less, with the accent on the last syllable). Cut to some young men with a homemade sign saying "Quebec on t'aime—BC" (Quebec, we love you—BC). Never had patriotism been taken up so ardently by this postwar, post-70s generation of white anglos. Nationalism was suddenly a corporeal matter of life, death and breath. As Marvin and Ingle write,

> Ritual elements are expressed in bodily terms.... As the referendum for Quebec independence approached, a newspaper headline proclaimed, 'Canada holds its breath as Quebec votes.' ... Ritual is creative; it seeks the unity of form and substance, which is embodiment. Thus, media are ritually driven to offer the illusion of bodily presence restored. (142–43)

As the language of the body increased to almost comedic heights, PQ leader Lucien Bouchard's body became more visually prominent. Bouchard has walked with a cane and a slight limp since he lost a leg to flesh-eating disease. His disability, usually tactfully ignored, was mentioned repeatedly in the last days of the referendum campaign. One CBC report described a consequence of Bouchard's battle with the disease: "Because of his charisma, because of his brush with death last year, Lucien Bouchard has been elevated into the status of a living martyr." Accompanying this voice-over was a waist-down shot of Bouchard, with cane, limping (*The National*, September 27, 1995). But it was on September 29 and 30, Referendum Eve and Night, respectively, that metaphors of ill bodies took over the speech acts of sovereigntists and federalists alike.

Referendum Night

> KEN DRYDEN, LAWYER: I haven't been feeling very good this week. It's like I have a hole in my stomach and it won't go away.... I want one Canada for me because I hate the hole I feel. Maybe you feel that hole too.
> MANSBRIDGE (AS YES VOTE EDGES UP TO 58.9%): There are a lot of stomachs nervous in a lot of different parts of the country and a lot of different parts of this province. (*The National*, October 30, 1995)

Candlelight vigils. Rallies across the country in support of the No side. Another squabbling couple ("she's for No, he's for Oui"). And a divorced couple, Peter Mansbridge and Wendy Mesley, anchoring the special October 29 and 30 coverage of the referendum.

The lead-in to CBC's October 30 special news program looked like a low-budget film trailer. As the hands of a clock appeared over a Canadian flag, Mansbridge's voice begins the introduction: "Thirty minutes before the ballot-counting begins. We know the stakes. We've heard the voices of the politicians." Over a shot of Quebec flags, Parizeau's voice was heard: "I think we'll have a country pretty soon." A man waving a Canadian flag, then a dissolve to a fleur-de-lys in the top half of a horizontal split-screen, a No rally in the bottom half. Chrétien in voice-over: "We have every reason to be extremely proud to be Canadian." More voices and images, and the sequence ends with the clock superimposed against a Canadian and a Quebec flag, and again Mansbridge's voice: "In thirty minutes we hear the voice of the people. Will it be yes or no?"

In the interest of full disclosure, I admit that when reviewing archival footage of referendum night I was no detached observer, even eight years after the fact. Like the audience for a melodrama whose genre I knew well, my heart was in my throat—to use another bodily metaphor. Though I knew how the story would end, I nonetheless wiped away a tear when the vote reached 50–50 and then again when the No side won by the slimmest of margins: 50.6 per cent to 49.4 per cent. Like anyone returning to the site of trauma, I wasn't crying for the lost object; I was crying for myself, for the memory of the intensities at the original scene.

As voting began in northern Quebec, a vertical line appeared on the bottom half of the screen: blue for Yes on one side, red for No on the other. The first poll to be counted was in Ungava, where the split was 50.5 per cent Yes, 49.5 per cent No. That almost equally divided red–blue line was hardly to change all night.

> MANSBRIDGE: Nervous? A little bit edgy? Well, you are not alone. The Yes side, the No side, all Quebecers and all Canadians are nervous …

As the evening wore on, newscasters worked hard to fill airtime, allowing for plenty of slippage and peculiar speech acts.[10]

> HANA GARTNER: I'm watching your blood pressure go up, Brian Tobin!
> TOBIN: I'm feeling not cocky but confident …
> GARTNER: Earlier, you were about to lose your dinner! (CBC round-table discussion, October 30, 1995)

Following Foucault, the body is a capillary of power; power flows into individual bodies affecting gesture, posture, utterance (*Discipline and Punish*). In these terms, the language of the demasculinized, romantic, pathological body (Quebec) flows back into the economic power relations of Canadian nationalism. This heterosexualized and feminized (and occasionally disabled) subaltern body is the one which the discourse of nationalism serves to preserve—but in a benevolent colonial fashion.

Massumi speaks of "a complex flow of collective desire" in which certain bodies stand in for certain images" (qtd. in Sawchuk 103). These are something different from unknowing Cartesian bodies.[11] These bodies know, to paraphrase Bannerji, the dark side of the nation. Some of them know it intimately; others know it from afar.

That night, Parizeau said, famously and bitterly, to a reporter, "We were beaten by money and the ethnic vote" (*The National*, September 30, 1995).

The Racialized Other

Mansbridge: Good evening. Canada is still here tonight—but just barely. (*The National*, October 30, 1995)

After the referendum and its aftermath disappeared from the television screen, I resigned myself to becoming a resident of English Canada in that most anglo of Canadian provinces, *British* Columbia. I had moved to Vancouver from Montreal mere months before the referendum. I traded the decadent *patisseries* of the rue Saint-Denis for the prosaic coffee bars of Commercial Drive; I went from being proudly allophone to shamefully "ethnic." Nonetheless, I still used French expressions in my speech; the message on my voice mail was still dutifully *bilingue*. I still had a vote (which I never made use of); as the vote reached the 50–50 mark on referendum night, I joked, in yet another corporeal metaphor, that the future of the country rested on my shoulders. I was, however, relieved that Quebec hadn't separated—not because I supported federalism but because, five years after Oka, I did not support the racism that seemed to be constitutive of the sovereigntist project.

Using the 1991 Mohawk standoff at Oka as a vivid example of Quebec's racism, social critic Himani Bannerji argues that racist incidents such as Parizeau's awkward utterances are used by English Canada to obscure its own racist project (Bannerji, *The Dark Side of the Nation*, 92). This might help to explain why the discursive legacy of the Quebec referendum debate has *not* been a more critical approach to the ideology of nationhood. It was, I would argue, quite the opposite: an increase in racially overdetermined ideas of the nation, underpinned by melodramatic calls to patriotic excess and the moral binaries of the genre.

WHOSE CHILD AM I?

CBC News was quick to adopt this trope. Reporter Tom Kennedy had this to say about Parizeau's comment, over footage of Parizeau chanting "Vive le Québec," followed by a shot of a young woman of colour looking dismayed: "If anyone expected healing words after such a divisive campaign, they didn't get it. Jacques Parizeau took aim right away at Quebec's minorities, who voted massively to stay in Canada" (*The National,* October 30, 1995).

Over reportage of Parizeau's comment and the fallout that ensued, there was a frequent and curious repetition of a particular image from Referendum Night: a South Asian man with a No sticker on his forehead, embracing a Canadian flag. People of colour, formerly bit players in the televised referendum serial, were marshalled back into the drama. According to Foucault, normalizing regimes such as federalism encourage conformity but also individualize each member by enabling precise classifications—in this case, measurable degrees of racial deviation from the norm (*The History of Sexuality,* Vol. 1).

Natasha Gauthier, the No-voting, mixed-race daughter of the present-day Plouffes, was pulled into the CBC studios and asked her opinion of Parizeau's comment. "It made my hair stand on end," she said. "I think it was a very unastute thing for him to say" (*The National,* October 31, 1995). In one of the most insightful commentaries I'd heard in weeks, *fille* Gauthier went on to say: "We'll have to see what the backlash does to the allophone and the anglophone communities, especially since Parizeau has singled them out." She recounted a conversation at a Yes party where someone said that if the No side won, a law should be passed like one in Belgium by which immigrants can't vote until the third generation. Said Gauthier: "He actually said that. People were going, 'Yeah, yeah, that's a good idea.' So you can't say that what Parizeau said was out of the blue and that it didn't reflect what Quebecers feel!"

In the days after Referendum Night, pain diminished to hurt—hurt being, as Sawchuk has pointed out, an indication that someone is responsible for the pain (104). On October 31, CBC's *The National* reported that Parizeau had resigned. Commented Mansbridge: "In defeat he had said words that *hurt.*" On November 13, 1995, when it became clear that Parizeau would not apologize, Mansbridge reported: "The Parti Québécois tried to reach out to the people the premier may have hurt." This somewhat less painful affect referred to racism, rather than separation.

National Time

We are "national" when we vote, watch the six o'clock news, follow the national sport, observe (while barely noticing) the repeated iconographies of landscape and history in TV commercials.
—Eley and Suny, *Becoming National* 29

According to implicit assumptions held by the CBC during its coverage of the referendum debate, Quebecers and Canadians did have one thing very much in common: a shared belief in the viability of nationhood. That this is a contested notion, both academically and historically, was never once broached in CBC coverage. Not once did I see anyone questioning the *idea* of sovereignty, be it that of Quebec or of Canada. Indeed, it seemed that affect was utilized in almost identical ways on both sides, as a way of naturalizing the imagined community of nation, and providing it with unquestionable stature. Sawchuk argues that federalists and sovereigntists had much in common: "Both sides understood their own position as real, but temporarily delegitimated, and the position of the other as inherently false or 'manifestly fictitious'. Both deploy the image of the human body 'to substantiate' or to lend an air of 'reality' to a shaky ideology" (99).

This ideological doubling brought these national bodies back together in a paradoxical manner. Lutz, following Neale, posits that melodrama insists upon both the imagined powerlessness and the imagined agency of the viewer: "The resolution of melodrama is always in important ways 'too late' for the characters.... our mourning for lost possibility and our demand for continued possibility combine to elicit tears" (200–1).

CBC responded to melodrama's demand for a continuous narrative for as long as it possibly could. A serial approach to the dilemma of a divided country continued well into the 1996 season. A March 1996 serial entitled *Remaking Canada* aired over several weeks and utilized some of the strategies of reality TV: "Twenty-five Canadians have seventy-two hours to remake Canada.... Tomorrow at 10." But by the end of 1996 the referendum debate had more or less faded from view in national media, thus fulfilling the imperative of serial melodrama. This fading away can also be seen as a kind of legitimation. As Roger Silverstone argues, "The gradual withdrawal of the reporting of the event into the regular news programmes is, once again, evidence of its incorporation into the familiar and hopeful, distancing and denying structures of the daily schedule" (17). The event of the Quebec referendum, integrated back into the TV routine, changed in meaning, then, from a traumatic rupture in the fabric of nationhood to historic proof of the nation's cohesiveness.

Neil Bissondath (a federalist South Asian Canadian writer who frequently appears as a CBC commentator), said during an interview: "I got for the first time in a long time the idea that Canadians were beginning to discover the possibilities of their own power. For the first time in my memory there was a huge and massive gathering of what we like to call ordinary Canadians all coming together to save their country for the first time taking the agenda away from the politicians ... so there's hope" (*The National*, November 2, 1995).

Here Bissoondath is referring to September's No Rally, held in Montreal. What Bissoondath fails to mention is that this rally was funded, produced, and staged by the federal Liberal Party. While Bissoondath here perpetuates a kind of fantasy narrative of a unifying nationalist community, Keohane asserts that it is, rather, antagonism—in this case, the antagonism of competing political parties—that continually reconstitutes the notion of Canadian unity (8).

Institutions, television among them, attempt to insert us into what Cathy Caruth calls "national time": the ebb and flow of commercialized festivals and national holidays. But this marking actually performs an erasure: "The arrival into national history ... erases not only her past but other nations as well" (33). The serial nature of CBC's referendum coverage ensured that this was an event that could be ordered into thirty-minute documentary "magazine" segments, some of which—the sequence on the Gauthier family in particular—ran as miniseries. Like audiences watching other miniseries, whether *Survivor* or *Canada: A People's History*, the intimacy and continuity of the format allowed the coverage to become embedded in the daily conversations, gestures, and habits of its viewers.

As Foucault has pointed out, the body too is temporal. Normalization is rooted in the concept of a temporal body. This body—one that rises, works, and rests at certain hours—is therefore more naturally suited to institutional regimes and, as such, to national time (*Discipline and Punish*). The respectively male and female bodies of Canada and Quebec became a machinic entity, connected to, and becoming, part of a national television schedule and thus of a national imaginary.

Ann Cvetkovich suggests, as have others (Berlant, Grossberg), that affect, with its passionate feelings located in the body, often stands in for social problems (156). The racialized nature of both sides of the Quebec referendum, and the (largely unmentionable) white-supremacist project of separatist leaders Bouchard and Parizeau, produced a provocative and unsettling emotional landscape, one in which hurt, pain, and disease were repetitively evoked. But as Berlant proposes, "the authenticity of overwhelming pain that can be textually performed and shared is disseminated as a prophylactic against the reproduction of a shocking and numbing mass violence" (qtd. in Cvetkovich 157). Perhaps, then, it was melodrama itself that "saved" the country from separation, in its constant deferral of an authentic struggle to do with race and nation. The feelings expressed so viscerally by both people on both sides of the debate may or may not have been authentic in and of themselves. Certainly contagion, governmentality, and mediality played their part. Certainly there were those, myself included, who experienced a range of real feelings: from grief, to pleasure, to excitement, to shame. In terms of televisual affect, however, racialized modes of nationalism became the way in which English and French Canada become conjoined—it's one thing they have in common. Canada was at risk of disappearing ("barely there") without its other: Quebec. But the final, almost-tied outcome ensured that the open-ended seriality of Canada–Quebec relations, as seen on TV, would endure.

FOUR

HAUNTED ABSENCES
Reading *Canada: A People's History*

All formations of memory carry implicit and/or explicit assumptions about what is to be remembered, how, by whom, for whom, and with what potential effects. In this sense, remembrance/pedagogies are political, pragmatic, and performative attempts to prompt and engage people in the development of particular forms of historical consciousness.
—Roger Simon, Sharon Rosenberg, Claudia Eppert, *Between Hope and Despair*

I ONCE SHOWED STUDENTS an excerpt from a 1996 CBC special, *Who Is a Real Canadian?*, a televised "town hall" debate about official multicultural policy in Canada programmed in the wake of the Quebec referendum of October 1995.[1] The debate had the predictably "balanced" mix of brown and white faces on the panel, with a carefully arranged wallpaper of TV audience faces behind them—white faces behind a brown face and vice versa.

I played the commercials for the students too. The commercials were highly racialized, while the CBC program was, perhaps, merely biased (I particularly wanted them to notice an Air Canada ad featuring rows of Japanese women in kimonos waving to the camera). But it was a bland Home Hardware ad that provoked the most interesting comment of the day. The ad featured two white people—a salesperson and a customer—engaged in happy banter about the paint selection at Home Hardware: "A rainbow of colours!," the lady salesperson shrilly exclaimed. As one student (Sargie Kaler) pointed out, it was in this ad that ideas about home—and, by extension, nation—were spelled out in a manner far more explicit than the complex ideological tennis match going on in the CBC town-hall debate. "Home" was awash with white faces and coloured walls. My student observed that the rainbow of colours would be applied by the white people—and just as easily removed.

Goods and services advertised in commercials circulate on a symbolic level throughout the super-text of the television schedule, allowing narrative pleasures that news programs on their own cannot fully provide (Browne). In this way, flow between ad and program is maintained, so that the ad becomes something more than an interruption. The Home Hardware ad addresses the "lack" in the question "Who is a real Canadian?," a question that can never really fulfill its desire to define the "real" of Canadian identity. Home renovation is a symbolic answer to the "lack" of racism and its threat to original (national) unity.

In this chapter, by way of an examination of episode one of the serial *Canada: A People's History* (CBC, 2000–1) as well as episodes from *A Scattering of Seeds* (Knowledge Network, 1997), *This Hour Has 22 Minutes* (CBC, 1996–) and *North of Sixty* (CBC, 1991–98), I note the ways in which Canadian television continues, post-referendum, to practise these forms of narrative rupture and closure, exclusion and inclusion. I attempt to analyze the workings of historical memory in its performative intersection with a Canadian national imaginary. Performative acts, writes Judith Butler, "are forms of authoritative speech: most performatives for instance are statements that, in the uttering, also perform a certain action and exercise a binding power.... Performatives tend to include legal sentences, baptisms, inaugurations, declarations of ownership.... (*Bodies That Matter* 225). Performativity, then, can be seen as the repetition of certain gestures to produce normalcy. Rather than looking at what certain words mean within nationalist narratives I am looking at the repetitive production, or performance, of certain utterances and tropes. I am also interested in the overlaps between certain theories: performativity, melancholia, and acting out. These modes have an inverse relationship to ethics, for, as LaCapra writes, "to the extent that someone is possessed by the past and acting out a repetition compulsion, he or she may be incapable of ethically responsible behavior" (*Writing History, Writing Trauma* 70).

Ghosts in the Narrative

Benedict Anderson's formulation of nation as an enacted space comprising roles and relationships of belonging and foreignness is now an academic truism (*Imagined Communities*). But his reference to space is worth pondering. In the past decade, the borders between Canada and Quebec and between Canada and the US have become increasingly porous. National space in this new world order is, then, perhaps not only enacted but also *acted out*, in the sense of a compulsive response to trauma and lack. This national space is always marked by absence: an absence haunted by the ghosts of history.

For Derrida, ethics and responsibility begin with the ghost. In spectral presences—traces, fleeting images—Derrida sees something that will always return. The ghost "begins by coming back" (*Spectres of Marx*, 11). The past, which returns to the future in the figure of the ghost, must inform the ethical responsibilities of the present. This ghost is not just history but also otherness—the other within ourselves, but also, I would argue, the other within the nation.

National memory is always selective, as much about forgetting as remembering; memory as performance, memory as interpretation. "Technologies of memory" (Hirsch and Smith 7) help us to feel part of a group, or of a nation. Here I look at several "technologies of memory," including Canadian television programs that have appeared on Canadian television since 1995. In doing so I examine trauma, genre, and repetition as they relate to the media representation of these issues. As Stephen Neale writes: "Genres … provide a means of regulating memory and expectations, a means of containing the possibilities of reading. Overall, they offer the industry a means of controlling demand, and the institution a means of containing coherently the effects that its products produce" (55).

In a similar way, there is a certain genre of immigrant narrative that repeats itself on Canadian television and seems to follow a religious format: confession followed by absolution; a cataloguing of shameful historical episodes in which the "victims" of these episodes are compelled to confess, followed by redemptive endings in which the victims realize they are better off than ever. One example of this is *A Scattering of Seeds*, a fifty-two-part independently produced made-for-television series that, according to its website, "celebrates the contribution of immigrants to Canada." The series description on the website itself is particularly instructive: "By personalizing the stories of immigrants, *A Scattering of Seeds* makes *the stranger immediately familiar* and the beginnings of this country, a shared experience" (*A Scattering of Seeds* official website, "About the Series"; italics mine). According to Ahmed, the stranger can *never* be made familiar, and instead must always function as a marker of boundary maintenance. The shared experience of nation relies on the fact of the stranger (*Strange Encounters* 22).

I briefly address one episode of *A Scattering of Seeds*, in particular "The Fullness of Time: Ukrainian Stories from Alberta," directed by Ukrainian-Canadian TV and film director Halja Kuchmij. Each episode of *A Scattering of Seeds* begins with a superimposition of a silhouetted (immigrant?) farmer sowing seeds against a black-and-white photograph of immigrants in ethnic costume. An accented voice recites the pledge of Canadian citizenship: obedience and governmentality are signified, situating the immigrant, as I have argued earlier, in an infantilizing system of tutelage.

This episode focuses on a Ukrainian immigrant named Harvey Spak as he recounts the life of his Ukrainian immigrant grandfather. Alexander Spak was run over by a train while taking a load of grain to town in a horse-drawn cart. The moral impact of the story hinges on the fact that Alexander died because, heroically, he wanted to save his horses. As Harvey has noted earlier in the episode, "life was tough ... food was scarce ... winter clothing was hard to come by." The stranger, less valued than livestock, has been erased by means of a naturalized social context in which the lack of farm aid, relief, and decent medical services for poor and isolated immigrants are not addressed. This tale of immigrant hardship and death concludes with the following monologue, overlaid with slow mandolin music, and spoken over montaged shots of a graveyard, a Ukrainian community dinner, and a prairie summer landscape:

> Despite hardship and tragedy, Canada was the promised land to the Ukrainian immigrants of my grandfather's generation. Its new frontier and freedom offered more than the uncertainty they had left behind in Ukraine. Their descendants flourished in a new land and became passionate Canadians, offering their spirit and vision to Canada, contributing to its greatness. [Fade out]

The tragic expulsion of the immigrant, whether by death, internment, or deportation, somehow becomes justification of Canada's greatness, because, as Ahmed has pointed out, that expulsion constitutes the nation, and must therefore always be represented in particular and specific ways (*Strange Encounters*).[2] The image of an unnecessary immigrant death, juxtaposed against a patriotic voice-over, is resignified as a necessary element of nation-building. One could also argue that individual trauma (death by train collision) here stands in for historical trauma; nowhere in Harvey Spak's story is mention made of the Canadian internment camps that imprisoned thousands of Ukrainians of his grandfather's generation.

This particular genre of immigrant narrative draws from the late-nineteenth-century novel with its racialized subtexts that ultimately provide proof of the superiority of the West (and, in this case, the North as well). Mackey traces this notion back to the ideas of the Canada First Movement, a nineteenth-century nationalist movement that sought to prevent Canada's assimilation with the US by promoting ideas of northern superiority and masculinity, in contrast to a South (the US) that was seen as inferior (30). This narrative may also bear the marks of such narrative tropes as the Horatio Alger story.[3] As such, this genre of immigrant narrative contains a strict knowledge–power relation. Following Foucault, it is not only that every description is somewhat "biased" but that the very terms used to describe something reflect power relations. Confession, no longer coerced, and occurring in a multitude of everyday situations, implicates the subject within a state power that both individualizes and homogenizes (*The History of Sexuality*).

Such immigrant narratives seek to reaffirm, as Mackey has pointed out, an idea that Canada has about itself: its "long history of benevolent forms of justice and tolerance" (77). As Sedef Arat-Koc has pointed out, tolerance is not the same thing as acceptance. And those who are tolerated are those who display gratitude. Ghassan Hage uses spatial terms to describe this process, in which tolerant nationalists see themselves as masters of national space, with immigrants or racial others as kinds of moveable objects within this space (*White Nation* 28). An inability to master national space is experienced by the nationalist as trauma, or loss.

In the case of Canadian history, I am speaking of a double-sided loss: the loss of a fantasy of a cohesive national imaginary juxtaposed with the actual loss of dignity, hope, and life for those who have suffered from the racism and xenophobia embedded in Canadian culture. Both ideas of loss are connected. Deborah Britzman writes about "the importance of working through both kinds of loss: the loss of the idea of the social bond and the loss of actual individuals. These losses must be considered as intimately intertwined" (33).

What happens when neither loss is explicitly acknowledged?

A People's History: Acting Out versus Working Through

Canada: A People's History (*CPH*) is a big-budget, sixteen-part historical series produced by the CBC in both official languages that premiered in October 2000 and continued into the 2001–2 season. The series had several spinoff products: children's books, CD-ROMs, and a documentary and book on the making of the series (Dick). In writing about how the program came about, producer Mark Starowicz describes coming home on the train from Montreal, where, with his daughter, he had witnessed the 1995 Quebec referendum first-hand. Wanting to give his daughter some historical idea of Canada in the wake of the near-dissolution of the federation, he suddenly had the idea for the series (*Making History*).

CPH was expensively promoted as the "real thing": an unflinchingly direct telling of Canadian history that claims to include the long-ignored ontology of the other. It offered, supposedly, a uniquely unbiased approach, written after highly touted consultations with scholars, activists, and historians of every stripe; indeed, its very title invokes a popular, collective Truth. Unlike the aforementioned episode of *A Scattering of Seeds*, more recent productions such as *CPH* don't, any more, exclude mention of traumatic historical events (as opposed to individual traumas). As Eva Mackey writes, "Aboriginal people are necessary players in nationalist myths: they are the colourful recipients of benevolence, the necessary 'others' who reflect back white Canada's self-image of tolerance" (2).

However, I argue that, following Freud, the shame, regret, or guilt these passing mentions represent are more constitutive of a collective melancholia, like the ego's idealization of the lost object, rather than actual mourning, where loss is actually integrated into the ego's—or the nation's—sense of self. Freud wrote: "Mourning is regularly the reaction to the loss of a loved person, or to the loss of some abstraction which has taken the place of one, such as one's country, liberty, an ideal, and so on" (243). Mourning, then, is conscious, while within melancholia "one cannot see clearly what it is that has been lost" (245). Here, loss becomes conflated with absence, like the absent presence of Ukrainian internment camps within narratives such as "The Fullness of Time."

LaCapra builds upon Freud's essay by extending his notions of mourning and melancholia to the collective process of nation-building. He creates a useful and pragmatic distinction by redefining melancholia as a form of "acting out" and mourning as "working through" (*Writing History* 65). Echoing Silverman, he describes how the acting-out process involves a repetitive performativity wherein "the past is performatively regenerated or relived as if it were fully present rather than represented in memory and inscription, and it hauntingly returns as the repressed" (*Writing History* 70).

Canada: A People's History is a historical costume drama, albeit heavily influenced by the tropes of both melodrama and documentary. Melodrama's primary characteristics—heightened dramatization, binaries of good and evil, explicit use of music and voice to mark moments of affect, and its repetitive form—make it well suited to the excesses of the melancholic acting-out mode. Peter Brooks writes: "melodrama at heart represents the theatrical impulse itself: the impulse toward dramatization, heightening expression, *acting out*" (xi; italics mine). Indeed, as we have seen in such national traumas as the Quebec referendum debate, the overflow of media information that seems to accompany national traumas seems to correlate with what Brooks has described as melodrama's "desire to express all.… Nothing is spared because nothing is left unsaid" (4).

CPH clearly makes use of dramatic elements—actors, costumes, sets—but its creators speak repeatedly of having created a documentary. This gesturing to the documentary genre is significant because documentary claims to represent a peculiar mix of reason and emotion. Peter Hamilton quotes various 1930s and 40s documentary photographers who attested to this dual function. He cites Edward Steichen: "a feeling of a living experience you won't forget"; and he cites Roy Stryker: "it must … tell the audience what it would feel like to be an actual witness" (83). Documentary's humanist project gives us ways of feeling national, as in Roland Barthes' classic example of a *Paris-Match* magazine-cover image of a Black soldier saluting the French flag, an image whose complex semiotic chain provides a sense of "Frenchness" that is both uncomfortable and comfortable with colonialism (*Mythologies*). I would further argue that the creators of *CPH*, in drawing upon this tradition, are attempting to naturalize the workings of authorities of delimitation—ways in which television can and cannot discuss these topics.

CPH, with its wall-to-wall voice-over, draws from the Griersonian documentary tradition, employing a highly authoritative off-screen narration. Largely discredited within critical debates over contemporary documentary, "voice-of-God" narration is nevertheless a common trope in such television genres as news documentary, reality TV, and, of course, commercials. Narration of this sort may be a way of enacting documentary's initial impulse (the integrating of art and industry) within an avowedly industrial, commercial medium. It is significant that the narrator is female (voice-of-goddess narration?), which could be seen as an attempt to diminish but not eliminate the authoritative, didactic tone of the voice-over.

CPH is usually described in terms of its success and its high, perhaps excessive, budgetary expenditures (rumoured to be about $25 million). Again and again, audience numbers are used to indicate this success, although these numbers are never substantiated in any empirical sense (Wright 147). But perhaps more important than launching into a debate over the program's success or failure is the mode of excess evident even within the discourse surrounding the program.

The official website of *CPH*, in describing the show, tries to reverse the traditional sorts of power relations that a costume drama might be seen to reproduce; here, it is the Europeans, rather than Natives, who are described as "strange":

> The opening episode of this 16-part documentary ranges across the continent, looking back more than 15,000 years to recount the varied history of the first occupants of the territory that would become Canada. From the

rich resource of Native oral history and archeology come the stories of the land's first people—how dozens of distinct societies took shape, and how they encountered *a strange new people, the Europeans.* ("Episode Summaries," *CPH* official website; italics mine)

It is not within the scope of this book to examine the entire span of *CPH*. With the aim of doing a close reading that could reveal the technologies of affect encoding the nationalist statements that *CPH* produces, I focus on *CPH*'s opening episode. The violin strains, haunting Irish and Japanese flute sequences, Native drumming and chanting, and synthesized crescendos of this episode provide us with an excess of affective high points that, as Lyle Dick points out, create a sense of false coherence "when historical facts failed to unify" (41–42). Using mostly dissolve edits (there are very few straight cuts), lush landscape footage, a slow, soothing female voice-over, maps and dramatic re-enactment, the opening episode takes great pains to assert the presence of the First Nations before European contact. The presence is a conditional one. A heavy emphasis on the Bering Strait theory positions First Nations people as immigrants, just like everyone else (Dick). Indeed, their presence is heavily mediated by special digital effects that produce a ghostly, shadowy, apparitional representation.

The episode begins in the nineteenth century. William Cormack, a Newfoundland-based merchant and naturalist, has an interest in the disappearing race of Beothuks, the now-extinct indigenous peoples of Newfoundland. He summons Shawnadithit, considered to be among the last remaining Beothuk, to his home in St. John's—she had been working as a maid in Exploits Bay. Cormack has Shawnadithit draw pictures for him of the Beothuk. Cormack tries to track down more Beothuks but has no luck. To eerie Japanese flute music and the sounds of lapping water, he says, "It was as if Shawnadithit had stumbled out of a land of ghosts."

At this point, the music changes to a mix of European strings and Native drumming, and the story segues back thousands of years to "the beginning of time." The line "they were the first people" is spoken twice in the voice-over narration. Past tense is significant here, as is the frequent linking of Aboriginal peoples with death. Such phrases as "creation legends spoke of survival and *death,*" "a people always balanced between life and *death,*" and "the cycle of war and *death* seemed endless" create an image of what Daniel Francis and others have called "the imaginary Indian," the product of a white imperial imaginary: "The Indian is the invention of the European.... The Indian began as a White man's mistake and became a White man's fantasy. Through the prism of White hopes, fears and prejudices, indigenous Americans would be seen to have lost contact with reality and to have become 'Indians'; that is, anything non-Natives wanted them to be" (4–5).

The Imaginary Indian emerged within representation in the mid-nineteenth century, just as Canada was beginning to establish itself as a nation. White Europeans in this northern territory had to create a new national identity for themselves, so the image of the Indian became crucial. As Francis writes: "The image of the Other, the Indian, was integral to this process of self-identification. The Other came to stand for everything the Euro-Canadian was not" (8). Canadian artists such as Paul Kane and Emily Carr and the American photographer Edward Curtis created an enduring image of a supposedly disappearing race. This was, I would argue, a kind of compulsive return on the part of the Canadian national imaginary: a ghost who constantly returns within representation. Aboriginal peoples at the time were, certainly, dying from alcohol poisoning and disease, but they were also assimilating, or attempting to become part of Canadian society, or they were thriving in their own self-sufficient communities. The Romantic idea of a dying breed of Indians that would not see the end of the twentieth century was attractive to artists such as Kane, Carr, and Curtis, not to mention those that viewed and bought their popular works of art.

Mark Starowicz, producer of *CPH*, has written a memoir-style account of the making of the serial that echoes some of the Romantic impulses of Curtis and Kane. In the chapter "How Not to Stalk a Muskox," which recounts the challenges of shooting Episode 1, he cites what he calls "the biggest challenge of all: conveying the twenty-thousand-year history of aboriginal nations that have left no written records" (128). The dubiousness of this claim and its disdain for oral histories sets the stage for subsequent forays into the white imaginary of the disappearing Indian race. Like Robert J. Flaherty's staged enactments of "Eskimo" life in his film *Nanook of the North* or Edward Curtis's highly constructed Indian portraits, Starowicz's book describes a white southern crew reintroducing "authentic" rituals to a somewhat bumbling Inuit community—they barely know how to hunt for muskox! He quotes *CPH* producer Gail Gallant, who says of the community: "At the end of the day we screened everything we had shot.... They looked wistfully at images of their own past. We knew we had captured the right thing" (129).

The final edited footage of *CPH* continues this durable romantic tradition. The Indians in the program are mostly nameless and faceless, often presented in silhouette, in long shots or long dissolves, in shadows or mist, or with long hair obscuring their faces. As Mackey writes, these representations, while indicating a certain recognition of First peoples, are a matter of expediency. They draw from a discursive tradition of building alliances with and promoting inclusion of First Nations that are part of economic self-interest and national identity, or what Mackey describes as "a push to construct a [Canadian] settler national identity perceived as innocent of racism" (25).

From genocide and disease to residential schools and the inner city, the history of the mistreatment of First Nations people represents an ongoing traumatic episode that ruptures the Canadian imaginary. In an interview with *National Post* reporter Elizabeth Nickson, First Nations activist David Dennis uses the terms of trauma and affect to describe his relationship to the Canadian nation:

> NATIONAL POST: Are all white people racist?
> DANIEL DENNIS: In any abusive relationship, whether it's abuse between a man and a woman, a parent and a child, there's an incredible amount of shame, and I don't think that Canadians in general have dealt with shame on a large scale towards our people. You look at some of the headlines that occur after, in our eyes, landmark decisions that advance our rights, and you hear ignorant rhetoric, fear-mongering and hate. (Nickson B2)

In this sense, there is, perhaps, a contingent relationship between national shame and national pride: one informs the other. Nathanson writes about what he calls the shame–pride axis, a balance between "the sort of hoped-for personal best that hovers as an unreachable image within most of us and the terribly feared personal worst that, when revealed, will trigger an avalanche of deadly shame" (20). He continues, "Shame—our reaction to it and our avoidance of it—becomes the emotion of politics and conformity…. Its influence in human civilization is paramount" (16). Within Canadian culture, this shame has been responded to through melancholia, or acting out, rather than the working-through process of mourning, constructing what might be seen as narratives that attempt to conform to dominant modes.

In Episode 1 of *CPH*, aboriginal actor Tantoo Cardinal plays a nameless storyteller recounting a creation legend in which women and men, initially separated, are brought together by the Creator so that they can procreate: "When they worked together they prospered … there would be families here for a long time to come." The widely documented presence and importance of two-spirited, or queer, peoples in Aboriginal cultures is never mentioned, but it is not long before anxieties about race enter the representational field by way of sexuality. As Gilman, Hart, and others have argued, the primitive body is often, within representation, conflated with the non-reproductive queer body to allay fears of the fecundity of the other ("families for a long time to come") and the demise of the white race.

Two scenes in particular from Episode 1 represent the ways in which representations of the other become the bearers of discourse, allowing for (contained) challenges to dominant fictions. Halfway through the episode we see the warring activities of Indian tribes before first contact. According to the program, Indian nations fought endlessly with one another (before they were, presumably, civilized by contact with Europeans). One scene depicts the capture and torture of one Indian warrior by another. The voice-over describes the arcane rituals that would attend such a capture, over a scene with homoerotic overtones. In a tight two-shot, the two warriors face each other in profile. The captor offers a last drink of water to his prisoner while slowly, tenderly, stroking the other man's face.

Historical trauma can result in interruptions to performativity, challenging the symbolic order, however briefly. Francis writes, "The Indian became the standard of virtue and manliness against which Europeans measured themselves and often found themselves wanting" (8). Here, queerness interrupts that masculinity but in a manner that is contained by our revulsion at torture and murder.

The larger containment to any sort of challenge to the dominant fiction (queer or otherwise) occurs in the series' inordinate and lengthy focus on war between French and English settlers. In the white settler wars depicted throughout the subsequent seven episodes of the first season, a kind of fetishization of masculinity stands in for the trauma of racism. The white soldier fights for his country in an excess of masculinity, of traumatized whiteness striving for supremacy. LaCapra describes this sort of trope as yet another symptom of acting out: "the dubious appropriation of the status of victim through vicarious or surrogate victimage" (*Writing History* 71).

An examination of the text of fandom as represented in the chat site on the series' official website reveals the ways in which audiences both accepted and negotiated this preferred reading of white innocence. Turk, a contributor to the site, had this to say:

> The TV series has given us a different viewpoint and allowed us to see the world as the people who lived then saw it. It has allowed us to see that no group was blameless when it came to cruel and unusual treatment of others. At various times during the documentary, I was angry at the French, the English, the Americans, the Natives, etc., etc. This indicates to me that this is a very balanced and thorough treatment of the subject.

Alvin Ying, on the other hand, posted to the same site: "I mourn of not able to learn about the diverse cultures that once were, such as the Hurons before decimation.... I mourn of all the wisdom that is forever lost in the ebbs of time. I mourn of those whose stories will never be heard."[4]

Yet another opinion comes from *Globe and Mail* columnist Russell Smith, who, in the only critical writing I have ever seen in mainstream media on *CPH*, describes the program as official art, because it meets the demands of socialist realism of the Stalinist era: "*ideynost* (ideological expression), *narodnost* (national character) and *partynost* (party spirit)" (R5). Smith writes further: "A great deal of government money, from various agencies and the CBC, went into the massive 'A People's History' documentary series.... This was seen to be worthy art with both and educational and a national character. It was broadcast on our own national, publicly owned network. It is official art" (D1).

Lyle Dick, in a detailed overview of the nationalistic elements of *CPH*, concurs on the paucity of critical response to *CPH*. He traces the ways in which industry competition, cutbacks to the CBC, and a highly ideological climate in the wake of the 1995 referendum contributed to the making of a series that eschewed ambiguity, serious analysis, or critique. He writes:

> By situating the narrative within an absolute past, it displays a remoteness from the actual contingency and possibility of substantive change in the future. Rather than engage the actual diversity of voices and perspectives on Canadian history, the producers opted for the valorization of selected historical figures and their perspectives, which they presented as models for advancing the series' overriding political objectives of shoring up the nation-state in its contemporary travails. (37)

But if we are to believe media reports, especially those from the CBC itself, *CPH* was an unqualified success. How to explain this popularity? Kaja Silverman writes, following Louis Althusser: "Ideological belief ... occurs at the moment when an image which the subject knows to be culturally fabricated nevertheless succeeds in being recognized or acknowledged as a 'pure, naked, perception of reality'" (17). She tries to explain how memory and ideology cohere: "events which never literally happened can assume the status of highly significant memories, while occurrences which might seem of first importance to a biographer may not even figure within the subject's psyche, since it is fantasy rather than history which determines what is reality for the unconscious" (18).

This reverse discourse can be seen again and again in *CPH*. One glaring example is the history of Black slavery in Canada, which goes unmentioned in the serial. Indeed, this absence is filled with the story of the Underground Railroad, by which means African American slaves found freedom in Canada. As

Maureen Moynagh has written (about *CPH*), "The myth of the nation that represents Canada as a place of refuge, tolerance and equality is dependant on the careful erasure of that earlier history" (104–5). Canadian popular culture is the site at which this erasure, or forgetting, is constantly reinscribed. Under what circumstances can popular culture be used to bring about empathetic unsettlement?

Empathetic Unsettlement

With the concept of empathetic unsettlement, LaCapra distinguishes appropriation of the traumatic experience of the other from empathetic unsettlement, which denies closure or transcendence. This position constitutes a will to truth rather than a will to knowledge, which could result in unsettling emotions and possibly secondary trauma. This response would be ethical, responsible, and open to challenge (*Writing History*).

At the level of representation, the comedic form may be particularly suited to this function. Indeed, LaCapra argues that the problem of representation (the reinscription of trauma) requires a consideration of the carnivalesque, "whereby impasses are somehow played out and existing norms or structures are periodically transgressed" (*Representing the Holocaust* 222).

Mikhail Bakhtin describes comedy as dialogic: it invites a multiplicity of voices and is opposed to closure and completion. He writes, "It is precisely laughter that destroys the epic and in general destroys any hierarchical distance.... Laughter demolishes fear and piety before an object, before the world, making it an object of familiar contact and thus clearing the ground for an absolutely free investigation of it" (23). In comedy, then, is space for the grotesque: a sense of otherness that is liberatory rather than oppressive. Central to Bakhtin's theory is the notion of carnivalesque reversal; the clown celebrates the "lower" functions of the body (eating, drinking, defecation, giving birth) and thus defies the "higher" regions of authority. Queerness is frequently sutured into the repetitive structure of the comedic, providing fertile ground for the return of the repressed.

This Hour Has 22 Minutes, a satirical newsmagazine program that premiered on CBC in 1993, has always had several ongoing and one-off queer characters and situations: lesbian-feminist academic Genoa Halberstam (a play on Camille Paglia) and working-class dude Dakey Dunn, to name two. *22 Minutes* may then represent the space of interruption within repetition that trauma (and, not coincidentally, the genre of comedy) provides, allowing space for challenges to the normal. The title, *This Hour Has 22 Minutes*, echoes the 1960s Canadian current-affairs program *This Hour Has Seven Days*, and, while differing in genre, the former has a similar, if more pronounced, critical edge. Geoff Pevere describes it as a show with "a clear affinity for the Canadian powerless over the powerful" (32). I would argue that its frequent queer content also functions as a site of ethics.

As I skimmed through tapes of *22 Minutes* from the years 1996–2001, I found only brief references to First Nations and immigrant histories. One recurring Native character, Joe, played by Cathy Jones, appears irregularly to deliver irreverent, ironic monologues full of deliberately clichéd wisdom. He is always depicted walking through a forest or sitting beside an artificial-looking fire. He seems to be an intertextual commentary (and a bit of an in-joke) on Joe Two Rivers, the Métis character in the 1970s Canadian series *The Forest Rangers* (played by Ukrainian actor Micheal Zenon) and, by extension, on the Indian as a white fantasy.

Generally, it is the image of the queer that becomes the bearer of discourse in *22 Minutes*. As Silverman points out, breakdowns in the symbolic order signal ruptures in national imaginaries. She writes, "History sometimes manages to interrupt or even deconstitute what a society assumes to be its master narratives … to undo our imaginary relation to the symbolic order" (55). In the character of "male correspondent" Dakey Dunn, Mary Walsh cross-dresses to play a male hustler-like character whose masculinity is in question at the literal level of the diegesis as well as at the subtextual level. Walsh's performance as Dakey Dunn is an ironic theatricalization of masculinity that makes use of a repetition of overtly masculine gestures; thus, to a lesbian audience-in-the-know, it becomes a drag-king performance. This is no clean-cut, normalized, made-for-TV gay neighbour. With her/his hairiness, large size, and gestures to the crotch, this is a grotesque, carnivalesque inversion of femininity. Dakey Dunn often laments the demise of masculinity, but her/his character also delivers trenchant political commentary and economic analysis in Newfoundland working-class vernacular. Here he/she comments upon transnational globalization, economic flow, and debt:

> I admit I'm a weirdo. I don't live, dream, and eat the cash.... Boy there's plenty a bucks out there, one trillion buckeens whizzin' around the globe every nighta the week bein' traded back and forth, and the high rollers are havin' a ball.... Every country in the world is up to its arse in debt. *To who?* Who do we owe this debt *to*? Do they have a debt they owes to someone else? Or do they owe a debt to us? Call a meetin', boy! Call the whole shaggin' thing off! Sure it's only a buncha numbers on a big computer terminal! Brazil don't pay us, we don't pay Japan. Japan don't pay— well, if they

don't owe any money, maybe they don't, I dunno, maybe we can promise not to drop anymore nuclear bombs in 'em or something, I don't know, I don't have my grade 11. (*This Hour Has 22 Minutes*, February 12, 2000)

22 Minutes' most radical commentaries frequently occur by way of lesbian affect. The butch lesbian, still too unreadable to be fully commodified, holds a deeply subversive charge. Like the butch lesbian, the drag king exists within the mainstream only in the most apparitional sense and always signifies lack: a white masculinity put in crisis by economic downturn, not to mention feminism and transgendered politics. Definitely unsettling and implicitly empathetic, Dakey Dunn (who also spoke out against the war on Iraq during the 2003 season) resists moral closure through the instability of his/her gender and class position.

However, *This Hour Has 22 Minutes* straddles the fence, managing both to unsettle and to affirm the nationalist project. Since the Quebec referendum of 1995, patriotism has been on the rise everywhere on Canadian television, including the renegade *22 Minutes*. A spinoff serial, *Talking to Americans*, which used hilarious streeter interviews by Rick Mercer to demonstrate Americans' deep ignorance of Canada, situates me as Canadian and nationalist at the very moment I recognize America as Canada's imaginary other. Interestingly, Mercer decided to end the serial after 9/11, and he also declined a nomination for a Gemini Award during that period.

Mercer's double-sided project could perhaps be seen as both an acting out and working through. These are not discrete entities; each requires the other. Following Freud, LaCapra describes melancholia as both a "precondition" and a "necessary aspect" of mourning (*Representing the Holocaust* 213). Failing that necessary mourning, are certain moments in Canadian history simply unrepresentable within the dominant fiction of Canadian cinema and television?

Can the most direct seeing of violent events in history occur as an absolute inability to know it? Cathy Caruth defines trauma as a response to an overwhelming event that, not fully known as it occurs, returns later in the form of flashbacks, nightmares, and so on. This not-knowing, she argues, is trauma's epistemology (92). For how else to explain the ways in which a nation has not fully narrativized its past?

"North of Sixty": Working Through

A now defunct dramatic series, *North of Sixty* (1992–1998), provides a sense of possibility through an intersubjective notion of "working through." It follows the daily life of Michelle Kenedi, played by Tina Keeper, a First Nations

(Dene) RCMP officer in the isolated town of Lynx River, Northwest Territories. The script, written in consultation with a team of First Nations elders, has a rough, immediate feel.[5] The primarily First Nations cast was a mix of Native professionals (including many who later appeared as unnamed Indians on *Canada: A People's History*). Linda Warley notes that this extraordinary program attracted a weekly audience of a million and a half viewers and was nominated for five Gemini awards. She writes: "This program has brought images of Native peoples into Canadian homes in a way that is unprecedented [and] … makes space for non-Native viewers by incorporating white characters into its narratives and by portraying relations among white and Native characters which, though fraught with the legacy of settler colonialism, are not necessarily limited by it" (173–74).

An article in *The Toronto Sun* quotes the reaction of American First Nations actor Michael Horse to the program:

> "I showed this show to a couple of Hopi elders that were staying at my house this weekend and they loved it. What happens on this reservation happens on any rural reservation everywhere," he [Horse] says. Although *North of Sixty* doesn't air in the U.S., Horse says it has a big Native following in border communities and among satellite dish owners. "What's interesting about this show is it doesn't play the cheap shot. A lot of the things that are written in the States have to do with the medicine man and the vision quest. This isn't." (Horse, qtd. in Bickley 82)

The plots of *North of Sixty* centred on conflicts between Kenedi and the somewhat anarchic, tragicomic Native-centred concerns of the town. Two things distinguished *North of Sixty* from other productions about Natives on Canadian TV. First, the memory of the residential schools continually haunted several of the town's residents. This traumatic memory was a constant presence in the chronotope of the show. Traumatic abuse memory was also, however, part of the characterization of a primary white character who experienced his own recovered memories of abuse at the hands of Catholic priests. If, as several trauma theorists (Herman, LaCapra) have implied, solidarity and wider notions of community are necessary for working through, this acknowledgement of abuse trauma inflicted upon both white and First Nations subjects would seem to create a larger discursive space for resolution. LaCapra writes: "Melancholia is an isolating experience … that validates the self in its desperate isolation. In the best cases it may allow for insights that bear witness to questionable conditions and have broader critical potential. To be effective,

mourning apparently requires a supportive or even solidaristic social context" (*Representing the Holocaust* 214).

Second, alcoholism (diegetically positioned as a result of post-traumatic
stress disorder from residential schools) was something that could be and was
overcome, through traditional healing practices and community support. Death
was often present in the episodes, but it was not thematically dominant in the
series. By representing traditional mourning practices the show made literal the
mourning, or working through, that was occurring in its storyline.

One episode in particular demonstrates this. In this segment ("Fair Trade,"
December 1992), both a temporary white resident of Lynx River and a long-
time Native resident (who is also the town bootlegger) need to bury their
dead. In the latter's case (Albert Golo, played by Gordon Tootoosis), the remains
have been in the possession of a museum in the south, a commentary on the
"salvage paradigm" that museums of anthropology represent. In the story, a
CBC camera crew flies up to video the reclamation of the remains and interviews Golo and the chief, Peter Kennedi (played by Tom Jackson)

> GOLO: It's enough for me that the remains of my ancestors are in their
> rightful place and that their spirits are free. Politics is unimportant.
> KENNEDI: It really is just the tip of the iceberg, though. I mean, the whole
> question of the inherent cultural rights of the Dene or, for that matter, all
> Aboriginal people has not been addressed.

The episode succeeds in pulling off an extraordinary intertextuality of the
discourses of anthropology, race, and televisual spectacle. At the same time, in
keeping with the polysemy of television (and particularly that of a state-run
network), the episode takes pains to depict the good intentions of white people. As Kennedi delivers this ideological message, a white museum curator in
a funky African hat looks on, from a porch physically positioned above the two
men. The camera cuts from a long shot of the men to a medium close-up of
her. "Times change," she says, and then adds, sounding appropriately folksy:
"You have to go with the flow." Certain First Nations critiques of the program
noted by Warley could be applied to this episode; for example, the program
avoids "really tough legal and constitutional issues, specifically the Native issue
of sovereignty, thereby effacing the threat to Canadian unity that Native political subjectivity represents" (Regina Harrison email, qtd. in Warley 179).

But the actual depiction of traditional mourning practices adapted to contemporary Native existence provides a means of "working through" for both
white and First Nations audiences. In a scene in the same episode, Golo explains
Dene mourning traditions to the younger Teevee (Dakota House). Mourning,

it seems, is open-ended; there is no recourse here to an idealized "lost" Canadian self. The final shot is of a mourning ceremony for both the white and the Dene characters' dead. To the sound of drumming and chanting, the camera circles the gathering. But the circle does not close. Here, specific individuals are being mourned, but the realization of other losses is ongoing and constitutes a powerful presence rather than a melancholic, structural absence.

This may have all been too much for the funders in the deeply conservative province of Alberta. Despite ninety successful episodes, many awards, and a loyal following, *North of Sixty* was cancelled in 1997 for lack of funding.[6]

Ghostly Return

LaCapra asks if the social conditions for a ritualized passage through the necessary state of melancholia exist, and argues for specificity in naming the object of mourning (*Representing the Holocaust* 213–14). A comparison between *CPH* and *North of Sixty* reveals stark differences between a melancholia to do with a vaguely defined Indian race (who or what is being mourned in such a generalized field of representation?) and the explicit details of cultural and political mourning practices in a Dene community. LaCapra writes, "the difficult problem for public education and practice would be to reorient both emotion and value in the direction of victims who are indeed deserving objects of mourning" (*Representing the Holocaust* 214).

Are there, nonetheless, phantoms that refuse to be laid to rest?

According to Derrida, ghosts are productive. They destabilize the binaries of past and present, self and other—perhaps, even, of east and west. This productivness, argues Derrida, is crucial to survival, allowing the past to live on in the future. But this is a disquieting position, analogous perhaps to LaCapra's empathetic unsettlement, for as Derrida writes, "Here we come closest to ourselves but also to the most terrifying thing. It is of the essence of the ghost in general to be frightening…. The most familiar becomes the most disquieting" (*Spectres of Marx* 142–46).

That ghostly invisibility, then, so crucial to the boundaries of the nation-state, always holds within it the potential to become present—Derrida's "imperative of a speaking that will awaken others" (*Spectres of Marx* 108). Television, as a marker of a contested Canadian national space, exists at the boundary of inside and outside space, protecting national subjects from outside forces at the same time that it seems to laminate them to these very forces. Cultural products like *Canada: A People's History* performatively reinscribe a melodramatic acting-out mode for the nation-state, while the unrepresentable "real" of First Nations genocide ghosts the edges of its representation.

FIVE

AN OTHERNESS BARELY TOUCHED UPON
A Cooking Show, A Foreigner, A Turnip, and a Fish's Eye

The meeting often begins with a food feast: bread, salt, and wine.... The one confesses he is a famished baby, the other welcomes the greedy child; for an instant they merge within the hospitality ritual.
—Julia Kristeva, "Toccata and Fugue for the Foreigner," *Strangers to Ourselves* 11

IN THE HEADY EARLY DAYS of official Canadian multiculturalism, my mother, like many of her generation of Ukrainian immigrants, became an unofficial publicist for all things Ukrainian. One January, she called up all her media contacts to inform them that January 6 was the "real" Christmas for East Europeans the world over and therefore a news item.

In point of fact, we celebrated both Christmases in a desultory fashion, each by half. The two halves never made up a whole, and it was perhaps these unsuccessful faux celebrations that made my mother want to produce and direct her own. Fair enough. But I hadn't anticipated that my mother would have a stand-in daughter for the media version: Maria, a girl from our church and a second-generation Ukrainian, blissfully free of the sullen resentment and ethnic shame that we children of immigrants possessed. Maria *loved* being Ukrainian. She was earnestly and smugly proud of it. She appeared at our door at the appointed time immaculately made up and coiffed and in full ethnic regalia—embroidered blouse, tunic, skirt, and flowered headdress. My mother promptly seated her at the front window along with my little sister Lydia, who'd reluctantly agreed to be similarly displayed. I was relegated to the kitchen to chop cabbage and beets. The camera crews were ordered outside for a better shot, and next day on the local news there was Maria with an annoyed five-year-old Lydia on her lap, solemnly looking out of the window of our sub-urban house for the first star, after which, according to my mother's apocryphal telling, the family would sit down to eat. Of course, it was a complete construc-tion. After that overly lighted tableau was dismantled, my father bellowed his dis-gust, I went and sulked in my room, and the "sacred meal" got cold.

Media images, of course, are never "real," and my mother understood this well. Whatever it was she was selling required a double, a stand-in, someone less foreign and more hyperreal, who could soften the grotesque edges of the immigrant's existence and yet, ironically, satisfy the audience's desire for the authenticity of the Native. One might assume that the picture in the paper was less for us and more for a white Anglo reader immersed in nostalgia for lost ethnic "multicultural" ontologies.

In this chapter I examine the televisual representation of multiculturalism through the lens of the ethnic cooking show. In order to explore the function of the immigrant, or the stranger, within media representation, I have a pop-ular cultural text—an ethnic cooking show—and Julia Kristeva's work on the foreigner interrogate each other. While I gesture to the several critiques of official multiculturalism and its representations that now exist (Ahmed, Ban-nerji, Hage, Mackey), I am also interested in the slippages and unintended effects that occur in the representation of the foreigner. It may well be that the curious position that Kristeva proposes, both for the woman and the for-eigner—"to make manifest her solidarity with other forms of strangeness and marginality" (*Strangers to Ourselves* 38)—is in excess of what the televisual narrative seeks. But it is perhaps these excesses and *not* the appeals to unity through an identification with the other that provide a way *out* of the nor-malizing regime of the host culture.

Official multiculturalism has existed in Canada since 1971, emerging out of the Bilingualism and Biculturalism Commission of the Pearson administra-tion. Multiculturalism is popularly described as having been a response to "eth-nic" groups that wanted official recognition, and it is seen as one of the major achievements of the Trudeau era. The policy meant that some eighty different ethnic or cultural groups could now apply for financial support to various min-istries, particularly the newly formed Ministry of Multiculturalism, to support culture and language programs (Mackey). But its adoption exactly one year after the October Crisis of 1970 points to its implicit aim of pitting ethnic against Québécois or, as Mackey puts it, "a means to undercut Quebec's demands for spe-cial recognition by bestowing recognition on other cultural groups" (64).

Multicultural policy performs other functions in a Canadian context. Canada has been criticized for leaning heavily upon its multicultural policy, both to manage cultural difference and to maintain appearances as a democracy (Bannerji, *Dark Side of the Nation*). Writing about Australia, which has in common with Canada an official policy of multiculturalism, Ahmed argues that acceptance of certain benign differences can obscure deeper cultural rifts (Ahmed, *Strange Encounters*). Certainly, as I have argued in previous chapters, official multiculturalism (and its imbrication in funding requirements) can lead to a plethora of problematic representations, from the absurdities of a character named Olga Perogy in the CTV variety show *Circus* (1977–84) to the more subtle but no less pernicious harnessing of the immigrant as advertisement for Canadian tolerance, as in "A Scattering of Seeds." In these cases, multiculturalism is as much a work of the imagination as it is of nationalism. Canada's deeply structured reliance on the other (immigrants, migrants, and so on) as a support for an imaginary Canadian identity demands such characters, who generally exist outside of television's everyday flow.

But I wish also to argue that the boundaries of multiculturalist representation are also horizons of possibility. If, as several scholars (Probyn, Sedgwick, Tomkins) suggest, pleasure and shame are inextricably connected, can the guilty yet somehow shameful pleasures of indulging in one's own stereotypes as seen on TV lead to some new ideas about the immigrant self? Following current cultural studies theory, Appadurai, in writing about the intersections of media and migration, describes electronic media as "resources for experiments in self-making" (3). Migrant representations, he argues, produce images and viewers not "easily bound within local, national or regional spaces" (4). For nationalism, as Appadurai points out, "is now itself diasporic" (160). Can certain "ethnic" representations, such as those on the Canadian cooking show *Loving Spoonfuls*, provide valuable insights into the transnational diasporic subject?[1]

Ethnicity, Sex, and Cooking Shows

Loving Spoonfuls (2000–3) was a weekly cooking show on W, the Women's Television Network. According to its promotional website:

> It all started in north-end Winnipeg. The concept behind the new docu-comedy *Loving Spoonfuls* came to creator Allan Novak as he sat in a tiny kitchen watching his favourite aunt cook her specialties while cracking jokes and telling tales.... Struck by the explosion of cooking shows, he conceived of a series that combined cooking, comedy, and quirky characters ...

authentic ethnic cooking, poignant real-life stories, and unscripted, spontaneous fun from a real grandmother. ("About Us: The Story of *Loving
Spoonfuls*," *Loving Spoonfuls* official website)

Loving Spoonfuls was shot in the actual kitchens of immigrant women of a
certain age who demonstrate favourite recipes from their country of origin.
Each episode is narrated and in a sense mediated by David Gale, a middle-
aged, somewhat effeminate, B-grade Canadian actor of Jewish heritage (though
this is rarely mentioned in the show).[2] Because the program is meant to be comedic,
Gale attempts to provide witty commentary throughout, while at the same time
translating the grandmothers' vague directions into actual measurements and
asking nosy questions about the traditions and history of the women's country of
origin. At certain points, a lurking husband or daughter is asked to contribute
arcane culinary tips or bits of ethnic lore. Gale's persona is rather uneasy and
sometimes even slightly hysterical as he tries, mostly unsuccessfully, to create
comedy out of the daily routine of an older immigrant woman.

 Loving Spoonfuls is part of an intersecting discourse on food that is specific to late-twentieth- and early-twenty-first-century food journalism but
that can be traced back to the domestic-advice manuals of the mid-nineteenth
century (Leavitt). The Food Channel, an increase in food writing, and the rise
of the empires of Martha Stewart, Jamie Oliver, and others have signalled an
unprecedented interest in representations of food and its preparation. The
televisual roots of this phenomenon go back to the 1970s. The bringing of
the chef to the home cook, and the transference of the aesthetics of public
restaurant space to the private realm of the home, can be said to have begun
with Julia Child's television series *The French Chef*, which first appeared on the
Boston television channel WGBH in 1962 (and which was recently re-released
on DVD). Martha Stewart—less white than Julia, with her peek-a-boo Polish
heritage—can be seen as a transitional figure in this continuum.

 Canadian cooking shows such as *The Galloping Gourmet* and *Loving Spoonfuls* would seem to invert Child's dignified legacy with a carnivalesque descent
into sex and bawdy ethnicity. One has only to glance at the onscreen antics of
The Galloping Gourmet (1968–72) to see how far we've come. Featuring a
boozy, leering host (Graham Kerr), this program set the scene for the associative
connection between food and sex on TV, upon whose legacy the food shows
Nigella Bites and *Loving Spoonfuls* are built. Levin writes: "Kerr was engaged
in a bizarre sort of lovemaking—with his audience, his food, his cooking uten-
sils, and even himself" (Kentner and Levin 64). Indeed, Kerr flirted continually with audience members while employing salacious metaphors that had,

until then, not been deployed to describe food: "Look at that lovely hunk of lobster, that lovely succulent beautiful portion, and brandy over that, and the whole thing runs over your mouth … it should be tender and melting, soft and sensuous" (*Galloping Gourmet*, December 24, 1970).

As Diane Negra has pointed out, food representations resonate with affect: "a channel for sincerity and emotional expressivity" (62). But they also speak to the body and to desire: "Food," she argues, "with its intimate connections to the body, is in many ways an ideal fetish object, taking up the place of sexual desire and hinting at the character of the experience of unified identification" (69).

A subset of the cooking-show phenomenon is ethnic food fiction. Negra notes an increase in media representations of ethnic identity, giving the example of films such as *Like Water for Chocolate* (1993), *Eat Drink Man Woman* (1995), and recent advertising campaigns such as that for the Italian restaurant chain Olive Garden. French chefs are reviving folk culinary styles. Even *Joy of Cooking*, that bible of Anglo-American cookery, now includes recipes for what co-author Marion Rombauer Becker describes as "such national culinary enthusiasms such as couscous … strudel, zabaglione, rijsttafel and gazpacho" (Rombauer and Becker, "Foreword," par. 2).

On television, cooking-show hosts Emeril Lagasse, Christine Cushing, and John Folse are forthright about their ethnicity, occasionally producing dishes inspired by their cultural backgrounds. Even the all-American Martha Stewart will, on occasion, display her mother, Mrs. Kostyra, cooking Polish dishes such as borscht and buckwheat. Negra argues that these ethnic tropes are ambivalent, substituting for real fears regarding questions of ethnicity that conflict with national identity. She writes: "The fetishistic depictions of food and food preparation work to recover the ethnic family, which is endowed with an emotional expressivity lost in late-twentieth-century white U.S. culture" (62). Thus, as Keohane, Probyn, and Stearns have pointed out, such representations are motivated in part by a sense of longing and desire, or what Negra calls "exhausted whiteness" (62).[3]

The politics of food on TV overlaps with the politics of imperialism. On reality TV shows such as *Survivor* and *Amazing Race*, contestants must inevitably have bodily contact with native foodways, imagined or otherwise. Bugs, slimy food items, and problematic beverages find their way into Western bodies, with disgust writ large in the contestant's grimaces and vocalizations. Survival, and perhaps even superiority (in the show, in the world), demands the ingestion of otherness. Disgust helps to negotiate proximity with the other (Ahmed, *Cultural Politics of Emotion*).

Unofficial Multicultural Discourses

Loving Spoonfuls is part of the repertoire of representations produced, in a sense, by a national multicultural discourse. While official multicultural policies have evolved from an ethnic-food and -dance focus to policies that encourage anti-racism education, I would argue that *unofficial* discourses maintain the circulation of such troubled terms as "diversity" and "tolerance." Ghassan Hage describes this premise as "enrichment." Referring to an Australian multicultural festival, he writes:

> The discourse of enrichment still positions [the white Australian] in the centre of the Australian cultural map. Far from putting "migrant cultures" … on an equal footing with the dominant culture, the theme conjures the images of a multicultural fair where the various stalls of neatly positioned migrant cultures are exhibited and where the real Australians, bearers of the White nation and positioned in the central role of the touring subjects, walk around and enrich themselves. (*White Nation* 118)

Hage posits a viewing relation in which immigrant cultures exist for the enrichment of Anglo-Celtic cultures. Importantly, he maintains that this relation is built upon a fantasy in which immigrant viewers of ethnic spectacles are erased: the spectacle exists only for the consumption of the anglo audience, which goes some way toward helping to explain the tropes of these narratives.

Keohane offers similar observations on Canada. Following Hegel, Keohane argues that the other provides affirmation of our enjoyment and allows us to hide the lack of national identity from ourselves. In this formulation, "Canadians derive enjoyment—have their enjoyment affirmed, certified, and approved as authentic, as it were—by seeing immigrants become more like themselves, but, note, not indistinguishable, not the same as themselves. The difference must persist in order that the reflection is from the Other" (25).

In *Loving Spoonfuls*, Gale's mediating presence is, then, essential to the genre. He filters the white gaze. He functions both literally and symbolically as the one who makes sure all the ingredients are measured and in the right proportions.

GALE: How much rice do you have there?
ZORKA (YUGOSLAVIAN GRANDMOTHER): Three cups.
GALE [LOOKS CLOSELY]: It doesn't look like three cups. Looks more like two cups!
ZORKA: Two cups—
GALE: And how much beef do you use?
ZORKA: Oh, use one pound, two pound, that depends, yeh.
GALE: Yeah, but that's not one or two pounds …

In this episode, Gale finds it almost impossible to get exact measurements for the making of Yugoslavian cabbage rolls. But he keeps trying, and his interventions fulfill both a comedic and legislative role.

The role of the grandmother forms a parallel function. Food films, for example, often depend upon a central older character whose role is pedagogical, demonstrating the importance of tradition. Thus the food and its preparation, argues Negra, become "a powerful form of 'emotional capital' for women.... We imagine the food we eat is the transparent reflection of the emotional commitment of a caregiver" (63–64). The grandmother reminds us of our own good fortune. Each episode of *Loving Spoonfuls* makes mention of immigrant hardship. In the Yugoslavian-grandmother episode, we see a cheerily coloured intertitle that says, "Zorka survived a forced labour camp in World War II. Most of her family was killed." Questions from Gale reveal that Zorka worked in a German munitions factory and never got more than a grade four education. Later, in the supermarket, she says to Gale:

> ZORKA: In Yugoslavia, we no have nothing, no shows, no clothes, bare feet. But today I have everything. I never dreamt I have house, little bit money. Today what I have, I'm millionaire.
> GALE: Compared to what you had, you're a millionaire. That's beautiful.

Here, Canadians can see an immigrant become "more like themselves" (Keohane 25)—more affluent, better clothed, better shod—but still with the accent that requires Gale's syntactical and ideological translation. Thus, Zorka's otherness could be seen not only as providing the pleasure of self (national) identity but as constituting that very identity in an Althusserian sense of calling it into being. Everything about her, then, is essential to this process: her accent, her cheap clothes, her memory of the camps, her chaotic, utensil-filled drawers, her grimy pots and pans.

Queer Affects

Gale seems to make no great effort to hide his queerness on the show; effeminate gestures abound, and he occasionally utters coded asides. The grandmother's foreignness, Gale's gayness, and comedy are intertwined. The queer body joins the racialized and gendered body as a border subject, a processual being whose essence lies in the act of becoming rather than being. Comedy, in turn, plays an important role in articulating such liminal positions, mapped onto the body. Within comedy's carnivalesque reversals, the clown (the foreigner or the queer) celebrates the lower functions of the body (eating, drinking, defecation, giving birth) and thus defies the higher regions of authority (Bakhtin). In other words, Gale is a kind of foreigner too—but only at certain comedic moments, as when he resorts to an effeminate campiness. At such moments the possibilities of queer's alliance with race become apparent. But when tragedy, in the form of a grisly war story, emerges, Gale takes on a more classical, less grotesque mien: he becomes an insider or, at the very least, an ethnic informant. This shift underlines, as I have mentioned, the fluidity of the radical meanings of queer and the ways in which queer can, as a subaltern term, become subsumed by normalcy.

At the end of every program, Gale sits down to eat the meal with the grandmother and her children and grandchildren. Only Gale and the grandparents are individually miked, however, and the camera, having gone wide at the opening of the sequence, mostly stays fixed on a two-shot of Gale and his new "mammi" or "baba" or "oma" during the meal. The relationship is in a sense completed as Gale eats the grandmother's food. Difference here is diminished and domesticated: it is the foreigner's absence, rather than their presence, which is being celebrated and fetishized here.

The website happily concludes: "Thanks to *Loving Spoonfuls*, David has collected 65 new grandmothers who have extended a standing invitation for Sunday dinner and are expecting a call once a week" ("About Us: David Gale—Biography," *Loving Spoonfuls* official website). As I watch the program, I have the uncanny feeling that some ideal, appreciative, happy son, unmarked by his parents' wartime trauma and consequent displacement from their homeland, has displaced *me*.

But perhaps this displacement is productive. Zorka's foreignness is uncannily doubled by Gale's queerness, producing an excess of signifiers of strangeness. In this instance, the overdetermined (multicultural) production of self and other becomes deterritorialized, freed of origin. During certain unscripted moments both the immigrant and the queer become, in their connection to each other, something else. Also active here are modes of visibility and invisibility, which have been primarily theorized in a lesbian context, as when Amy Villarejo writes of "the slippery movement that lesbian appearance reveals and conceals between sexual difference and social relations" (27). Gale's momentary "appearances" as queer, then, have the potential to reveal the particularly vexed nature of an immigrant's or a queer's relation national belonging. Perhaps, at those moments, to paraphrase Appadurai, the program begins to think itself outside the nation (158).

The Figure of the Foreigner

Julia Kristeva has done much to trouble the figure of the foreigner. In the chapter "Toccata and Fugue for the Foreigner" from *Strangers to Ourselves*, Kristeva outlines certain categories that the foreigner, to avoid annihilation, must attend to: "the wise," "the just," or "the Native." Drawing upon the experience of her clients in psychoanalytic practice, as well as psychoanalytic theories of the other, Kristeva's figure of the foreigner becomes the other within the self, as well as a way to mediate between the demise of religion and the rise of the nation-state: "Between the man and the citizen there is a scar: the foreigner" (*Strangers to Ourselves* 97–98).

It can be surmised that there is an autobiographical strain to this essay. Kristeva was exiled from her native Bulgaria for almost twenty-five years and has written about her sense of foreignness in what she sees as an extremely xenophobic climate in France, both as a woman and as an immigrant (Smith). One could see Kristeva's foreigner, then, as somehow between the semiotic realm of the maternal, which can be seen as mother tongue and motherland, and, on the other hand, the fixed identities and laws of the symbolic, which can be equated with masculinity and fatherland, the country of exile.

What Kristeva ultimately proposes is the thin possibility of all people recognizing foreignness within themselves: "Living with the other, the foreigner, confronts us with the possibility of not of being an other. It is not simply—humanistically—a matter of our being able to accept the other, but of being in his place, and this means to imagine and make oneself other for oneself" (*Strangers to Ourselves* 13). A program such as *Loving Spoonfuls* is built upon this premise: that there is a certain virtue in audiences being exposed to different cultures and that through the ministrations of the ethnically (and sexually) indeterminate host we the audience might also feel part of the grandmother's family and, by extension, the larger human (Canadian) family.

This furthers, to borrow Kristeva's musical metaphor, the notion that different voices would create a harmonious, if polyphonic, composition. For the purposes of this chapter, the composition could be seen as analogous to Canada's policy of official multiculturalism, which attempts to recognize ethnic diversity within the boundaries of the nation-state. This policy has been described as a mosaic, a decorative pattern created from small, usually coloured pieces, perhaps a kind of visual parallel to the fugue. It is no coincidence that the mosaic is a metaphor drawn from the realm of the aesthetic. As Lisa Lowe writes, "multiculturalism … aestheticizes ethnic histories as if they could be separated from history" (9).

Does Kristeva herself participate in this aestheticization? Her thesis in *Strangers to Ourselves* has been criticized by some as being focused on the individual within psychoanalysis and thus less relevant within the field of social relations, let alone the politics of race and racism. As Ewa Ziarek writes: "Kristeva's thesis is bound to disappoint as an answer to the political violence of nationalism and xenophobia. The idea of welcoming others to our own uncanny strangeness not only appears individualistic, it also risks psychologizing or aestheticizing the problem of political violence" (4). While I find this critique useful in placing a certain discursive limit on Kristeva's expansiveness, I find Kristeva's own excesses within the text to be the excesses of the foreigner, which productively rupture the harmonizing logic of her thesis, as when she writes: "Melancholy lover of a vanished space, he cannot, in fact, get over his having abandoned a period of time. The lost paradise is a mirage of the past that he will never be able to recover. He knows it with a distressed knowledge that turns his rage involving others (for there is always an other, miserable cause of my exile) against himself" (*Strangers to Ourselves* 9–10).

How can these excesses possibly be harmonized? The foreigner is enraged against others, against herself. The foreigner's friends include *paternalists, paranoid persons,* and *perverse people.* In an episode of *Loving Spoonfuls* featuring a Greek couple, a horrifying story of wartime displacement is told, almost casually, by the grandfather as he's basting a rack of lamb. Gale winces and then doggedly continues trying to be funny: "An otherness, barely touched upon, and that already moves away" (Kristeva, *Strangers to Ourselves* 13). The foreigner's story is in excess of what the televisual narrative seeks. But it is perhaps these excesses, and *not* the appeals to unity through an identification with the other, that provide a way *out* of the normalizing regime of the host culture. The slippages, the falling-between-the-cracks of fatherland and mother tongue, provide spaces where even an immigrant audience can find pleasure.

Pleasure, and the Anticipation of Failure

The exile is a stranger to his mother. He does not call her, he asks nothing of her. Arrogant, he proudly holds onto what he lacks, to absence ... the foreigner, thus, has lost his mother.
—Kristeva, *Strangers to Ourselves* 5

The first generation in the new country must reject its mother tongue and perhaps even its mother's food. Gale, outside of the symbolic order and therefore a kind of failed phallus, stands in for that lack, obscuring but not quite erasing it. The actual child of the featured ethnic woman could not be present to narrate the mother's story—for shame, as Sedgwick has asserted, is about self-effacement—so Gale becomes the child, but a child who must erase the mother by eating her (her food), and by moving onto a different mother each week. "They welcome me, but that does not matter.... Next ... It was only an expenditure that guarantees a clear conscience" (Kristeva, *Strangers to Ourselves* 11).

We know Gale won't be coming to the family meal each Sunday, even though he has a standing invitation, for it is part of the generic structure of television comedy to forget the previous week's failures and try something new.[4] Genre provides a means of regulating audience memory and expectation and, in terms of representation, of making use of, but also containing, the potentially grotesque aspects of the comedic. The laughter of comedy, as Neale points out, turns on an anticipation of failure (for example, the failure of the fall guy to resist the danger of the banana peel). The women profiled on *Loving Spoonfuls* ultimately fail at the seamless representation that the genre of the cooking show demands. The turnip for the Finnish meal is ridiculously huge and requires an axe; the fish is laid onto the platter with its eyes intact, and, what's worse, when dared to do so by Gale, the grandmother actually *eats* one of the eyes. Wartime stories are told casually, too casually, in the kitchen or on the way to the deli. We recognize this genre by what it is not: it is *not* Julia Child, much less Martha Stewart, and this inevitable failure is meant to produce laughter.

The laughter is a kind of rejection. We know that these women are not really Gale's grandmothers and that in order to *not* be seen as a foreigner he must embrace them with exaggerated endearments and wildly affectionate gestures. The true son or daughter would be more restrained, would certainly be shamed by the turnip and the fish eye.

Ambivalence: Double Vision

At the end of each program there is always too much food. Negra notes that such excess marks a hunger "that is not merely physical but emotional as well" (68). As Gale swallows the food that has been painstakingly prepared with an excess of ridiculous gestures and actions, including acrobatics (the Finnish grandfather showed David his knowledge of circus tricks), singing, and folk dancing, Gale incorporates the otherness of the family into himself, just as we will if we try the recipes available on the website. Certainly there is a utopian potential in this. Bakhtin, for example, argues for the importance of the act of eating as a way of representing the unfinished body and its interface with the world: "The body transgresses here its own limits.... Here man tastes the world, introduces it into his body, makes it part of himself" (281). There are few instances of actual eating on television; while the Galloping Gourmet of the 1960s regularly sat down for a boozy meal with a pretty female audience member at the end of each episode, today's cooking shows usually satisfy themselves with a meager nibble. But David's thin, classical (if effeminate) body belies this promise. The focus on his own appropriated blood relationship with the mother at the expense of the blood family's inclusion denies a possibility of an image of community (Gale as friend, or as Jew, or as queer) that would truly recognize difference.

I would argue that a program such as *Loving Spoonfuls*—or indeed any number of Canadian TV programs that claim a sensitive representation of the foreigner, the ethnic, or the immigrant—is still very much engaged in the production of a normative power that allows for a diversity of individuals but keeps watch over those who are excessive and exceptional. In this sense, their representations are ambivalent, in the way that Stuart Hall describes as " the double vision of the white eye" ("The Whites of Their Eyes" 22). That ambivalence produces a kind of shameful fascination for me even as I watch these programs for the third or fourth time. I worry that the grandmother is being made to look foolish, with her grimy bowls and her crude measurements. I decide that this spectacle, like that long-ago newspaper photo of Maria and Lydia, is not for me but for the non-ethnic, for whom pleasure arises out of nostalgia for culinary ways that are part of my ontology but not theirs.

I know that these recipes are like secret spells and won't be reproduced successfully by anyone else. How many times have I tried, and failed, to reproduce my own Baba's *perohy*? Even Gale finally admits this:

GALE: So there's no official recipe. You just throw in what you think you need.
ZORKA: Yeah.

Anne E. Goldman, in analyzing the autobiographical writing of ethnic-cookbook authors, uses the term "masked resistance" to describe this deterritorialization. While the narratives usually begin with what she calls "a characteristically feminine humility," a closer look reveals "a critical awareness that is often at odds with the status quo" (xix). The cookbook author and the ethnic grandmother may indeed be putting themselves on display for epicurean tourists. But Goldman argues for the agency embedded in complicated old-world recipes: "the series of imperatives the exchange of any recipe requires—the 'cut' and 'soak,' 'simmer' and 'season' ... gesture toward a sense of authority. These directives—orders, really—bespeak a kind of command" (8).

Indeed, as Sneja Gunew points out, the precise and often incomprehensible rules of ethnic cooking are meant to maintain boundaries:

> Once we enter the modern period of diasporas we are indeed haunted both by the structures and strictures of the paradigmatic Jewish diaspora, which often lead diasporan groups to retain rules and the maintenance of social regulation because of the overwhelming fear of being, precisely, overwhelmed and assimilated. However, diaspora is intrinsically as much about breaching and blurring boundaries as about their maintenance, and cultural purity, like Lacanian desire, can actually never be attained. (228)

Like the Ukrainian children looking for the first star in an urban sky polluted by street lights and satellites, that purity is ever elusive. It is imagined at the site of whiteness, as one of its pleasures—but it is imagined by the foreigner too.

Subversive Pleasures

Still, subversive pleasures are to be had for the ethnic spectator. The dirty stained bowls and pots are history, says my mother: "That's her life story. She's been *using* those bowls!" Zorka's similarity to my own Baba pleases me; I enjoy that tough bitterness overlaid against a wilful and charismatic hospitality. Here I would disagree with Hage in his argument that these images exist solely for the white spectator. These immigrant stories are campy performances[5] and they provide fantastical pleasure for the immigrant viewer too. Canadian immigrants, insists cultural critic Sherene Razack, have taken the small representational space afforded them "to resist, to make claims, to convince ourselves that we have not disappeared" (Druick, "Sherene Razack in conversation with Zoë Druick" par. 19). My mother claims that *Loving Spoonfuls* is more "relevant" to an ethnic audience; she can't imagine why English people would be interested. While she's dismissive of Gale, she says the grandmothers "aren't stereotypical ... you really get a sense of the individual."

As I discuss the program with my mother, over my tea and her pastries, I envy her lack of ethnic shame. But it is that very shame that fuels my critical work and burns at the very roots of my creative practice. For shame, like power, is also productive. It marks sites of love and passion. Probyn reminds us that shame happens when you care deeply about what others think (*Blush*). I wouldn't feel such embarrassment about a newspaper photograph from thirty years ago, or a contemporary TV show that displays my culture, if I didn't *care* so much. And I wouldn't be so deeply aware of the aspects of camp and queer affect if my pride and my shame did not coexist in such a frictive, passionate way.

For shame to be *creatively* productive however, is another matter (Sedgwick, "Queer Performativity" 135).[6] The shame—like Kristeva's foreigner, perhaps—must be acknowledged and folded into the creative act, thus nullifying or reversing its effacing power. And this, perhaps, is the moment where multiculturalism could be overlaid onto transculturalism. At this moment the borders between self and other, between local and global, and perhaps even between shame and creativity become more porous. Such hybridized representations—alongside their evident limitations—may occasionally allow us opportunities to (to repeat Appadurai's compelling prase) "think ourselves beyond the nation" (158).

SIX

NATIONAL MANIA,
COLLECTIVE MELANCHOLIA
The Trudeau Funeral

If you ask anyone they will tell you that I do not cry easily but by the end of the yulagy [sic] I was very near tears.
Chloe Donahue, Victoria

When Justin stopped at his father's casket and wept, I joined the country in its sorrow and wept too.
Veronica Dignard, Halifax

When Justin Trudeau said his amazing speech that really moved me and I burst into tears.
Liz Daniele, Toronto

I have been moved. We all have.
Peter Mansbridge, Toronto

Canada weeps.
Mr. and Mrs. Ed and Norma Ryder, and Tim, Lethbridge
— *From the books of condolences, posted on a Government of Canada website 1*

As a child in the 1970s, I was too young for Trudeaumania. My mother, in her late thirties, was perhaps a tad too old. Nonetheless, it was from her mouth and through my ears that I experienced this particular affect that was sweeping the nation.

Trudeaumania is the name popularly given to the extraordinary public appeal of Pierre Elliott Trudeau, Canada's fifteenth prime minister, and is thought to have lasted from approximately 1968 to 1972. George Radwanski writes, in a biography about Trudeau:

> In [an election] campaign that often seemed like a joyous coronation, crowds gathered by the tens of thousands, not to hail his past accomplishments ... but simply to see the man—and preferably to touch him. Wherever he met he was mobbed like a pop star; fingers grasped toward him for a handshake, a touch, or a snatched souvenir; at one stop his watch was ripped from his wrist, and late in the campaign pubescent girls took to trying to pluck hairs from his balding head. (96)

Touch, proximity, and the contagion of manic excitement are all ways in which affect manifests as collective national sentiment. In this chapter, I examine Trudeaumania and the televised state funeral of Pierre Trudeau, as phenomena in which the body, affect, and ideas about the nation intersected.

Silvan Tomkins would perhaps classify Trudeaumania as interest-excitement, but to me it sounded like pure delight, a strangely thrilling mix of glamour and patriotism; the distant and the proximate, flashing across the surface of my mother's white teeth and Max Factor red lips. My Ukrainian immigrant Mama always looked and sounded beautiful when she spoke French, and so it was when she repeated what Pierre Elliott Trudeau had said to her at a Parliamentary reception: "*J'suis enchanté de faire votre connaissance.*"

My mother learned French from the nuns at her convent school in a small Franco-Albertan town; *that convent,* she always said, *was like heaven to me.* But my mother's piety was transformed into bubbly patriotism the day she met Trudeau. That Mama could shake hands with a prime minister, that mother tongue could become so enchanted, was enough of Trudeaumania for me. Then and there I resolved to speak French some day, and the word "Trudeau" became one of pleasure, promise, and opportunity.

Deleuze and Guattari write: "There is no mother tongue but a seizure of power by a dominant language within a political multiplicity" (*Anti-Oedipus* 13). If I couldn't have mother tongue in a country that no longer had practical use for its East European settlers, if Slavic mother tongue had become so shamed that it couldn't fully inhabit anglo mouth, then another (francophone) tongue, more enchanted and only slightly less strange, would inhabit it instead.

National Figures, Collective Affect

This chapter attempts to grapple with the ways in which power operates to produce national figures and collective affect toward them, particularly on television. What is the process by which Trudeau's face and body—both in life and in death—became emptied of actual historic meaning and overly coded with excess? What affective processes of longing, excitement, or shame create the process of belonging to the nation? How does such a queer-looking, queer-acting body such as Trudeau's become reterritorialized as a heterosexual national body?

In October 2000, Canada mourned the passing of one of its former leaders, Pierre Elliott Trudeau. Prime minister from 1969 to 1986, Trudeau was perhaps Canada's first (and last) small-l liberal government leader and a figure of nostalgia for Canada's baby-boom population, including myself. One of Trudeau's first actions as minister of justice was to modernize divorce laws and eliminate anti-sodomy laws. "The state," he famously pronounced, "has no business in the bedrooms of the nation" (Stevens 1967, 1). Son of a wealthy industrialist, aristocratic yet frugal, Trudeau managed to embody a diverse array of despotic and countercultural signs, produced by print and electronic media. Sexuality played a large role in managing these contradictions. Trudeau's frequently alleged bisexuality was an open secret, but it was his infamous marriage to the impetuous Margaret (née Sinclair), nearly thirty years his junior, that captured media attention around the world. That troubled, flamboyant union, the libidinal imperative of Trudeaumania, and Trudeau's own predilection for gay icons such as Barbra Streisand further served to queer his image and expand his celebrity status.

Zoe Sofoulis has written about the ways in which people map their lives onto celebrities; thus, the loss of a celebrity becomes a loss of part of themselves. Celebrity funerals, she writes, become "a collective attempt to re-make the world, and to reconstitute it, both through shared media consumption of the event (people making dates to watch the funeral together) as well as public, physical and emotional acts ... (waiting to sign condolence books, queuing to put down flowers, lighting candles etc.)" (17). The virtual community of the Canadian nation was unified and embodied in its simultaneous consumption of the televised Trudeau funeral. The funeral, then, in Deleuze and Guattari's terms, became a desiring-machine (*A Thousand Plateaus*), in which an insatiable desire for images and memories of Trudeau produced other desires: for an imaginary historical moment of democracy and justice; for an alterity that predated the hegemony of globalization; for the innocence of the 1960s with its summers of love. That the funeral occurred just weeks before a federal election also meant that, for a time, the current (Liberal) prime minister running for re-election could, despite a history of conservative legislation regarding immigration, free trade, and health care, feed on and embody these desires without even gesturing to their fulfillment.

Trudeau's funeral was heavily covered for five days by both of Canada's major English-language television networks, CTV and CBC. His body lay in state in the parliament buildings of Ottawa, Canada's capital city, for several days. Large numbers of Canadians lined up to view the Trudeau casket and to write comments in government-organized "books of condolences" across Canada (later reproduced on a government website).[1] The casket then travelled by special train to Montreal, accompanied by Trudeau's two sons, Justin and Sacha— recalling the posthumous train ride of another liberal countercultural figure, Bobby Kennedy. At the funeral, the all-star cast of mourners included England's Prince Andrew and former US president Jimmy Carter, complemented by the countercultural cachet of honorary pallbearers Leonard Cohen and Cuban president Fidel Castro.[2] The highlight of the funeral was a melodramatically declaimed eulogy by Justin Trudeau that presented a sentimental, child's-eye view of a prime minister's life and produced tears and applause inside and outside the church (eerily echoing the applause at Diana's funeral).

Certain collective performances of mourning—such as the Trudeau funeral—are conflicted sites where the nation in a partial and unsatisfactory way tries to integrate loss through the process of melancholia or, in Dominic LaCapra's terms, "acting out" (*Writing History* 1). However, within Canadian television, this consciousness is constantly deferred or displaced. As at Princess Diana's funeral some six years earlier, it was racialized citizens who enacted an entire nation's tragic structure of feeling, expressive of the unnameable sorrows and griefs of Western culture (Ang). The Trudeau funeral had many uncanny similarities with Diana's, from flower-strewn public grounds to applauding crowds. Aerial views of mourners on Parliament Hill recalled even grander aerial views of mourners at Kensington Palace, a kind of colonial overlay.[3] British newspapers noted with pride the multi-ethnic composition of Diana's mourners; here in Canada, the presence of a multicultural society (supposedly Trudeau's invention) at his funeral, too, was much remarked upon. The process of mourning Trudeau was mapped over the surface of those feminized black, brown, yellow, and even queer faces—this was even more proof of forgetting, since very few of those othered bodies were actually *inside* the church at either funeral.

Deleuze and Guattari distinguish between two kinds of memory: "Short-term memory understands forgetting as a process; it does not merge with the instant, but with the collective rhizome.... Long-term memory (family, race, society, civilization), traces and translates, but what it translates continues to act within it" (*Anti-Oedipus* 35). Long-term memories (those connected to the national imaginary) captured Trudeau's statesmanlike movements, like a film still, or a trace. Short-term memories were more like the space *between* film frames, sliding past our eyes: tanks on city streets, refugees in jail cells. In the act of national mourning, the two kinds of memories merged: we did not know sometimes why we were weeping. As Françoise Gaillard writes (about Diana's funeral): "Since it is easier to weep together than to live together, emotion of this sort may come increasingly to stand in for the social bond" (167).

Also like Diana's funeral, there was a subtle queerness to this event, in the generic sense of queer as outlaw, or non-normal. Trudeau's alleged bisexuality was never mentioned in the mainstream print or television media except, briefly and ambivalently, on CBC's satirical newsmagazine *This Hour Has 22 Minutes*, by two recurring old-lady characters played by Mary Walsh and Cathy Jones.

> JONES: I heard it said he was fruity as pink ink!
> WALSH: Yes, as gay as eighteen balloons, they said.
> JONES: But I don't believe it!
> WALSH: No, no me neither!
> JONES: He was a goer! Sure, he went out with that Kim Cattrall.
> WALSH: Who's that?
> JONES: She's the one who plays the slutty one on that there *Sex and the City*.
> WALSH: Sure, how can ya tell with a crowd of high-heeled harlots!
> JONES: Yes, a good time was had by all kind of girls.
> (*This Hour Has 22 Minutes*, October 2000)

The newspapers coyly played along: endless photos of Trudeau in capes and femmy hats were printed and reprinted. Seated in the front row of Montreal's Notre-Dame Basilica during the funeral service was a less-than-normal family: Trudeau's two unmarried sons, his ex-wife from twenty years ago, his one-time mistress, and his illegitimate daughter, whom Trudeau sired in his seventies.[4] This was a kind of double funeral; also present was the ghost of Michel, Trudeau's youngest son, from whose tragic death a year earlier Trudeau had never recovered—more like a mother than a father, really, in his inconsolable grief.

If nationhood is a masculine construction, then Canada has always existed outside of that symbolic order. From comedic references on *The Simpsons* and *The West Wing* to George W. Bush's significant omissions, Canada's subservient relationship to the US is legendary. As Arthur Kroker writes, "The essence of the Canadian intellectual condition is this: it is our fate to be forever marginal to the 'present-mindedness' of American culture" (8). This marginality, then, can also be seen as un-masculine, producing an uncanny structural similarity to queerness.

One is tempted to surmise that Canada's infamous absence from global discourse (except for Canadarms in space and hockey games against Russians and Americans) and Canadians' legendary self-deprecation is a result of melancholia or acting out: an inability to resolve its historical trauma. Freud notes that while melancholia results in, among other things, "utterance in self-reproaches and self-revilings, and culminates in a delusional expectation of punishment," mourning significantly avoids this "disturbance in self regard" (244). As Silvan Tomkins states, in a phrase that anticipates Dominick LaCapra's notion of acting out, "If negative affect is too punishing, biologically or psychologically, it may be worse than the alarming situation itself, and it may hinder rather than expedite dealing with it" (qtd. in Sedgwick and Frank 111).

But this acting out can be occasionally redeemed. Thus, the televised funeral of a queer-acting elder statesman, with all of its pauses, its funny unmentionables, and its melancholic idealization of a lost part of the national "self," also represented a limit, and a line of flight.

Proximity, Contagion, and Affect

The theories of Deleuze and Guattari provide some exciting possibilities for the project of television criticism, with its complex intersections of cultural studies, sociology, and cine-psychoanalytic theory. Moreover, as television criticism begins to grapple with digitality and the shifting movements of industry and audience, there is a need for theory that does not create a fixed object of the viewer. While critiques of psychoanalytic theory vis-à-vis film theory are, these days, innumerable, Steven Shaviro's use of Deleuze and Guattari's terms to carry out this critique is useful for the purposes of this chapter.

As an erstwhile lecturer on film and cultural studies in a women's studies department, I found that the pessimism of feminist cine-psychoanalysis folded too neatly into female masochism: the camera lens an evil eye, the female body on the screen a bad object of desire. Shaviro pinpoints distance as a primary problem: filmic images that are theoretically "isolated, like dangerous germs" (16). He argues that "lack" stands in for fear, that what the sacred film-theory lineage of Christian Metz through Laura Mulvey is afraid of "is not the emptiness of the image but its weird fullness" (16). In short, he makes a case for proximity: "the image is not a symptom of lack but of an uncanny excessive residue of being that subsists when all *should* be lacking ..., the insistence of something that refuses to disappear" (17).

Perhaps television, even more than cinema, is peculiarly suited to notions of proximity and of the excessive affect that proximity can encourage and give flight to. More than a schema of behavioural cause and effect (for example, crime shows cause violence in children), this proximity is one of body and machine, skin to skin.[5] *I was glued to the set,* I said to people during the five-day coverage of Trudeau's death and funeral. I spoke of being unable to take my eyes off the screen and my hand off the remote. I cried when Justin Trudeau gave his eulogy, and I got a lump in my throat when I recently replayed the tapes. My neighbour and I congregated on her deck or in my living room to laugh together about Margaret's drama-queen hauteur and compare notes on the different stations we'd been watching. Radio-Canada (CBC's French-language network) was excited, almost giddy, about Castro's presence, whereas the American networks demonstrated barely veiled contempt. My students and I chatted about our Trudeau memories, while photos of people standing together in public areas to watch TV coverage or bursting into spontaneous renditions of the national anthem appeared in the papers. At these moments, the crowds standing in vigil at TV shops or sports bars need the amplification of the crowds standing in vigil on Parliament Hill (Gibbs, "In Thrall"). Trudeau was a machinic exercise with molecular components: a pre-election Liberal government, state-owned media, bodies longing to be part of a nation next to bodies (such as my own) that had long since abandoned the project of nation, the hyperreality of a famous family conveying its private emotions and gestures to the public.

Another affect-related notion pertinent to television is that of contagion. As Shaviro writes: "Mimesis and contagion tend to efface fixed identities, and to blur the boundaries between inside and outside. The viewer is transfixed and transmogrified in the consequence of the infectious, visceral contact of images" (53). Shaviro goes on to speak more specifically of the horror film, but one could as easily think about, as Robert Stam does, television tropes such as reality TV that construct an impression of intimacy and viewing power across all TV formats—even state funerals (Stam 24). Thus, in our proximity, rather than identifying with the image, we are *touched* by it. With various speech acts (for example, headlines such as "The Nation Mourns") the nation becomes embodied as a person with feelings. The nation becomes both the subject and object of feeling, with affect circulating between and through bodies. Affects become attached to other affects: love of the elder statesman becomes a reason for grief but also a reason for hate as we remember those (Quebec separatists) who did not love him as we did (Ahmed, *Cultural Politics of Emotion*).

Marshall McLuhan has described television as, "above all, an extension of the sense of touch" (333). Using the assassination and funeral of John F. Kennedy as an example, he writes convincingly of the power of this new medium to touch and implicate the body:

> No national event except in sports has ever had such coverage or such an audience. It revealed the unrivaled power of TV to achieve the involvement of the audience in a complex process. The funeral as a corporate process caused even the image of sport to pale.... The Kennedy funeral, in short, manifested the ability of TV to involve an entire population in a ritual process. (337; italics mine)

Indeed, the Kennedy funeral has become synonymous with televised spectacle, in that it was the first such event covered by television in real time. It contributed to the idea that an event on television *could and should* touch and move bodies to painful affect.

"I was moved. We all were," wrote CBC news anchor Peter Mansbridge in a book of condolences. This pronouncement is another example of the doubled, uncanny affect of the hyperreal. Mansbridge, a paid employee inside TV, is there to move us; outside of TV he is there to be moved. His job is to infect us with grief and, therefore, an insatiable desire for images of the departed; our job is to pass this on to others with our conversations in classrooms and offices and living rooms, with our hugs and tears and gestures. "Desire is a machine," write Deleuze and Guattari, "and the object of desire is another machine connected to it" (*Anti-Oedipus* 26). In the case of the Trudeau funeral, it is the media that becomes a desiring-machine: it is not the need for images of Trudeau that produce desire for them but rather desire that produces need. This desire is productive. As Deleuze and Guattari write: "In group fantasy the libido may invest all of an existing social field, including the latter's most repressive forms" (30). On the twentieth anniversary of the October Crisis—which coincided with Trudeau's death—the traumatic memory of Trudeau's invocation of the War Measures Act became reterritorialized, incorporated into the national body of Trudeau, of the nation, and transformed from shame into pride.

Bodies pressed against bodies lining up in an autumn chill, hands pressed against pen, writing in books of condolences, tearful eye catching tearful eye. These contagious affects give us a sense of belonging—if not to the nation then to the virtual community of television watchers and newspaper readers. But, as I argued earlier, the impossibility of full belonging can produce shame.

The desire for home, for roots, for fixed and stable meanings, is a function of a prelinguistic psychic space. Does it not, sometimes, feel shameful, to long for that secure and prideful zone?

The War Measures Act, with its sweeping powers, gave rise to many episodes in Canadian history that are now conventionally considered shameful. This legislation (now known as the Emergency Measures Act) is Canada's most notorious and long-standing anti-terrorist legislation. Initiated in 1914 as a means of rounding up and interning itinerant East European immigrants during wartime, it was later used to intern Japanese Canadians during World War II and, more recently, to quell Quebec separatism in October 1970. When invoked, it gives the government extra-legal powers of surveillance, arrest, and detention, as well as the ability to call in military forces. The invocation of the War Measures Act functions as a site of traumatic memory for several generations of Canadians. That this despotic term could have been transformed into a site of national pride at the moment of Trudeau's death provides an interesting example of a nation seeking to increase its own shame–pride balance.

'Just Watch Me'

"Just watch me," said Trudeau in a television interview on the eve of invoking the War Measures Act in response to separatist uprising in Quebec. Trudeau, ever conscious of the camera, used the FLQ Crisis of October 1970 to the benefit of his (and Canada's) international image. Overnight, Canada and Trudeau were masculinized by the panoptical all-seeing camera eye. With those words, Trudeau affirmed and amplified his scopophilic appeal: his body becoming-TV, becoming-military, becoming-machine. The shame of a weakened federation giving in to terrorist threat was averted.

Years later, Trudeau cited his friend Eugene Forsey in his memoir: "In my judgment [Trudeau] saved us from Baader-Meinhof gangs and Red Brigades" (148). Adds Trudeau on the next page: "It should also be noted that in the quarter-century that has followed the October Crisis, the country has seen no resurgence of terrorism" (149). The spectre of a dark, Germanic insurrection coupled with the image of Trudeau as saviour is monumental. Monuments mark spaces of remembrance and forgetting, and perhaps also of shame. A leader so monumentalized can only be the product of arborescent histories, what Deleuze and Guattari have called "organized memories" (*Anti-Oedipus* 36). I argue instead for a rhizomatic notion of the "semiotic chain" of "diverse acts" (*Anti-Oedipus* 12). This notion speaks to the flow between the different meanings of the Trudeau legacy; rather than being contradictions, Trudeau's effeminacy and his assertion of masculinity during October 1970 are offshoots of each other. For, according to Deleuze and Guattari, any point of a rhizome can be connected to anything else. From Trudeau's rebellious, faggy pirouette at Buckingham Palace to his militaristic quashing of dissidents, it is this non-linear sequence of diverse acts that would seem to form the Trudeau legacy.

The Driveways of the Nation

There was a strange proximity to the October Crisis of 1970 in our modestly middle-class Ottawa neighbourhood. First there was the television, sputtering earnestly in black and white: mug shots of FLQ (Front de Libération du Québec) cell members with their flowery names (Rose and Cossette), and Trudeau in gunslinger mode, playing to the camera. And, second, there was my neighbourhood, and the presence of army tanks on our very own street, with its own flowery name, Featherston Drive.

I was in grade seven, and seriously working on my popularity. I had never felt more self-conscious, more watched: by my eagle-eyed mom, by mirrors and reflections in store windows, by girls, and by boys. I had just started to be courted by a group of bad girls, who invited me to allegedly girls-only basement sleepovers, where boys were daringly smuggled in like contraband, long after the moms and dads had gone to bed. Spin the bottle and long boring bouts of necking now occupied the site where girl talk, Ouija boards, and makeup sessions had once deliciously reigned. Those kisses felt interminable to me: unpractised boyish lips like wet washcloths, skin that smelled like running shoes. Mouths again, but without language this time; or perhaps it was a completely new language that I could never inhabit but which, for many years, I would try desperately to speak.

It was at one of these awkward basement parties that we heard about Quebec Labour Minister (or "minister of unemployment," as the FLQ dubbed him) Pierre Laporte's assassination, on someone's pink transistor radio. Was it before or after that tanks rolled into our neighbourhood to protect some low-level diplomat living in one of the "colonial-style" prefabs that lined the treeless street? As I wrote later in a film narration:

> In our suburban Ottawa neighbourhood, everything seemed so calm. Army tanks were parked in front of some of the better homes, and the Moms brought the soldiers coffee or tea. When the Dads came home, family snapshots were taken in front of the tanks, which had very quickly become status symbols. Clearly, we were protected, with or without the tanks: by our

whiteness and innocence, by our willingness to speak English, by the size of our very green lawns. *(Unspoken Territory)*

Perhaps we also felt protected by Trudeau, whose masculinity and paternalism were suddenly no longer in question. On some level, I could relate. I too had just left behind an innocent same-sex milieu. The state had been banished from the bedrooms of the nation only to reappear in its driveways. The world would never be quite the same again.

Affect and Trudeau

I feel that the Canadian people and I did dream together for such loves in challenging times—love for ourselves, love for our country, love for more peace and justice in the world.
—Trudeau, *Memoirs* 368

In the minds of most Canadians, it would seem to be affect that most defined Trudeau. References to him after his death—in popular media and in the books of condolences—make frequent use of such words and phrases as *exuberance, passion, love, excitement, charisma*. It was perhaps the exoticization of English Canada's other—Quebec—that allowed this image to develop so durably. Perhaps Trudeau stood in for Quebec, or at least for Montreal, a place anglo Canadians can go and be all the things they are not in Moose Jaw or Winnipeg or Saint John: passionate, excited, exuberant, in love. Quebec's exoticism, represented by the wide, acrobatic motions of the tongue and mouth and hands and arms, the poetic cadences of the French language, the drinking of French wine in smoke-filled (*smoke!*) bars until three in the morning.

And it was affect that most defined Trudeau's funeral: the slightly deranged grimaces of Margaret; Fidel behind her, providing a Latin beat; the tear-filled eyes of those not generally seen as emotive—former prime ministers John Turner and Joe Clark and former cabinet minister Marc Lalonde. And finally there was Justin Trudeau's eulogy to his father, which *The Vancouver Sun* described in theatrical terms: "It was Justin Trudeau who brought the entire church to their feet with applause and tears in their eyes" (Baxter et al. B1). Television cameras and editing helped frame Justin Trudeau's affect-laden and perhaps affected performance with slow dissolves to the coffin, weeping statesmen, and the somber-looking crowds outside:

My father's fundamental belief never came from a textbook. It stemmed from his deep love and faith in all Canadians and over the past few days, with every card, every rose, every tear, every wave, and every pirouette, you returned his love…. He left politics in '84. He came back for Meech. He came back for Charlottetown. He came back to remind us of who we are and what we're all capable of. But he won't be coming back anymore. It's all up to us, all of us, now. "The woods are lovely, dark and deep. He has kept his promises and earned his sleep." *Je t'aime, Papa.* (October 4, 2000)[6]

Upon completing his eulogy, Justin Trudeau descended from the podium at Notre-Dame Basilica, walked over to his father's flag-draped casket and bent to kiss it, his shoulders suddenly wracked with sobs. With his childlike locution—*Je t'aime, Papa* (I love you, Daddy)—and his tears, Justin became a child in relation to the ritual gestures of the nation (reminiscent, again, of Diana's flag-draped casket, crowned with an envelope with the word "Mummy" scrawled on it in child's handwriting). As Marvin and Ingle write, "The flag that wraps the casket transforms shed blood into the community seed ritually planted at the fertile centre … ritual gestures and language represent [the flag-covered coffin] as an infant with regenerative power" (149). Indeed, as rumours immediately began to circulate about the possibility of Justin entering political life, his body—with its own potential for regeneration—stood in (by way of his father's body) for flag and nation.

Television footage of this eulogy invariably produces embodied feeling: tears, goosebumps, lumps in throats, chills down spines. Justin's voice sounded eerily like his father's, albeit more heavily laden with emotion. With television, sound is generally seen as more important than image—it calls to us even as we head to the fridge for a beer during a commercial; it fills the room and compensates for our distracted glance. Anna Gibbs writes of televisual sound: "the emotional tone of a voice will come to the foreground, as meaning slides into the background" ("Mixed Feelings" 3). The effect is not unlike that of melodrama, a genre itself heavily marked by sound. Although one is deeply familiar with the genre (and perhaps even ironically detached from it), its performative repetitions cannot help but produce an affective response.

This response is at least partially rooted in normalcy. According to Silverman, "social formations depend upon their dominant fictions for their sense of unity and identity" (54). Following Freud, she argues that groups of people, perhaps even entire nations, can protect themselves from trauma by, in a sense, repressing the memory of the traumatic event and participating in collective identifications that attempt to create closure and fixity of meaning. The trauma in this case would entail not merely the death of an elderly former prime minister but personal as well as collective or national traumas. These identifications usually involve the repeating of the forms and gestures of a particular genre. The genre of melodrama, for example, participates in the compulsion to repeat but then also tries to close over the wound of pain that these traumatic events represent.

Jostein Gripsrud has traced the many uses of melodrama as well as its historical roots in relation to television. She insists upon melodrama's "moral urgency ... and its ambition to speak of what was actually unspeakable" (246). Its repetition, she claims, is pleasurable, providing audiences with moral lessons that they want repeated again and again. Citing Peter Brooks, she posits melodrama as a secular way of explaining the world to peasants and nobility alike, "a textual machine designed to cope with the threatening black hole God left after him when he returned to his heaven" (244). The excessive affect inherent in melodrama stands in not only for religion but for politics: "a popular resistance to abstract, theoretical ways of understanding society or history" (Gripsrud 245). Perhaps this is one way of understanding the enormous effectiveness and contagiousness of a eulogy so visibly produced and so melodramatically declaimed. Justin's words superseded those of the priests and the politicians who spoke; his face loomed larger and more beautifully than the majestic gothic arches of Notre-Dame Basilica. The lessons in the eulogy were ones of morality, not ethics; of acting out rather than working through.

But affect is also about the need to see oneself as fully human and of this world and, therefore, affected. Sofoulis writes (about Princess Diana's funeral): "By participating in a global mourning, individual people make the claim of belonging to another world, a world of affects and performances that are interlinked with but also exceed icons and narratives. Some participants in the flower-laying or funeral were not particularly emotional about Diana; they just wanted to be part of this major historical event" (18).

Since 9/11, amid the circulation of images and ideas about mourning those who died in the World Trade Center, this interrelationship—of celebrity death, affect, and citizenship—has never, it seems, been more active. The ability to mourn these celebrity deaths—Diana, Trudeau, the dead of New York— became a mark of normalcy. However, in *Planet Diana*, Rosanne Kennedy cautions that "identifications generated through dominant media images are so exclusionary that we are prevented from grieving for some of the people in our local communities. How many of us, for instance, have grieved over the ruined lives of stolen children [in Australia]?" (52) And what of those bodies *not* invested in the nation that shed tears for neither Diana nor Trudeau? For a member of the 1970s generation, conventional markers of citizenship would seem to hold no cultural capital. But perhaps the very act of watching TV was where consumption became citizenship; in Kroker's words, "the profound paradox of a modern technology as simultaneously a prison-house and a pleasure palace" (125). That pleasurable grief, so thinly satisfying, was then compounded by a deeper sadness, an encounter with the limits of consumer culture and the spectacle of celebrity.

The National Body

Dear Justin, Sacha and Sarah: Every day in my work as a Co-Operative Housing Manager, I see the faces of people who are here largely due to the vision of your father. People like Alvaro, who fled death threats in Colombia and the families from Afghanistan who fled the violence there. Today they are Canadians, helping to contribute to the country your father loved so much, due to his efforts to embrace the peoples of the world to help this country grow.
—Linda Phillips Kelm (Newmarket, Ontario), from a book of condolences

Hi, I am 10 years old. I might not have seen him before. I do know that he was a great man. My parent's are from India. If it wasn't for him, I would not be here in Beautiful British Columbia.
—Annu Grewal (Terrace, B.C.), from a book of condolences

As the funeral week continued on TV, the screen became like the face of a corpse, drained of colour. Black-and-white images of the "Trudeau years"— the late 1960s to the early 80s—flickered in my living room day and night, organizing my own, and the nation's, memory. These are the images that pierced through the self-absorbed miasma of my teenage years—ersatz images of hope amid soulful depression and the writing of much bad poetry. The TV documentaries about Trudeau's life and the special memorial sections in the Saturday papers were pleasurable, nostalgic, drawing me into the phantasm of an arboreal community, a tree with a single set of roots, an intact family with normal parents who didn't have East European accents. *Je t'aime, Papa.*

In the week of homage, Trudeau was credited for an astonishing number of achievements, from a more open immigration policy to widespread Canadian facility in the French language. And yet there certainly cannot have been any single author of bilingualism and multiculturalism. In the nation's need to fix authorship, Trudeau's body became overly coded, bearing excessive signification. His body thus became a national body, but, as Deleuze and Guattari write, "each of these becomings [assures] the deterritorialization of one of the terms" (*Anti-Oedipus* 20). The becoming-queer of the national body; the becoming-national of the queer. In the week's coverage of Trudeau's death, sexuality was, of necessity, in constant play with nationalism.

"He could have danced all night," reads the headline of a *Globe and Mail* photo spread (Griffiths R14). Trudeau is all waving hands and swaying butt here: "1989: Trudeau does the bump in Montreal"; "1981: a jive dance threatens to turn into a pirouette"; "1982: fancy footwork with a Macedonian dancer." And more proximity. Playwright and actor Linda Griffiths (known, incidentally, for playing a lesbian in the 1970s film *Lianna* and for playing both Margaret *and* Pierre in a one-woman play in the late 1980s), snuck into a Governor General's ball for the purposes of doing research. She managed a dance with Trudeau, describes "his slightly tense shoulders, the angle of his head, the touch of his *small hand* on my back" (Griffiths R8; italics mine). Small hands, skin to skin, a body constantly in contact, a body that is a contact zone. This is a body that could dance with anyone, "an individual varying in an infinite number of ways" (Deleuze and Guattari, "Ethology" 625), a body of diverse gestures, a limit text. Writes Griffiths: "I realized the entire country had danced with Trudeau. And some felt dropped like old high school flames, and some still felt beloved. It doesn't matter how it went. What we felt for Trudeau was true love, and true love never goes away; it stays in the heart and mind forever" (R8).

Two years after Trudeau's death, CBC produced a miniseries entitled *Trudeau.* In it, the former prime minister (played by Colm Feore) is portrayed in a florid, populist manner: Trudeau as sexy philosopher-king, Trudeau as pop star. More importantly, production of the program *itself* was portrayed, by both CBC executives and dominant media, as something akin to statesmanship. In a *Vancouver Sun* article entitled "Trudeau mini-series 'nation-building,'" CBC network programming head Slavko Klymkiw described *Trudeau* as "nation-building, larger-than-life" television (Strachan A4). Trudeau's body had indeed become national, and those invested in its monumentalization had become heroicized.

How do we constitute a map of this national body? Two bodies, perhaps, French and English, passion and reason, queer and straight, with one white face, with a grin that reveals nothing, that was never so expressive as at his son's death. A face deterritorialized from a body, from orifice, from the grotesque. The national body is unsettled, made grotesque, by folding into an image of the queer. Branches, movements, and flows. A friend sends me a newspaper article tracing the origins of Trudeau's pirouette—ballet lessons in the 1960s. Margaret's face at the funeral, head bobbing, smiling at no one, an excess of affect in danger of spilling over, a horizon, about to explode. Justin delivering his eulogy: Margaret's face mapped onto Pierre's. The tragic face of Jacques Hébert, rumoured to be Trudeau's former lover, back in the seventh row, deterritorialized. Nostalgia. For my youth and my mother's. A displaced mourning for my own father, the rags-to-riches refugee. All of this on a single page.

"Dead ends should always be restructured on the map," write Deleuze and Guattari, "and in that way opened up to possible lines of flight" (*Anti-Oedipus* 31). In the year after the Trudeau funeral, only one other TV event has drawn me in as obsessively. The images are beautiful, really: the billowing pale grey smoke of tear gas, the sinewy bodies of anarchists dressed in black, throwing stones and tear-gas canisters in wide graceful arcs, the phalanx of cops like the advance of blue-black insects with hard, shining carapaces.

Friends of ours are in Quebec City, demonstrating against the policies of the G7 nations gathering nearby. The screen disappears, we enter into it, we are immanent. We are becoming light itself, a rearrangement of pixels on a digital plateau, visual persistence breaking down the hastily erected concrete wall, the TV screen.

In the space between frames there are trace memories of other moments of resistance; among them the black-and-white flicker of Trudeau on TV, in a trade-union march against the Algoma Steel Corporation, circa 1949.[7] "I think trade union people across this province should rise up in arms," says the young Trudeau in a TV interview (CBC Digital Archives). Cut to images of young men throwing rocks at Quebec provincial police more than fifty years ago, charging at police cars and factory walls.

If desire produces reality (Deleuze and Guattari, *Anti-Oedipus*), then these desiring bodies, struggling at the concrete border of public and private, of the corporate and the democratic, are also bodies belonging to the nation.[8] This nation, then, becoming these bodies.

SEVEN

HOMELAND (IN)SECURITY
Roots and Displacement, from New York
to Toronto to Salt Lake City

impossible citizens, / repositories of the city's panic
—Dionne Brand, *Thirsty* 40

ON SEPTEMBER 11, 2001, broadcast and print media around the world narrated the destruction of New York City's World Trade Center, and the deaths of thousands of its occupants. This chapter examines the ways in which Canadian television and its appendages (the telephone, the cellphone, the Internet, the newspaper) operated to organize the discursive meanings of this traumatic event. I propose that between September 11 and the February 2002 Olympic Winter Games in Salt Lake City, Utah, ideas about home, roots, and rootedness (and their others—foreignness, homelessness, nomadism) operated as a discursive mapping of that which could otherwise not be mapped or fully grasped. From the demonization of those nomads, migrants, and others moving across borders, to the triumphant Roots logos on the uniforms of British, American, and Canadian Olympic athletes, roots, in a sense, became the unrepresentable "real." How did television, then, in its liminal function as portal to both the inside and outside of the home, narratively organize the spatial boundaries of private and public, local and global? More specifically, I examine how Canadian television worked to mediate the trauma of boundary dissolution in both a literal and a representational sense. Following recent trauma theory, I ask: How does a nation itself experience common symptoms of trauma? And can such trauma—for example, the perceived trauma of the nation being violated—become unrepresentable in and of itself, so that the metaphor of home and roots stands in its place?

The use of the words "homeland" and "homeland security" erupted in the US almost immediately after September 11, and the meanings of the word "home" became delimited by unspoken racialized binaries.[1] These days, race crises often operate without reference to race and can speak through culture rather than through the skin and bones of biology (Gilroy). Thus, *Heimat* and home can stand in for a desire for whiteness. The terminology of *Heimat* also served to reiterate earlier racialized utterances as well as to produce new ideas about self and other. The US, as an imperial power, has long projected its borders across space. But as Hannah Neveh writes, colonizing notions of distance and proximity acquired new meanings after 9/11:

> September 11 has violated and shattered the confidence of the United States in the total security of its territorial body. The sense of being violated has permeated U.S. domestic space by and large—every "place" as well as every "in-between" has become suspect of infection: the work space, the leisure space, the home space.... Yet the ultimate and illuminating transformation, which conceptualizes America's new sensitivity, is the creation of a federal agency for "Homeland Security." (451)

In Canada, 9/11 produced a new proximity to the US. Canada, its identity historically defined as *un*like that of the US, now had to redefine otherness. Wray writes, "Canadian nationalist sentiment remains inextricably and completely bound to a 'not-American' status. Marking and remarking upon differences (even, perhaps especially, where they do not exist) ensures the articulation of an English Canadian imaginary in the face of an otherwise invisible 'otherness'" (165–66). Essential to this imaginary is the notion of tolerance. Indeed, Canada's belief in itself as tolerant is one of the primary ways in which Canada defines itself as different from the US (Mackey). Thus, Canada's new *in*tolerance for refugees and foreigners, post-911, created even more ideological synergy with the US.[2]

9/11 provided useful insights into how television networks operate within a knowledge–power relationship. 9/11's excessive flow of information, among television and phone and Internet and street, produced, in Foucauldian terms, "an uninterrupted play of calculated gazes" (*Discipline and Punish* 177). At that moment, discipline operated relationally: hegemonic discourse passed from ear to ear, digital to analog, and back again. In this sense, television did not operate alone; never had it been more a part of a discursive network. As the entire nation became a single contact zone, it seemed at first that affect had

*this is the key point I need to make

never been so contagious and so conservative. Every person who ventured an opinion about the terrorist attacks was part of this network—either for or against the US call to war—but those who proclaimed "our" innocence and "their" infamy made it to air and in turn influenced those who hadn't made it to air, becoming part of a multiplication of small-scale judgment and disciplinary authority. In Canadian media, an increased emphasis on notions of home occurred in news stories about those (Canadians) *staying* home more on one hand and those (foreigners, immigrants) being told to *go* home on the other.

Since 9/11, several news reports of Canadian- and American-born people being "sent back" to homelands they'd never been to have circulated in the media. Morley writes, "the nation is idealized as a kind of hometown writ large, a sociogeographic environment into whose comforting security we may sink.... The over-valuation of home and roots has as its necessary correlative the suspicion of mobility" (33). This fantasy of hometown roots rewrites the actual narratives of peoples displaced by globalization not once but many times in their lives. The desire to send undesirable others home becomes constitutive of nationalism. In feeling that desire, national subjects express their own desire for roots and home. As Hage puts it, "In the desire to send the other 'home,' subjects express implicitly their own desire to *be* at home. In every 'go home,' there is an 'I want to and am entitled to feel at home in my nation'" (Hage, *White Nation* 39–40).

Home and *Heimat*

An overt national focus on notions of home and homeland carries with it the disturbing echo of the German concept of *Heimat* (Morley). Celia Applegate defines *Heimat*, which originated in the nineteenth century as an expression of the "feeling of belonging together" (x), in which sentiment stemming from shared roots become part of an essential identity. German Jew Jean Amery writes scathingly about the ways in which the meanings of *Heimat* permeate the meanings of home: "One would like to dispel the embarrassingly sweet tones that are associated with the word home and that call forth a rather disturbing series of concepts: regional arts and crafts, regional literature, regional foolery of all kinds. But they are stubborn, keep close to our heels, demand their effect" (48).

Amery here refers not to all local crafts and literatures but to the ways in which German fascism capitalized on the idea of roots by integrating "*Heimat* associations"—traditional expressions of German communalism such as youth groups, hiking fellowships, and singing clubs—into Nazi culture. As Applegate writes, "club activities ... could and did legitimate the Nazi regime by giving it an appearance of *rootedness* in the structure of everyday life" (203; italics mine). At the same time, however, the Nazis were centralizing all operations, negating the *Heimat* idea of local organization and fellowship (205). *Heimat* became nothing more than a symbolic notion, which, through the Nazi practice of encouraging folk customs, was a means of imagining cultural roots that were racially pure (217). We might also relate this to contemporary debates on globalization, in which a loss of the local can lead to an uncritical valorization of hometown roots and homespun values.

In *A Thousand Plateaus*, Deleuze and Guattari ponder postmodernity's vexed relationship with roots, which they dub the "fascicular system."[3] They imply that the root system has its origins (roots?) in the classical era—"noble, signifying" (5), and perhaps even despotic: "It is odd how the tree has dominated Western reality and all of Western thought, from botany to biology and anatomy, but also gnosiology, theology, ontology, all of philosophy ... the root foundation, *Grund, racine, fondement*. The West has a special relation to the forest, and deforestation" (18).

Deleuze and Guattari map a symbolic connection to fascism with the notion of the fascicle—"a bundle-like cluster," according to the *American Heritage Dictionary* (477), but also the etymological root of the word fascism—which in a sense "bundles together" state, corporate, and nationalist interests. This coming together of local and global forms of capitalism is vividly evident in the ways in which television operated within domestic space during and after 9/11.

Festive Viewing

"Home is where the heart is," goes the expression. Home is at the heart of post-9/11's excessive nationalisms, on TV and outside of it. Television schedules are one of the things that help create a sense of home; thus, home is not only space but also time (Morley). Thomas Dumm, taking this idea further, argues that the prime-time viewing schedule is an instrument of discipline: "I have known for some time how much hinges on regularity, how the creation of the modern soul, to borrow from Foucault, now depends as much upon television as it does on a prison schedule" (315). Indeed, several feminist television theorists (Modleski, Probyn) have discussed the ways in which television regulates, and in some sense oversees, women's housework schedules. In this sense, the home is a space of discipline.

According to Foucault, certain disciplinary apparati work upon the body as a locus of power, producing the repetition of bodily movements and gestures (*Discipline and Punish*). We might think, at a time of national crisis, of the body's movements from remote to telephone to television to Internet and back again to TV. The event's very mediality, its instantaneous reproduction through cellphone cameras, texted messages, emails, as well as radio and television reports, can be seen as exacerbating the possibilities for an ideological reading of the event. As Grusin writes: "In today's world, in the current geopolitical environment, governmentality and mediality work hand-in-hand. If governmentality is the way in which biopolitical power controls and manages (and also makes possible particular forms of) people, bodies, cultural and economic practices, and so on, then mediality necessarily participates in this project through all forms of media today—including but not limited to film, TV, print media, the World Wide Web, email, video games, mobile phones, MP3 players, radio, theater, or art" (par. 9).

The call to turn on the television, even in final phone calls between hijacking victims and their wives, even by those who were watching the event firsthand, is one of the things that marks 9/11 as a moment of mediality, located primarily in the home. I heard about a young man who watched the towers start to go down from his Manhattan rooftop. As they were in mid-collapse, he left the rooftop to go inside to turn on his TV, hoping it would make him "understand." Even if the subject knows that much of what he or she is seeing on the screen is fabricated, belief is produced as a result of what Kaja Silverman calls "orchestrated corporeality" (17).

Television's ability to suture together one's own fragmented observations and then to repeat them over and over can undercut local and personal experience (Morley). While this has been true of many national and international events, 9/11 is generally considered to be unique in that the entire event was covered live and in real time by TV.[4] As such, television took on a totemic importance, connecting itself to people's emotions through ritualized utterances and generic forms.

When regular broadcast scheduling collapsed during and just after 9/11, I felt a sense of disorientation and a kind of relief—the relief one feels, perhaps, when temporarily away from home. Perhaps it was the same feeling one gets on a holiday: Monday no longer means work, a weekend may no longer mean certain social pressures. But it was also that there was now a seamless, seemingly undisciplined, flow of television, which one could watch endlessly, without the irritating interruption of commercials or TV shows one disliked. This flow was, of course, only a different sort of disciplinary apparatus. Daniel

Dayan and Elihu Katz, writing about televised historic events (state funerals, inaugurations, and the like), use the term "festive viewing" to mark a broadcasting genre that is, to their minds, by definition not routine (334–35). Dayan and Katz's typology, which lists such things as "reverence and ceremony," "the almost priestly role played by journalists," and "a norm of viewing in which people tell each other that it is mandatory to view, that they must put all else aside" (336–37), recalls televisions playing in every store and workplace I entered that day, or New York firefighters (the secular saints of the occasion) standing at attention as stretchers were carried out of the rubble. Pseudo-religious invocation permeated the earliest breaking news of the event, as in this morning broadcast by CBC Newsworld as the second of the Twin Towers collapsed: CBC newscaster Mark Kelley: "Oh my God ... [silence]. Oh my God [silence] ... if you can imagine the situation get any worse it just got worse, that was the second tower of the World Trade Center collapsing before our eyes.... Unspeakable horror in Manhattan."[5]

Processes of decoding also shifted (Hall, "Encoding/Decoding"). For the first few hours of 9/11, there was little need to prefer one thing over another, no need to engage in a decoding process, to negotiate the text beyond its preferred readings. All of the wall-to-wall coverage was, in a sense preferred.[6] Since all stations were broadcasting the same images, there were few choices to be made. TV became less like home—with all of its banal routines—and more like a trip, a being-away-from-home, but one, ironically, that one had to stay home for (grounded flights notwithstanding).

Flow is one of the foundational ideas of television scholarship: the idea that television programming, rather than comprising bounded narratives, flows within itself (for example, the flow between news segments), from program to program and from program to commercial. Further, television programs are structured narratively so as to hold the viewer's attention (and maintain flow) between commercial breaks[7] (Williams, *Television* 93). In more recent television writing, this idea is expanded to include the routines of everyday life, so that one may theorize, for example, a flow between the soap opera, the home, the freeway, and the shopping mall, in the sense of these as narrative and physical spaces dominated—in the daytime at least—by women and by forms of female address (Morse).

Flow operated in an almost hyperreal sense on September 11 and the weeks that followed. There was an *overflow* of information and imagery; there was an endless, constantly churning *flow* between and across the spaces of the home, television narratives, the Internet, the cellphone and telephone, and the street. Sometimes you couldn't distinguish what was on television from what you saw on the street. As John Updike wrote in *The New Yorker*: "From the viewpoint of a tenth-floor apartment in Brooklyn Heights ... the destruction of the World Trade Center Twin Towers had the false intimacy of television, on a day of perfect reception" (28). *Tears flowed*, on TV and off, in the privacy of the home and in public. Žižek described the spectacle as reality TV: "even if the show is 'for real,' people still act in them—they simply play themselves" (*Welcome to the Desert of the Real!* 12).

There was also considerable *flow between* television and cinema. Television's form of address is generally seen to differ from that of the cinema in that film is more spectacular and television is more fragmented and generically mixed (Houston). Where moviegoers are fixed in a single gaze toward a narrative, television watchers, watching from home, are constantly distracted, getting up during commercials, talking on the phone, dealing with a flow of advertising, news, drama, and so on. Cinema is said to produce the "gaze," television "the glance," but on September 11 and 12 television became something else. Its set of cultural competencies, theorized amid a control group of half-hour programs—schoolchildren on a normal day with normal amounts of homework, and housewives with feeding and laundry schedules (Modleski)—was nowhere to be seen. Everyone, it seemed, was channelling CNN, as monolithically positioned as Laura Mulvey's visually transfixed cinema-goers. For a time, resistant readings had little or no currency; everyone was locked into the American gaze.

Indeed, cinematic metaphors were constantly evoked by television hosts at a loss for words—the phrase "it's like a movie" was repeated many times. CBC anchor Peter Mansbridge groped for words: "It just ... it's just ... almost too hard to comprehend. If you'd watched a movie like this in a theatre you'd say this could never happen" (*CBC News*). *New Yorker* writer Anthony Lane pointed out that the duration of events—the bombings and the towers' collapse—lasted about two hours, the approximate length of a Hollywood action movie (79). Lane also enumerates the extent to which people's televised responses to 9/11 came from blockbuster movie scripts like *Independence Day*, *Die Hard*, and *Armaggedon*. His citing of the 1998 thriller film *The Siege* most accurately sums up this uncanniness, as when Denzel Washington's character says, "Make no mistake—we will hunt the enemy, we will find the enemy, we will kill the enemy" (79). But this was a made-for-TV movie, a movie seen in the home. Its cinematic qualities—including the lack of commercial breaks on September 11 and 12—were what helped to produce a gaze that sutured spectators more precisely into a national narrative.[8] That *unheimlich* gaze, so unlike home TV-viewing and the theories that attend it, produced a series of cinematic looks. The look of the camera, searching through rubble for surviving friends, fellow cameramen, and reporters; the voyeuristic gaze of the audience that scanned the screen for falling bodies, that fetishized body parts, that hungered for images of suffering to substitute for a lost national self.

Global media operate by means of the resignification of products and images: the transforming of the Hollywood action film *Independence Day* into an actual event, the recycling of the actual event into an episode of the TV drama series *Third Watch*.[9] McLuhan was perhaps one of the first to acknowledge this process. "The content of any medium is always another medium," he wrote. "The content of writing is speech, just as the written word is the content of print, and print is the content of the telegraph" (8).

Guattari's "semiotic pillage" is a system in which capitalism "manages to articulate, within one and the same general system of inscription and equivalence, entities which at first sight would seem radically heterogenous: of material and economic *goods*, of individual and collective human *activities*, and of technical, industrial and scientific *processes*" (235). The Twin Towers reproduced themselves in movie metaphors, in war preparations, in the pledging of Canada's loyalty to the US, in TV images that repeated the bombing sequences over and over. The insatiable need and hunger for news and images about the bombings was produced in large part by the media, a neediness that became literally and metaphorically contagious, even as anthrax spores appeared at major news sites.

Watching 9/11, One Year Later: The Traumatic Dream

One year after 9/11, I reviewed CBC's coverage of the first eight hours of September 11, 2001. I experienced some guilty pleasures. There was raw beauty in those images, in the novelty of erratic camerawork, of dirty lenses, and unedited footage on TV. Cameras became as expressive as bodies: tilting quizzically, jerking in painful surprise, dilating or tearing up like human eyes. I enjoyed seeing what should have been edited out: the ellipses, the space between the frames. I was moved by the chiaroscuro of billowing clouds as the towers collapsed, by cameramen thinking they'd died and then come back to life, frail pinpoints of light convincing us (and them) of a second chance to live, to set things right with their wives, their kids, their lives. More than anything else, I was struck by the repetitiousness of the footage and the stunning lack of empirical information provided by the pictures and commentary from announcers and interviewees.[10]

I was, of course, watching this footage in a controlled setting (CBC Archives), without the overlapping texts of phone calls, emails, channel-flipping, newspaper, and radio. This was a radically different viewing situation from the one most of us experienced on the day. I wasn't at home, I couldn't phone a friend or walk away (I had brief and limited access to this footage), I couldn't *look* away. I was in a good position to notice what one couldn't possibly have picked up on the day it happened: the stutters, utterances and speech acts, the return of a repressed abject national self. Indeed, the representations and utterances I watched seemed to me to resemble the early stages of trauma as delineated by Judith Herman's classic accounting of the characteristics of post-traumatic stress disorder, *Trauma and Recovery*. Following Bessel van der Kolk, she argues that trauma can return humans to a prelinguistic stage that privileges the sensory and the iconic. Furthermore, the subsequent replaying of the Twin Towers' collapse (every few minutes on the first day, every few hours for months afterwards, and then every six months) seemed to enact the compulsion to repeat that characterizes post-traumatic stress. The compulsive return speaks to an unconscious desire to return to the state of trauma. By repeating or returning to unpleasurable experiences, the traumatized subject unconsciously hopes to achieve mastery and thus to return to pleasure.

The repetitive, compulsive televisual representation of 9/11 on Canadian television provides interesting insights into the relationship of Canadian and American national identity, the porousness of Canada's representational borders, its abjection in moments of crisis, and its concomitant desire for (national) boundary maintenance. All of these factors made 9/11 different in its impact from, say, the crises in Somalia and Rwanda. This was not something happening to a faraway foreign neighbour; this was a relational experience that evoked not just horror but also moral superiority, empathy, and fear.

Flow functioned as both a connection to a national home and a departure from it. At the outset of CBC's 9/11 coverage, American and Canadian images and voices were almost indistinguishable, an almost seamless weaving together of national narratives. In an eerie parallel, Trueman writes about CBC's use of American Vietnam War footage, in which it failed to identify footage that was being fed from US stations. He implies that this technical merging led to ideological synergy: "the CBC, tempted by dramatic American battle footage, found itself parroting the line taken by most American correspondents about the morality and progress of war … the message was American, its outlines dictated too often by the Pentagon" (17).

On September 11, CBC received a news feed from an American affiliate, WABC, and the voice of Mark Kelley, a CBC journalist who happened to be on air that morning, flowed in and out of the voices of journalists in New York. This provided me with a unique opportunity to compare American and

Canadian reactions to the event. By 9 a.m., WABC's announcers had named the event as a terrorist attack; it would be hours before Canadian broadcasters even attempted to draw such a conclusion.

> UNNAMED AMERICAN ANNOUNCER (WABC): Now it's obvious I think that there's a second plane just crashed into the WTC. I think we have a terrorist act of proportions that we cannot begin to imagine at this juncture.... My goodness. A second plane now has crashed into the other tower of the World Trade Center [*sigh*]. Obviously a suicide terrorist attack on the World Trade Center—what we have been fearing for the longest time here apparently has come to pass.
>
> MARK KELLEY (CBC): This is live coverage coming out of Manhattan, the scene of horrific, horrific—well, some people are calling it an act of terror, we're not sure.

Attempts at national boundary maintenance functioned at the level of delay, an echo, or a trace. Later that morning, US President George W. Bush delivered his speech to the nation, in which he declared, in ultra-colloquial terms, "We will hunt down and find the folks that did this" (WABC). In a kind of unconscious, traumatized repetition, the Bugs Bunnyish word "folks" began recurring in Kelley's speech: "This tragedy just continues to get worse, folks." "I may add, folks, that thousands of people work in these two buildings." "Clearly, folks, things are not under control." Thus, a Canadian TV announcer's repetitive utterance of the word "folks" on 9/11, after Bush's speech, performatively sutures him back into American normalcy and recalls earlier utterances of the phrase: the nostalgia of Warner Brothers cartoons ("That's all, folks!"), the unified subjectivity of the German Volk, the down-home comforts of folk music and folklore.

Sianne Ngai describes the drastic slowing down of language that can occur in the wake of trauma: "a proliferation of precise inexactitudes" (255). Her evocation of particular moments that combine the diametrically opposed affects of shock and boredom would seem to apply to 9/11: "Astonishment and boredom ask us to ask what ways of responding our culture makes available to us, and under what conditions. The shocking and the boring prompt us to look for new strategies of affective engagement and to extend the circumstances under which engagement becomes possible" (262). The repetitiousness of the footage and its commentary (perhaps no different from that of a state funeral), as well as its attenuated quality, have us paradoxically wanting more. The two affects are in a circuit, it would seem: as boredom rises, the need for shock rises too.

By 11 a.m., Kelley had caught up with America and was describing the situation as "a terrorist attack beyond belief." By 11:30, John Thompson, director of the right-wing Canadian think tank the McKenzie Institute, was on air saying, "This is not terrorism anymore, it's war." And "It's too soon to point fingers ... but I think you might follow the strings all the way to Afghanistan." At about noon, a CBC graphic appeared that read "Attack on the USA," with a star-spangled blue background. Peter Mansbridge, the CBC's chief news anchor, took the reins with gusto, and his unscripted comments fell in with those of the US president:

> MANSBRIDGE: As we heard from someone else today, it's almost wrong to be discussing this as terrorism, this is war. [*cut to shot of collapsing tower*] We have a country under siege, a city in devastation just south of us in the United States. These are not pictures from some far-off and distant land. This is our neighbour, and this is New York City, today, September 11, 2001. (*CBC News*)

As the vocabulary of war entered the day's repetitious language, new associations were conjured. Gilroy writes about the use of war as analogy, and its associations with immigration, crime, political protest, and alien invasion ("One Nation under a Groove"). In a similar vein, Mary Pat Brody notes that the War on Terrorism's "narratives of emergency" recall utterances and terminology used in the earlier War on Drugs, suturing the notion of an attenuated, masculinist, and institutionalized war into normalcy (446).

Mansbridge's responses are correlative with dissociation, with what Judith Herman has described as an inability to integrate memory. In this dissociative state, the replaying of the Twin Towers' collapse takes on the form of "traumatic dreams." "They often include fragments of the traumatic event in exact form, with little or no imaginative elaboration. Identical dreams often occur repeatedly. They are often experienced with terrifying immediacy, as if occurring in the present" (39).

The phrase "We are all Americans now" erupted days afterwards in the media. Canada's border with the US—long touted as the longest undefended border in the world—became porous and blurry almost overnight. "In Canada, pain has no borders," read a *Globe and Mail* headline on September 15, 2001 (Sallot A14). In that article, the US Ambassador to Canada, Paul Cellucci, was quoted as saying to Canadians: "You truly are our best friends" (Sallot A14). The sense of US as other, so integral to Canadian identity, was significantly diminished, as Canada and the US became embodied as friends with shared affective capacities. Shame, frequently harnessed at times of national crisis, was an integral part of this equation, producing what Nathanson has termed "the emotion of politics and conformity" (16). Shame here operates on several levels: the shame at the moral superiority one feels (the school bully has been chastened); shame, even, at the pleasure one might feel about the bully's tragedy; but perhaps, most profoundly, shame at the need we have for this bully to be our friend.

As the US became less and less Canada's other, foreigners and migrants became more othered. As home became more important, *homelessness* became evidence of questionable morality. Canadian television worked hard to bring grainy, criminalized images of Muslims and Arabs into the familiar surroundings of the home, drawing and building upon a nation's xenophobia. As Morley writes,

> The common location of the television set, in the very center of the home, profoundly integrates televisual experience into the time of everyday life. As a result of this, via television's transmission into the home, the coevalness of alterity is more strongly established than ever before, as that which is far away is made to feel both very much "here"—right in our sitting rooms—and precisely "now." (182)

The longing for a Canadian connection to terrorism was a vicarious traumatization. The impulse to imagine a Canadian connection was the trauma of *unheimlich*; the temporary loss of the maternal realm of belonging and incorporation, of home becoming not-home. On October 10, 2001, Peter Mansbridge announced the arrest of the first of several supposedly *Canadian* terrorists, in a trial-by-media that was to damage unnumbered lives and livelihoods: "Another possible Canadian connection to tell you about tonight. This man's name is Ahmad Sa'id Khadr. He's a Canadian, a former aid worker, and the FBI is hunting for someone with the very same name, listing him as a suspect in the attacks of September 11th" (*CBC News*, October 10, 2001).

When Canadian media wanted to present the "other" side of the story—that is, stories of racist attacks on Muslims—they would feel the need go to the US to do so. On December 16, 2001, CTV news anchor Sandie Rinaldo announced this story:

> RINALDO: This week, Americans watched in horror and anger as Osama bin Laden boasted about the attacks on the World Trade Center. But for Muslim Americans, there is fear the videotape will spark another round of hate crimes. Since September 11th, many Muslims have been harassed and victimized. CTV's Allison Vuchnich met with one family trying to cope with the hostility.

ALLISON VUCHNICH (REPORTER): Watching the Heshmat's prepare dinner, you would never know that this American family is living a nightmare.
YASSER HESHMAT: No one should accept this situation.
VUCHNICH: The Heshmats are Muslim and since the September 11th attacks, they have been harassed and victimized in their own home....
ALIAA HESHMAT: I don't think it's fair, because we are American. We are American citizens, and as I told you we don't know where else to go. This is our home.

Only an immigrant would have to say such a thing: "This is our home." If you have to enumerate nationality or to strive for a sense of home, you can be fairly certain that home will always be denied to you in its entirety (Hage). Ahmed concurs: "the narrative of leaving home produces too many homes and hence no home" (*Strange Encounters* 78). These Muslims are "bodies out of place" (78); they are not really expected to have a safe home. For Canadian viewers, the Muslim experience of "hostility" is at several removes, placed safely away from home and framed by the idea that these Muslims will have to keep moving. "In such a narrative journey, then, the space that is most like home, which is most comfortable and familiar, is not the space of inhabitance—I am here—but the very space in which one is almost, but not quite at home" (Ahmed, *Strange Encounters* 78). Or, as Amery puts it, "One must have a home in order not to need it" (46).

Anthrax and anti-terrorism were discursively linked in the media, the anthrax standing in for foreign elements, which in turn stood in for terrorism. As Henrik Herzberg wrote in *The New Yorker*: "They [the terrorists] rode the flow of the world's aerial circulatory system like lethal viruses" (27). Canadian television, in its desire to be part of this larger world of contagion, was quick to provide a national anthrax story that conveniently appeared the same day that new anti-terrorist legislation was announced:

A contamination scare spread fear on Parliament Hill today. Biohazard crews rushed to the scene after opened mail was found to contain a suspicious powder. The scare came as the Chrétien government launched its sweeping legislative assault in the war on terrorism. The controversial security bill would rewrite the law to give authorities new powers to hunt down suspected terrorists. It would allow for arrests without warrants in certain cases, expand police access to wiretaps, and impose stiff new sentences, up to life in prison, for those convicted of terrorist activities. (Lloyd Robertson, *CTV News*, October 15, 2001)

Canadian and American news became a kind of phantom limb of the Twin Towers, endlessly acting out its melancholia. News of the arbitrary imprisonment and deportation of over a thousand Muslims and other "foreigners" began to leak out through television's appendages: the Internet, the alternative press, and the occasional op-ed piece in newspapers. An American Press article on March 9, 2002, ran with the headline "Hundreds of September 11 Detainees Still in N.J. Jails," and reported on the mass detentions that had left many Middle Eastern men behind bars on immigration charges and with no evidence linking them to terrorist actions (Parry). Many hundreds more had already been deported.

The fantasy of roots, of a home that is fixed in time and place, was noted as early as 1882 by Ernest Renan, citing the French, who, claiming themselves as national, have no memory of earlier migrations or displacements. More recently, Liisa Malkki has written of the invention of homelands in the face of globalization's routine displacements (434). This fantasy of nativism became a fantasy of first-, second-, and third-generation immigrants who are made to go home, to a mythical place that is not *here*: "the condition of being a stranger is determined by the event of leaving home" (Ahmed, *Strange Encounters* 78). The border had opened up only for those who felt at home and were intent on staying there.

These were not new, or entirely American, positions. Canada has a long history of racial profiling and anti-terrorist legislation through its use, three times during the twentieth century, of the War Measures Act to forcibly imprison and deport immigrants, dissenters, and others. In fact, as Roy Miki and others have pointed out, the constant invocation of 9/11 as a repressive moment risks reinforcing the idea that anti-terrorist initiatives are entirely new (Miki, conference discussion). In a similar vein, Žižek points out that such oppressive moments recur as the unrepresentable real, a "return" of "the same traumatic kernel in all social systems" (*Welcome to the Desert of the Real!* 50).

The Olympics: Triumph of the 'Will to Totality'

The Olympic Winter Games at Salt Lake City, in February 2002, provided false closure for the national traumas of 9/11. According to Silverman, a person's or a nation's normalcy can be constituted through the repetitious work of particular genres, producing national narratives that are simultaneously known to be false and believed to be real. The genre of the sports spectacle is particularly effective in producing such narratives. Indeed, sports programming and coverage of national crises have certain generic similarities, not the least of which is the production of collective affect. Hage writes: "The national 'we' magically enables the 'I' of the national to do things it can never hope of being able to do as an individual 'I'.... Through this magical quality, all collective national identities work as a mechanism for the distribution of hope" ("Globalization, Social Belonging and the Political Economy of Hope" par. 11). *Village Voice* journalist Richard Goldstein wrote recently about similarities between sports coverage and the war in Iraq:

> Only one event drove Iraq off the front page last week: the grand-slam homer by Yankee slugger Hideki Matsui, a/k/a Godzilla. When I first read the Daily News headline "Godzilla Roars!" I thought it referred to the marines. My confusion was understandable. The Fox-inspired style of war coverage owes a lot to ESPN. Data streams, tech talk, retired pros calling the plays, and the battle equivalent of helmet cams all create a confluence between sports and combat. ("War Horny: Victory Is the Ultimate Viagra," par. 6)

At the Salt Lake City Olympics, the reassertion of hope through national boundaries was an admission of a limit to hybridity. As the flags of nations were triumphantly carried into the stadium by athletes, discrete borders of the nation-state were reasserted, if only for seventeen days. "Another Ice Age Begins," ran a headline in the February 9 issue of *The Globe and Mail* over a photograph of white Canadian athletes in their Roots uniforms, a Canadian flag filling almost half of the frame (1). Ice plays an iconic role in a Canadian national imaginary that foregrounds white settler values of agency and survival, which become rationales for colonization. In such constructs as that provided by the *Globe and Mail* article it is as though, as George Elliott Clarke writes, "the primeval frontier and the white body become one" (107). In a kind of televisual postscript to this trope, Wayne Gretzky, coach of the Canadian Olympic men's hockey team, appeared in an ad for General Motors that aired in December 2002. Against shots of neighborhood kids playing hockey, cars, Christmas trees, and, finally, an off-the-TV shot of Team Canada's winning game, Gretzky says: "What's there to celebrate about life in Canada? Celebrate ice. Trees. Determination. Celebrate hard work that pays off."

The signifiers of a traumatized American nation took centre stage at the Olympics. Canadian sports commentator Terri Libel said, "We arrived in Salt Lake City and discovered a nation still in mourning" (CBC Olympic coverage, February 12, 2002). Incessantly patriotic throughout the seventeen-day broadcast, she mused upon who would carry the "red and white" at the opening ceremony, another unconscious echo of an American speech act. The tattered

flag from the World Trade Center was displayed by New York City firefighters. A young American gold-medallist skater performed a memorial dance
for the victims of 9/11, complete with voice-over: "My name is Sarah Hughes.
I am sixteen years old. This dance is in memory of those innocent people who
lost their lives on September 11th" (CBC Olympic coverage, February 13,
2002). The much-touted innocence of those victims stood in for US victimhood and innocence, as when American folksinger Willie Nelson sang the
words to "Bridge over Troubled Waters": "I'm on your side / when times get
rough / and friends just can't be found" (CBC Olympic coverage, February 8,
2002). Nelson's ordinariness, his dishevelled hair and informal clothing, became
a poignant signifier of Middle America and its peculiar notion of victimhood.
As Ahmed writes, these kinds of representations are far from benign:

> [They signify] the ordinary as in crisis, and the ordinary person as the real
> victim. The ordinary becomes that which is already under threat by imag-
> ined others whose proximity becomes a crime against a person as well as
> place. The ordinary or normative subject is reproduced as the injured
> party: the one "hurt" or even damaged by the "invasion" of others. The
> bodies of others are hence transformed into "the hated" through a dis-
> course of pain. They are assumed to "cause" injury to the ordinary white
> subject, such that their proximity is read as the origin of bad feeling: indeed,
> the implication here is that the white subject's good feelings (love, care, loy-
> alty) are being "taken" away by the abuse of such feelings by others. ("Affec-
> tive Economies," 118)

The huge costly spectacles of the opening and closing ceremonies reinscribed
this fantasy of pure family and pure nation again and again: Donny and Marie
Osmond sang "We Are Family"; giant dinosaurs emoted: "We all share the
same planet, and after five billion years we're still one family." Silverman (following Ernesto Laclau) has called this kind of statement a "will to totality": a
societal mechanism that serves to forget and obscure cultural difference (54).
The figure of the family is central here, combining, as Silverman argues, both
sexual and economic normalizing regimes: family as node of symbolic order
and mode of production (33).

With the mythology of nation-as-family stronger than ever in the US, the
Roots logo, visible on the chests and foreheads of the US, British, and Canadian athletes, became subtextually resonant. This was a corporate branding not
only of athletics but also of normalcy, with its demonization of rootlessness.
The Roots-designed red Canada jackets (available to athletes and consumers
alike) had a vintage feel, reminiscent of my brother's peewee hockey jacket

from the 1960s. There was a big maple leaf on the chest, with "Canada" scrawled underneath in retro script, hearkening back to a time before Quebec separatism, before Bill C-36, Canada's brand-new anti-terrorist legislation. In Canadian media, much was made of the fact that it was a Canadian-based (albeit American-owned) company, Roots, that designed the uniforms for the Canadian, American, and British athletes. During the Olympics, Rebecca Eckler of the *National Post* entered a Roots store and purchased full Team Canada regalia. She wrote: "I looked like I belonged on a podium. Or in a mental institute. Who, in their right mind, would advertise their country to this extent?" (Eckler B6). Eckler interviewed Michael Budman, co-founder of Roots, who told her, "This is the greatest moment in Roots history.... We're just ecstatic how well Americans are receiving our products, all of which are made out of Toronto" (B6). According to Eckler, Budman credited Roots with making Canada "the star of the games" (B6). This was an interesting reversal of the actual situation. In fact, it was Canada that had made Roots the star of the games. Corporate branding had once again been re-territorialized as patriotism.

The enactment of nationalism, be it specifically Canadian or a brand of uber-Americanism, comprises a host of details. More specifically, the accruing of cultural styles, products, and positions can produce a sense of national belonging when overt gestures of patriotism will not (Hage, Keohane).

On a weekend trip to Seattle in January 2002, my friends and I delight in noticing the peculiarities of American behaviour and ritual. The almost aggressive friendliness of the waiter (he sits down with us to chat before taking our orders) reminds us of our own mythical Canadian *politesse*; the hundreds of flags we notice everywhere become proof of an overly determined patriotism that is not our own. But it is the similarities, the common symptoms of this nationalist hysteria, that are more difficult to notice and pin down. While much of 9/11's collective affect echoes earlier episodes, such as (in the US) presidential assassinations and (in Canada) the Quebec referendum, there is a different quality to the signifiers of Canadian national belonging after 9/11.

On a Sunday afternoon in February 2002, as I emerge from the cocoon of a three-day conference (ironically, a conference on hybridity), I am taken aback by the sound of cars honking and the sight of Canadian flags waving from car windows, worn as capes, and painted on faces. The streets of Vancouver, usually so staid and quiet, so *readable*, are filled by revellers of many races and all ages. A group of young women stand on the sidewalk, holding up flags and homemade signs as cars go by, echoing the posture of New York citizens as they hailed firefighters immediately after September 11. A man walks by, holding an empty Molson's Canadian carton aloft like a flag. Canada has defeated the US in the Olympic gold-medal hockey game. Suddenly, we are no longer Americans. Canada has regained its autonomy and perhaps its virility through sports. As Mansbridge announces on that day's evening news, over shots of people shouting "Ca-na-da!" we were "a country united and feeling good all over" (*CBC National News*, February 24, 2002).

This feel-good Canada was a folksier nation than we had seen in some time. This was a Canada different from Collins's earlier postmodern notion of a fragmented national televisual identity that found little or no link between "national interest, identity, survival, and communication, and cultural sovereignty" (18). This was a Canada of a single grand narrative, a Canada that confidently expressed its *Heimat*, its "feeling of belonging together" (Applegate x), through a valorization of the local (as in TV commercials that took us to the athletes' hometowns) amid an unprecedented centralization of state and global power in the form of anti-terrorist legislation and new controls on immigration. As Collins writes, "the appeal of old-style nationalism, with its seductive prospect of a national domestic hearth, a national family, and walls to keep the warmth and family in and the cold and foreigners out, maintains a powerful claim on the imagination of Canadians" (22). Such a retro, small-town Canada could reclaim its origins only in an earlier nation formation, one with a single set of roots and a burgeoning fascicular system. Indeed, as Silverman has argued, the signifiers of "town" and "nation" exist in ideological relation to other binary oppositions, such as male and female, and are integral to the formation of the dominant fiction (35).

Impossible Citizens

Anniversaries recur, with their deep compulsive need to repeat the trauma of loss. In the wake of the various tragedies of 9/11, the telling and retelling of the story becomes a way to return to an emotional ground zero, to the homeplace of grief.

As I attempt to watch a week's worth of anniversary footage of 9/11, I finally reach a necessary limit. It is not just that the documentaries, the interviews, the reflections have been harnessed to the service of Bush's invasion of Iraq. It is also that it is only two months since a death in my own family. The faces of New Yorkers mourning the loss of their husbands, wives, daughters, and brothers are suddenly familiar to me: they look like my face or the face of my mother. The television has become a mirror-machine, and I have reached a limit: of skin stretched taut, connecting New Yorkers' experience to mine, connecting theory and affect, private and personal. My brother, my father, my grandmother: my own dead, my flesh and blood, my skin and kin. The unrepresentable real has folded into the reality of personal grief. Theory for here, affect for there, layers of skin on skin, multiple points of connection: to justice, to power, to sentiment, to a false collectivity, to community, to the repetitive, compulsive home-place of grief.

My deceased brother's body is returned to his birthplace for burial: to a sun-bleached plot of prairie land. His real home-place was in Vancouver's Downtown Eastside. The DTES provided for my brother, as for many others, a site of ethics and community built from the ground of trauma. The grid of eight scarred city blocks amid which he lived is a place of roots shallowly but firmly placed, of memories of origin that rise in dreams and drug-induced hallucinations like hands choking throats, or like something someone else dreamed for you. Like de Certeau's *Wandersmann*, my brother played music on, and walked, the city's streets and alleys daily, obsessively, one of those "whose bodies follow the thicks and thins of an urban text" (93). But this was a text that, despite his daily presence in it, could not include him in its syntax, its organization. Impossible citizen: *vichnaya pamiat*, eternal memory, eternal unbelonging.

As Jill Bennet has pointed out, psychoanalysis-based trauma theory assumes a world in which the context surrounding the trauma is a normal one to which one can eventually return. She cautions, however, that "for those who live in violent communities, there is no stable backdrop" (347). The Freudian possibilities of mourning, in which trauma is worked through and located in the narratives of present-time, found a limit, in September 2003, in my own mourning process, in that of nations bent toward war.

De Certeau's Twin Towers were rooted, immobile, looking down upon nomadic populations: "the dark space where crowds move back and forth" (92). Panoptic, all-seeing, the World Trade Center represented a will to knowledge rather than a will to truth, an illusion of empiricism and purity. That those differences could and would erupt, in the form of terrorists, aliens, and foreigners, was, to some, inevitable. For de Certeau, the "clear text of the planned and readable city" was a palimpsest, overlaid with the text of the nomadic city, *heimlich* becoming *unheimlich*.

One of the things that television did on September 11, 2002, was to remind us that in the face of trauma the home always has the potential to become unlike itself, to become not-home. This was the trauma of the *unheimlich* with its uncanny Twin Towers–like doubling—reality that could be mistaken for cinema, Canadian TV that could be mistaken for American. Ghosts and doubles everywhere: the memorialized dead of Washington, Pennsylvania, and New York, the unmemorialized of poverty, neglect, genocide.

Trauma, writes Bennet, "seeks home not just in language but also in the body ... when one has the realization 'I am in this scene, it affects me, I am a witness'" (348). It is at that moment that the possibility of a public, rather than private, memory of trauma can unfold. Without that moment of inhabitation, traumatic memory remains privatized, a politics of individualized sentimentality in which the trauma of airplanes crashing into towers stands in for truth. "Over-addicted to pain," writes Berlant, in describing an American politic built on an epistemology of pain, "virtuous in the face of bad power" (335). And it is upon such a foundation of trauma and forgetting that twenty-first-century national citizenship depends.

Television, purveyor of ghost stories across the borders of inside and outside, made of each home a mirrored house of horrors. This home, as I have shown, was achieved through the demonization of migrants and immigrants crossing borders. Television and its appendages played a large role in this. At the same time, the desire for home, for roots, for fixed and stable meanings, as a function of a prelinguistic psychic space, came to the fore. People couldn't find words to describe what had happened. Instead, they sought security, a stable place, longed for a fullness and completeness; the only recourse, during both 9/11 and the 2002 Olympic Winter Games, seemed to be escape to the larger home of nation.

CONCLUSION
Empty Suitcases

For what makes nationhood? A sense of heritage. [shot of Mountie statue] That shared past—both of ordeals, and of good times. [dissolve to people square dancing, dissolve to man and son tobogganing] Common values. And family. [dissolve to mountains and geese, dissolve to cityscape] A geography one comes to feel. [dissolve to prairie, dissolve to ocean/lighthouse] That touches mind and heart. [front porch, dissolve to man in store window—European Textiles] Culture at all levels. [dissolve to Inuit coming out of igloo, dissolve to Black boy with white boy, dissolve to boys in cowboy hats] And a sense of place that finally says home to all.
—"Thinking the Unthinkable" (*The Magazine*, CBC, February 13, 1996)

AT THE PIER 21 MUSEUM IN HALIFAX, suitcases are the first thing you see— a small pile of them, battered, old, covered with stickers, juxtaposed against a sepia-toned photo montage of smiling white immigrants and ships. "Pier 21: Remembering Canada's heritage," reads the slogan beside these images. When I first laid eyes upon those empty suitcases, the sight filled me, a daughter of immigrants, with an odd combination of affects: anger and nostalgia.

Certain television texts such as *Canada: A People's History* and *Loving Spoonfuls* are perhaps not unlike these exhibits. As Irit Rogoff argues, "they [the suitcases] are on display as part of the signification of a postwar policy of dealing with the past.... a display strategy that wants to insist on driving home both its quite natural disapproval of what took place, but also its hope that this act ... serves as a kind of amend" (44–45). Rogoff further argues that these kinds of memorial acts end up negating the very history they claim to preserve (43).

Such memorials insist upon the nation as a site of closure, a final return to home. But home is a modernist construct. As I have mentioned earlier, the post-9/11 push to demonize the homelessness of the migrant is also, in its reification of *place*, a retreat from postmodernity.

Following the trajectory of postmodern theorists of diaspora, Caruth muses upon the notion of diaspora as a scattering of peoples who hope to return to their country of origin. She asks, "In what way is the history of a culture, and its relation to politics, inextricably bound up with the notion of departure?" (13). A return, she argues, may be available only through trauma.

My father's return was certainly thus. In a dissociative episode he could not later recall, he packed a small suitcase early one morning in his sixty-seventh year, a half-century after the end of the Second World War. In it he placed some random articles of clothing, his passport, and a Ziploc bag of radishes and salt. What did the contents of that small suitcase signify? (My father, a chronic overpacker, with three suitcases when one would do, now become spartan.) That suitcase was prepared for sudden flight, but this would be a journey *away* from the safety and bounty of this Western suburb. The suitcase was a gesture and a memory that, for all its pathology, was my father's final attempt to reclaim memory, to fabricate a ghostly return.

That my father's attempted return seemed to negate the achievements of the West and his own place in that narrative is, I think, what makes the story worth telling. It would be a "difficult return," as Simon, Rosenberg, and Eppert have termed it: "to live with a return of a memory that inevitably instantiates loss and thus bears no ultimate consolation, a learning to live with disquieting remembrance [and] the limits of a consolatory assurance that the past can be discursively integrated" (4).

But does a politics or a theory of trauma lead to agency or ethics? For many scholars, including myself, there is an ethical or reparative impulse at the root of our work, at the end of our day. To re-envision the world rather than merely (like those empty suitcases) memorialize its losses, to acknowledge (to paraphrase Deleuze ["Ethology"]) that *we do not know what theory can do*.

In the introduction to his book *Symptoms of Canada*, Keohane tries to offer a way out of critical theory's tautologies, gesturing toward reparation: "I want to locate the moments of openness in identities and the ways in which they might be attuned to one another. I am interested in the particular idiom of boundary transgression and reintegration of antagonistic identities in contemporary Canada" (12). For Keohane, there is hope that those othered figures in the archives may enter into Canadian nationalist discourse. But does such an impulse merely point to a longing for closure, to a desire for home, to a representational site of identity, no matter how fragmented those identities may be?

Amery asserts that there can be no return (*At the Mind's Limits* 50). Too much time has been lost. He discovers, in the process of resistance to Nazi oppression, that "my home was enemy country.... We ... had not lost our country, but had to realize it had never been ours" (50). Can a televisual representation of a First Nations community struggling with the legacy of residential schools (*North of Sixty*) be reparative of all the years of Joe the Indian and other such representations? Indeed, can reparation be considered within such a commercial undertaking as television?

Tinic sees the project of representing difference on Canadian television as something more than inclusion or reparation, arguing that cultural difference is integral to national identity. She writes, "In a world of flows—of images, people and ideas—multiple sites of identity and allegiance cohabit the physical space of the nation" (157). An understanding of the workings of affect in relation to nationalism can, I think, help to advance this project. Discerning the difference between the embodied intensities of state funerals and hockey finals and citizenship itself might, I hope, result in a more critical reading of racialized narratives in Canadian media. Acknowledging that there is no single logical flow between excitement and patriotism and between passion and love might well allow for unpredictable, unusual, and unconventional responses to media, unsutured from its restrictive text.

Media, East and West: Remembering Trauma

My father passed away before the Internet could, supposedly, accelerate his contact with those he had left behind in "the Old Country." I remember the letters that arrived every week in our mailbox, from his sister, my Aunt Marusia, in Ukraine. Peering over my father's shoulder, I could barely decode the spidery Cyrillic handwriting on blue parchment-like airmail paper, every inch of space used up. Those pages were full of detail and yearning.

My Kyivan cousins, Maksym and Roxolana, correspond intermittently with me by email. At the time of my visit to Ukraine, Roxolana worked for a private television station, funded, no doubt, by multinationals. Her television work was an intervention, a new, unbounded space of possibility, post-Communism. When I visited Kyiv for the first time, in the summer of 2001, she proudly handed me a video copy of a piece she did on Andy Warhol, on the occasion of a recent retrospective of his work in Kyiv. I watched it when I got home to Canada. It looked like early TV, full of representational possibility. In that as yet unregulated moment (somewhere between Soviet Communism and post-Soviet capitalism), it seems my cousin was able to say what she wanted, enlarging sites of ethnic and sexual identity *within* the space of capitalism.

At the beginning of this book I posed the rhetorical question "Can national television be otherwise?" The word *otherwise* gestures toward representational possibilities, or what I have also dubbed "ethical becomings"—the ways in which conventional speech acts or everyday practices in media can lead the viewer to question the ethics of these very acts and practices. Using a primarily text-based methodology, I have, in this book, outlined the ways in which Canadian television largely occludes hybrid representations, at the same time that it, confusingly perhaps, *includes* the foreigner (the immigrant, the person of colour, the queer) in that project. Certainly the occlusions can provide sites of resistance among audiences. However, I have concluded that Canada's increasing need to pose as a sovereign body—in obvious contradiction of its current status as a bit player in the project of American globalization—requires an unremitting nationalist stance embedded in affective codes of global consumption. National culture is never, anymore, just national, but is imbricated into the economic and political exigencies of globalization. We are all, claims Grossberg, "coerced into globality" (24).

As the Joe Canadian rant demonstrates, US dominance became an object of Canadian nationalism in the 1990s.[1] This was as much the result of popular struggles as of Canadian corporate concerns regarding loss of revenue from free trade. Ultimately, consumption frames both our resistance and our compliance. The text of the 1996 television news documentary "Thinking the Unthinkable" (*The Magazine*, CBC) cited at the beginning of this chapter reads (and looks) like a TV ad. It's not advertising a consumer item but rather is using the tropes of consumption (voice-over, dissolves, affective modes) to advertise the nation. Browne claims that television utilizes consumption as a solution to the problems of everyday life. Keohane argues that these pleasures of shared national consumption are amplified by antagonism.

Many scholars point to the pre-satellite, pre-digital Trudeau years as the halcyon days of nationalist representation on Canadian television (Beaty and Sullivan, Collins, Mary Jane Miller). Thus, while it cannot be said that the period between 1995 and 2002 was the high point of Canadian nationalism on television, it can be surmised that one of the discursive legacies of the televised Quebec referendum debate was an increase in highly coded representations of (or allusions to) consumer modes that stand in for the unrepresentable "real" of Canadian identity.

As corporations acquire more rights than humans, they acquire more roles. Corporation as producer, corporation as auteur.[2] In late-twentieth-century Canadian culture, it was Joe Canadian—a young, white, probably heterosexual male—who was the speaking subject of nationalist practice.[3] But Joe was, of course, only a stand-in for a corporation. Molson became the speaking subject that is, in Foucault's terms, "accorded the right" to proffer the truths of nationalist discourse (*The Archaeology of Knowledge* 50). These days, the corporation is accorded not only human rights but also human affect. Television, as a consumer medium, is the ideal surface of emergence for these affected truths.

Jill Bennet has argued for the healing possibilities of a *public* remembering of trauma. Is there such a possibility of a public unfolding of the narratives of Canadian history? Derrida's words, cited earlier, are cautionary: "this institutional passage from the private to the public ... does not always mean from the secret to the nonsecret" (*Spectres of Marx* 2–3).

Can there be such a thing as an ethics of representation on Canadian television, some sixty years after its birth? Through the prominent placement of certain critical programs such as *This Hour Has 22 Minutes, Rick Mercer Report, North of Sixty, The Border,* and one-off documentaries and dramas, the CBC manages to produce a series of descriptive and seemingly contradictory statements: *Canada is unique. Canada is just like the U.S. Canada is peaceful, self-effacing, and tolerant. Canada has racist immigration policies.* These contradictions must also be seen as part of Canadian nationalist discourse. Ethical closure through content seems elusive, but the contradictory ways in which affected bodies relate to content can open up horizons of possibility.

In the deconstructive tradition, ethics must remain non-prescriptive, resisting closure. Peter Baker asks whether it is possible to meet Derrida's "impossible" ethical demand but then locates an ethical position in the very act of questioning: "The deconstructive task then is to find ... an ethics that maintains an openness to the other as truly other, not merely an other who is the same." Deconstruction can never become a set of self-transparent rules for thinking or conduct, but the challenge it poses to thinking and conduct nonetheless maintains the force of an ethical demand (115–16).

In a 1982 interview, Foucault discourages the impulse to produce ethical closure, or what he calls "a call for prophetism." A single book, he argues, does not have to provide ethical principles at the same moment that it offers analysis. It is important to allow for readerly agency: "People have to build their own ethics, taking as a point of departure the historical analysis, sociological analysis and so on that one can provide for them" ("Foucault: An Interview by Stephen Riggins" 132).

Fragments of ethical becomings appear in the public but still very much underground, and perhaps secretive, realm of the video screen. Video art has always been television's poorer relation, making use of the technologies and lexis of television but rejecting its industrial mode. In a voice aching with sadness and anger, Vancouver-based Hunkpapa Lakota artist Dana Claxton invokes a litany of colonial abuse against the women in her family. She narrates the tragedy of her mother's and maternal grandmother's early deaths and her great-grandmother's migration to Canada, and she asks, again and again, "I want to know why" (*I Want to Know Why*, video, 1994). Hawai'ian Canadian artist Ruby Truly reads from a 1950s manuscript manual for Canadian missionaries teaching English to the Cree of northern Saskatchewan, a reference to the brutal history of the residential school system. She starts reading slowly but speeds up to the rhythm of a pulsing backbeat (... *And the Word Was God*, video, 1987). As in the Claxton video, repetition sutures the videographer into a circular trauma narrative. Such negative affect can, following Sedgwick and Frank's formulation regarding shame, be productive; it can radicalize notions of home and *Heimat*.

Movements Between and Across

I didn't ever feel at home in Kyiv. Nothing matched my father's memories or my grandmother's stories—not the architecture, not the language, not even the food. I stopped referring to myself as Ukrainian, for that only confused people. Instead, I learned to describe myself, in both Ukrainian and English, as simply "diaspora"—which is how others in Ukraine referred to me. As I walked the wide, leafy boulevards of Kyiv, I could feel the proper boundaries of skin and identity eroding. I was becoming a diasporic subject, something between East and West, something that would either never belong in either or would always long for one or the other.

Sara Ahmed describes the space in between homes as a space of belonging (*Strange Encounters* 77). A new generation of antiglobalization and antiwar activists call transnational communities "home." For many Canadian youth, an ironic appreciation of myth, still rooted in consumption, takes the place of overt displays of nationalism (Wright 187). Origin has become *unheimlich*, and destination is always unstable. Home represents an impossible yet yearned-for future rather than a stable past.

As I travelled by train and bus through the scarred social and geographical landscape of Ukraine, I wondered if my elders' recollections of the old country had been mere projection. Where were the lush green steppes and hallowed birch groves we had sung about as children? National narratives, as I argued earlier, compensate for the failure of individual memory.

National narratives become undone in that space in between. I have come to the conclusion that the ethical becoming of mourning, or working through, occurs across media. In an age of convergence, television can no longer be spoken of in isolation from other media. Audiences develop their own latent forms of media interactivity and meaning-making that the creators of these media may not have envisioned (like tweeting as a way to organize political interventions). Riposte, commentary, humour, scathing critique—all are available on the Internet: Rabble.ca, Znet, Frontlines.com, even YouTube. On the CBC Newsworld program *Inside Media*, a Black campus-radio host says his "ethnic" audiences shun CBC TV—not necessarily because of racism but because of what he calls its "polite anglo sound." He considers Radio 3, CBC's (youth-oriented) online presence, to be a much cooler and culturally diverse location (*Inside Media*, February 24, 2004). Such sites collude with the latest in digital consumption: laptop computers, scanners, CD and DVD burners, BitTorrent downloads, cellphone text-messaging systems, social networking sites, blogging programs, free online software shimmering with ads. Nonetheless, Beaty and Sullivan posit some interesting affective flows emerging from new technologies when they write, "The face of television is changing from the classical model in which images flow from the screen to a mass audience. In its place is a model that finds the flow originating with audience itself, as they deftly manipulate the fullest limits of the medium and adapt it to their needs" (24). This mastery of scheduling, format, and site of reception unique to audiences of digital media opens up new possibilities for affect to circulate among bodies as audiences share digital downloads in sites less vulnerable to government regulation or corporate influence.

McLuhan wrote, "the content of any medium is always another medium" (8). He would perhaps insist that the content of the Internet is television and the content of television in turn evokes both radio and print media. The Joe Canadian rant is curiously similar in language and cadence to the poem "I Am a Canadian," by Chippewa poet Duke Redbird, published in 1992 in *An Anthology of Canadian Native Literature in English*. Interestingly, the poem, by an Aboriginal Canadian, uses a positive construction: "I'm an easterner / I'm a Westerner / I'm from the North / And I'm from the South / I've swam in two oceans / And I've loved them both." The poem ends, "I am French / I am English / And I am Métis / But more than this / Above all this / I am a Canadian and proud to be free" (120–21).

In Deleuzian terms, I would suggest a two-way (at least) flow: Internet becoming TV, and TV becoming Internet. Currently, the Internet is highly dependent on television for content and vice versa. Even on YouTube, that highly touted alternative to television, the most viewed clips are TV shows, while television commonly uses YouTube footage in its news coverage.

Canadian television becomes more fluid, more interactive, at the borders of media. Molson's website bulletin board is an unwitting site of resistance, as when an anonymous writer declaims, in response to Joe Canadian's rants:

> I want my identity back ...
> Because my country's Identity has sold it's [sic] soul to corporate power
> Because consumerism and beer consumption has become our National religion
> Because we have forgotten the true meaning of being Canadian!!!!
> And BECAUSE CANADIAN NOW MEANS A BEER
> I AM not a demographic
> I AM not a consumer
> I AM who I AM and I AM not a beer.
> (June 25, 2003, Molson Canadian official website)[4]

The self is still constituted in fixed notions of purity, still at the site of the nation. But it does talk back to the TV screen. Bhabha argues that the atemporal disjunctiveness of the Internet, "the move from organic temporality to disjunctive, displaced acceleration" (x), is more suited to the exilic mode. Television, so rooted in national time, must be seen as being in dialogue with digital media's asynchronous time: the fragmented optics of video art, the Internet, YouTube clips passed on through Facebook.

Post-National Imaginary: The Twenty-First Century's Affective Turn

In the early years of the twenty-first century, affect, I would argue, increasingly structures the narratives of TV news and entertainment media.

Reportage about Operation Thread—during which twenty-one Arab and Muslim men were arrested in September 2003 and then released months later for lack of evidence (all but three were deported)—is described in affective terms: the government is merely red-faced, embarrassed. Once again, embarrassment (laminated onto the grainy image of the ethnic, or the exile) stands in for shame, precluding the possibilities of working through.

These contradictions come up in news reportage of migrants and immigrants, with their recurring themes of revulsion, fear, and half-hearted tolerance.

Encounters between strangers can involve surprise, a challenge to the familiar. Unfamiliar bodies become sign systems that are only partially readable, causing unease (Ahmed, *Strange Encounters*). The bodies of Fujianese migrants arriving on Canada's shores, for example, were indeed surprising bodies, arriving without warning on "mystery ships." They were young, in contemporary dress, and their faces did not assume the deferential expressions of the docile immigrant. Thus it was, in part, television's job to reorganize our encounter with these "strange" bodies: to frame them in wire fences and overlay the images with words such as "squalor" and "filth." At the same time, it was necessary to deny their suffering and to celebrate the achievements of a singular Chinese immigrant, Adrienne Clarkson, Governor General of Canada from 1999 to 2005. This mode of inclusion, so characteristic of Canadian television in the contemporary era, serves to prove a nation's tolerance and may also provide brief access to strange and exotic cultures.

Affect has also become a means of expressing political will. The 2008 election of Barack Obama was a moment of contact, of bodies affecting bodies: of tears, relief, excitement, and hope. This wave of thrills and chills was ushered in months earlier by a music video produced in 2008 by Black Eyed Peas member will.i.am. Entitled "Yes We Can," the piece was composed entirely of excerpts from Obama's concession speech at the New Hampshire primaries. It portrays Obama in split-screen with various celebrities echoing or harmonizing to his words. Scarlett Johannson, John Legend, Sarah Wright, Kareem Abdul-Jabbar, and others mouth words like: "It was the call of workers who organized / women who reached for the ballots / a President who chose the moon as our new frontier / and a King who took us to the mountaintop / and pointed the way to the Promised Land / Yes we can." The overlaying of political oratory with advertising (the music video), the use of Web 2.0 digital technologies, and the central role of celebrity provided a multiplicity of contact zones in which pride, excitement, and despair could flourish.

A post-national imaginary (Appadurai 177) may be an imaginary unbounded by the conventions of particular media. Ethical gestures may occur in the movement *between* television and Internet. Just as there may no longer be as direct a link between anger or fear and social action in this era of transnational capitalism (Ngai), there may not be a single unitary flow between social site and social action. Worldwide demonstrations against the invasion of Iraq were organized by email, through Facebook and Myspace, through blogs and cellphone text messages. Their passion, artistry, and rage can scarcely be captured by the TV camera, let alone their digitally liminal modes or organization. Television, for all of its flow, may, in moments of national or transnational crisis, limit us to a "one-way gaze" (Gregg). Digital technologies have more potential for cross-demographic and transnational flow, whether through Web-based social networking tools or forms of digital storytelling. Rather than isolating us, as many theorists claim, the proliferation of screens increases desires for connection and creates new possibilities for empathetic affects.

2004. I attend a demonstration in support of female Fujianese refugees (from the same "migrant ships" seen on TV) organized by a women's centre in Vancouver. I am there to videotape the proceedings in case of police violence. Television reporters merely perform themselves at this event, their bodies and cameras colonizing the activist space. Later, watching the news, we don't see ourselves: the demonstration is not mentioned on a single local or national news broadcast. So the story gets told and remembered orally, and photographs are passed on by email, in JPEG files. I transfer my digital footage of the demonstration to VHS tape and mail the cassette to a fellow activist doing legal support. Somehow she finds a way to show the tape to the incarcerated refugees.

A more recent story. January 2009. A group of Jewish women occupy the Israeli consulate in downtown Toronto to protest the Canadian government's inaction at the occupation of Gaza and the killing of over a thousand Palestinians. After several hours, the women are arrested and taken away by police. Again, not a single local or national news channel carries the story. A few days later, a video of the occupation, shot and edited by local filmmakers John Greyson and Cathy Gulkin, is uploaded to YouTube. Non-linear transmission, multiple flows. It receives some 20,000 hits and the organizers receive calls from news services around the world.

I imagine the Fujianese women laughing and crying as they watch the tape. I recall the YouTube link about the embassy occupation passed on through Facebook, a contagion of passionate affect. I have chills down my spine thinking about it. This fragmented national narrative, this displaced televisual space. And a transmission of contagious, transnational affects, body to body, country to country, screen to screen.

CODA
Fascinating Fascism: The 2010 Olympics

No government or corporation told us to feel this way—we just did it on our own.
—Lloyd Robertson, 2010 Olympic closing ceremonies, CTV, February 28, 2010

IN 1935, an ambitious young German filmmaker was commissioned by Germany's Ministry for Propaganda and Enlightenment of the Third Reich to create a promotional film for the Games of the XI Olympiad, to be held in Berlin the following summer (Sontag).[1] The filmmaker's name was Leni Riefenstahl, and her film, now as controversial as it is infamous, was called *Olympia*. Currently owned by the International Olympic Committee, the film draws heavily upon Nazi iconography and the notion that a superior German civilization was the rightful heir to an "Aryan" culture of classical antiquity. (Indeed, only Aryans were allowed entry onto the German Olympic team.) Swastikas are everywhere in the film, on flags and on German athletes' uniforms. More pointedly, as Sontag has argued, the themes of Nazi ideology are evident in the very aesthetic of Riefenstahl's films: "the contrast between the clean and impure, the incorruptible and the defiled, the physical and the mental, the joyful and the critical" (39).

Seventy-five years and many Olympics later, extracts of *Olympia*—with the swastikas and *Heil Hitler* salutes edited out—were shown on the official Olympic buses shuttling Olympic flame torchbearers to their spot on the route.[2] It was this incident and many others that made me want to write an afterword to this book about the televised opening and closing ceremonies of the 2010 Olympic Winter Games in Vancouver. Not unlike *Olympia,* these televisual spectacles were simultaneously an advertisement for the nation, a branding of a city, and a highly affective social conversation about consumption, elite sports, and elite pleasure that were deployed, both literally and metaphorically, as metonym for a superior country and race. I had never seen anything like it in my lifetime, on or off Canadian TV.

The Olympics are considered to be the most widely watched television spectacle in the world, and they have, since the Los Angeles Olympic Winter Games of 1984, used the opening and closing ceremonies as a way to promote the superiority of Western capitalist values. The LA Olympics occurred at the height of the Cold War. The US had boycotted the 1980 Moscow Olympics, and the Soviet Union and its allies in turn boycotted the 1984 games (Tomlinson). The 1984 games set the standard for mass spectacle as well as for private-sector support of the games, signalling a shift in meanings from the purely nationalist and imperialist to a merging of nationalist, globalized, and commodified ideals. In this matrix of signifiers, competition operates on a metaphoric level as a representation of capitalist truths: level playing field, self-interest, individuality, survival of the fittest (Wernick).

The opening and closing ceremonies of the 2010 Olympics, broadcast in Canada on CTV, followed a similar paradigm, with an affective impact multiplied by globalized technologies (Neubauer). The variety and proliferation of screens, upon which patriotic crowds and athelets could be viewed, created of the entire nation a contact zone. As Ahmed has argued, this national contact zone provokes an affective reading that must discern between bodies-at-home and the strange bodies of others (Ahmed, "The Skin of Community").

For the purposes of this book, the 2010 Olympics produced a vivid and unique case study of the tie-in of consumption, affect, and nationalism. Consumption was visible in a long chain of signifying meanings and practices, from the purchase of tickets, the lining up outside The Bay for souvenir items, patriotic advertising, and the hybridizing of genres. Sports broadcasting recombined with melodrama and reality TV, as when Neubauer writes:

> Sport for this purpose [televised broadcast of the Olympics] is no more but no less distinctive than reality survival shows or *American Idol.* Each meets the demand for an arranged progression from the many to the few, from contenders to survivors, in an open cycle of repetition that favours the continual re-supply of heroes and stars, who in the current consumption cycle (the analogy to a production cycle) recreate novelty out of the familiar, with each portion of the cycle producing a targeted marketing niche. (15–16)

As in reality TV, this hybridization produced tension between the "real" and the simulated. Are these real bodies or artificially produced bodies? Is this business of erupting into the singing of national anthems a performance for cameras and tourists or a "real" expression of national pride? Is this excessive production of *Heimat*, that feeling of belonging, of shared roots and racial identity, imaginary or constructed? In a postmodern sense, none of this really mattered. The opening and closing ceremonies played on this blurring of truths and inauthenticities while also drawing on a racialized set of signifying practices hearkening back to 1930s Germany.

Metonym for the Nation

If you listen carefully you can hear it, feel it. It's growing—every day—from the smallest hamlets to the biggest towns. Canadians everywhere are starting to believe. They believe our athletes will perform like never before. This country will shine like never before. And they believe that the world will come to realize all along: Canada is amazing!
—from a CTV ad for Vancouver Olympics coverage, February 12, 2010

Garry Whannel makes the argument that "there is no such thing as sport" (10). What is and isn't sporting practice is constantly changing—why gymnastics and not dance? javelin but not darts? Sport, he argues, is a creation of media. With its ephemerality and low-culture status, he writes, sport has eluded extensive scholarly study. Perhaps this vagueness of definition is why sports fandom stands in so easily for patriotism, becoming a metonym for the nation (Matheson). Metonymy, in its proximation of signs, is highly productive of affect (Ahmed, "The Skin of Community"). The televisual representation of the Olympics allowed for a series of things—bodies, signs, highly desired commodities—to be in constant contact. Ads for McDonald's, Coca-Cola, and CTV became almost indistinguishable from the coverage of sporting events themselves. It was this very contiguity, multiplied on innumerable screens and platforms—a mandatory festive viewing—that allowed an imaginary unified Canada to emerge as never before.

As Allison argues, it's rare to have complete national identification with a team; loyalties are more often split according to a country's multinational composition. How, then, could the reportage of national emotion not allow for the Jamaican Canadian rooting for her own bobsled team, or even folks like myself, who teared up not for the Canadians on the podium but for the Ukrainians? Matheson argues that sports broadcasting can create the illusion of deeply felt group identity in a way that other genres cannot: a cultural theatre "where the values of the larger society are resonated, dominant social practices are legitimized, and structural inequalities reproduced'" (D. Sabo and S.C. Jansen, cited in Matheson 139). Sports broadcast commentary is a rich zone of unguarded racialized commentary, that racialization being essential to national unity (Bannerji, Hage) and to a cohesive national discourse (Matheson). Seventeen days' worth of athletic events was narrated in an imperial tone by the various sports broadcasters and sports stars. Figure skating became one of the most popular sites of the kind of racialized commentary that TV sports can both highlight and get away with. Of a Japanese skater: "She's had a hot dog named after her!" A nod to the Russians, "known for their outrageous costuming"; the Chinese are "absolute tricksters." This imperial tone is justified by Canada's supposed inferiority ("The world will come to realize all along: Canada is amazing!").

And what of the (literally) faith-based advertising for the Olympics? The theme song for the 2010 Olympics was called "I Believe" ("I believe in the power that comes / From a world brought together as one / I believe together we'll find / I believe in the power of you and I"). Performed at the opening ceremonies by anglophone Québécois sensation Nikki Yanofsky, it accompanied CTV's opening sequence for every new event covered throughout the seventeen days. Ads for CTV's coverage of the Olympics, quoted above, delivered inspirational monologues by such luminaries as Canadian-born actor Donald Sutherland: "It's time to believe." Television spectatorship of the games become, in this ad, inextricable from patriotism. Other ads had athletes asking, in direct camera address, "Do you believe?" The CTV Olympics store also featured "Believe apparel"—everything from hoodies to scarves emblazoned with the word "Believe." Television sports fandom had become a belief system, with spiritual, or at least magical, overtones. In this instance sports and religion shared a way to make sense of a nation deeply divided about its participation in torture and war in Afghanistan and the contested funding of family planning overseas. Not watching the Olympics hoopla, or not participating in it, became far more than just not watching and not participating. It meant setting oneself apart from a national community of believers. Indeed, those of us who maintained our activist stance about the games found ourselves shunned by more than one Facebook friend or sports fan. Thus, shame, shaming, and even disgust appeared to be the underside of belief and national pride.

But it wasn't just activists who indulged in or provoked ugly feelings (Ngai). A controversial article by Dave Zirin of *Sports Illustrated/CNN* described a scowling Vancouver populace made cranky by exorbitant Olympic ticket prices, cost overruns, public service cutbacks, and increased homelessness in the Downtown

Eastside. A *Vancouver Sun* poll revealed a surprising number of negative affects when Vancouverites were asked about the doings of the Vancouver Olympics Committee (VANOC), which had by then run up a massive deficit: "37 per cent felt disgust, 32 per cent anger and 21 per cent shame" (Hall).

However, Ngai makes the point that disgust has been deployed much more successfully by the right than by the left. Early disgust at the excesses of the 2010 Olympics expressed by activists and ordinary folk was successfully extinguished by faith-based media propaganda. It was, however, the occasional links made to the Berlin Olympics (both by critics and unwittingly by VANOC's reviving of *Olympia*) that made shame and even disgust an *acceptable* affect for people of all stripes. Even a reporter from the *Fort Worth Star-Telegram*, overwhelmed by Canadian patriotism, made the comparison:

> I didn't attend the '36 Olympics, but I've seen the pictures. Swastikas everywhere.... What on earth were the Canadians thinking? An Olympic host is supposed to welcome the world. This one was too busy being (their word) "patriotic." "Now you know us, eh?" chief organizer Furlong said. We thought we did two weeks ago. Now, I'm wondering if Canadians can even recognize themselves. Nice party. But so was 1936. (LeBreton 2)

Opening and Closing Ceremonies

The prologue to Olympia combines Wagnerian operatic romanticism with a highly nostalgic and pointed evocation of Greek antiquity. Amid Riefenstahl's trademark mists, panning shots of barren landscapes and ruins settle on a statue of a discus thrower dissolving into a German athlete (Erwin Huber). An interlude of nearly nude male and female dancers culminates in the lighting of a torch by another Aryan athlete. A torch relay of more such athletes culminates in a lone blond male athlete running the torch through contemporary Europe, "a powerful statement of Germany's putative role as the heir of ancient Greece" (Guttman 74).

The opening ceremonies of the 2010 Olympic Winter Games began, not unlike *Olympia*, with a mythic, elegiac prelude. In a televised sequence that was also shown at the opening ceremonies, one figure—Vancouver snowboarder Johnny Lyall—negotiated a near-barren landscape of snow-capped mountains, as dates and locations of previous winter Olympics were recalled in voice-over. Panoramic aerial shots followed Lyall in his spectacular feat. At the conclusion of this semi-animated sequence, Lyall himself entered BC Place Stadium, site of the opening ceremonies, bursting through Olympic rings down a ramp exploding with snow and ice. He was applauded by an enthusiastic audience of 60,000 people clad in white ponchos (the better to perform as a screen for projectors overhead). Goose-stepping Mounties carried in a Canadian flag. Soon after, a set of three faux white totem poles rose out of the floor, robotic arms emerging from the poles. A coterie of First Nations from across Canada appeared in traditional dress, performing their tribal dances, contained by a ring of white-clad Olympic volunteers. Spectators beat white cardboard drums bearing Native designs. This was followed by a song called "Hymn to the North." As fake snow fell, performers in white pseudo-Arctic regalia danced around amid simulated Northern Lights.

Adrienne K, author of the blog "Native Appropriations" had this to say about the Native presence at the opening ceremonies:

> I am very happy that they decided to include the First Nations in the games overall—it's rare, even in 2010, to see such a strong Native presence in a national event.... HOWEVER. The extensive involvement of Natives in the games in the ceremonies gives off the impression that Canada has an equal, open, and strong relationship with its First Nations communities. Most outsiders would think that Canada is an indigenous Nation, with its peoples having equal recognition in government ... practising their sovereignty, etc.—when this is not the case. Canada, like the US, has not signed the UN Declaration on the Rights of Indigenous Peoples ... (http://nativeappropriations.blogspot.com/2010/02/vancouver-opening-ceremonies-honoring.html)

The northern world that snowboarder Lyall negotiated, and that was reproduced within the stadium, was a transparent, knowable, and sublime world, redolent of the fortitude of settlers and the innocence (and ultimate disappearance) of the primitive Native. As Adrienne K points out, this absence is occasionally rectified, but the illusions it creates contribute to a language of imperialism. Dyer has written about of this sort of image as a language of white superiority: "the North is an epitome of the 'high, cold' places that promoted the vigour, cleanliness, piety and enterprise of whiteness" (118). Canada, he argues, is particularly amenable to this discourse, with a mythology of a white settler population formed by the cold North into a "distinct white national character" (21).

As I mentioned earlier, Canada has a history of such racialized configurations, such as the Canada First movement of the nineteenth century. How can landscape lead to imperialism? As Ngai points out, what is sublime is not actually the landscape of BC, the prowess of the snowboarder, or even the beauty of all nations gathered together, "but rather the self's pleasurable and emotionally satisfying estimation of itself, its transcendance of reason, its dominion over nature" (*Ugly Feelings*). In short, its superiority.

Opening Olympic ceremonies condense a nation's idea about itself and construct an international consensus regarding its national mythology (Traganou). These constructed narratives are often rootless and ahistorical and (perhaps for that very reason) less than riveting. I return again to Ngai's invented affect, stuplimity, with its opposing circuits of shock and boredom. Both are "sudden in onset, brief in duration, and disappearing quickly." Indeed, the shock, chills and stupefaction of the opening ceremonies, with the *Olympia*-like opening sequence, with angry protestors outside and an elite gathering of fans, dignitaries, and performers inside, with its attendant indignations, quickly gave way to boredom. A massed gathering provides equal measures of awe and stupefaction, but perhaps the more obedient and regimented the crowd the greater the cause for anxiety. Sontag describes the crowds that fill the frame of both *Triumph of the Will* (a Nazi propaganda film Riefenstahl directed in 1934) and *Olympia*: "a characteristic pageantry; the massing of groups of people; the turning of people into things; the multiplication of things and grouping of people/things around an all-powerful hypnotic leader or force" (40).

Sontag wrote her canonical essay "Fascinating Fascism" in the mid-1970s, just as the right was starting to gain prominence in the US. She warned of the re-popularization of Riefenstahl's films: "their longings are still felt … their content is a romantic ideal to which many continue to be attached" (43). Are we in another such time? And cannot such eras of repression also produce proliferation—of resistances and alternate discourses? Stuplimity offers no transcendance but provides us with small moments of resistance (Ngai). In an interview on CBC Radio's *The Current* (I am there as an academic "expert" to speak to Olympics news coverage), it is the interviewer, not I, who references the Berlin Olympics. Carefully, soberly, I reply: "Nationalism always rests on a unified 'we' and an excluded other," to which Anna Maria Tremonti, a veteran CBC journalist, replies, indignantly, it seems, "Well, why do we need a unified 'we'?"

As the dirty secrets of the Harper government—its complicity in the torture of Afghan detainees, its entrenching of a law-and-order regime—become more and more apparent in online news sources, news satire, political blogs, and activist Twitter feeds—it becomes, perhaps, more and more difficult for standard media to hold its patriotic ground.

The 2010 Olympic Winter Games ended as this book began, by quoting the Joe Canadian rant from the 1999 Molson's Canadian beer ad during the closing ceremonies. Appropriately, for an American-owned beer that originated in Canada, three Canadian-born stars living in the US delivered awkward and unfunny versions of "The Rant." Michael J. Fox declaimed: "My name is Mike and not only was I born in Canada, I was raised in B.C. On a bad-hair day I wear a toque …" The other rants, by Catherine O'Hara and William Shatner, were just as heavy-handed, never achieving the casual, banal nationalism of the original.

The nation, once again laminated to space, consumption and affect, faltered.

NOTES

Introduction

1 For more on space in relation to Canadian identity, see Razack.

2 Collins makes a literal connection between the railway and communications, describing both the building of the railway and the simultaneous development of a cross-country communications infrastructure as a response to threats from the US (5–6).

3 Other earlier important surfaces of emergence for Canadian nationalism were (and perhaps remain) the educational system, art between the wars, and the military.

4 For more on cultural subsidies in the Trudeau era, see Edwardson.

5 See Chapple and Kattenbelt for a more detailed analysis of how television seriality interpellates viewers as agents in a process of mediating fictional and non-fictional worlds.

6 Throughout this book, I refer to Trudeau as "queer-acting" or "queered." Drawing upon the notion of queer as challenge to the normal, and the queer cultural studies tradition of open-ended readings of celebrities' sexual subject positions (Dyer, Doty), I read Trudeau's rumoured and alleged bisexuality as a text amenable to queer interpretation.

Chapter One: Affect Theory: Becoming Nation

1 A reference to the title of Eley and Suny's book, *Becoming National*.

2 This notion also recalls the Latin root of the word, *afficere* (to do to, to act on) and in particular its first-person-singlular meaning, *afficio*, "to connect" (*American Heritage Dictionary of the English Language* 28).

3 The ethical *limits* of deconstruction have been critiqued by some as a retreat from the politics of race, gender, and identity that entered the academy via student uprisings and social protests of the 1960s. Speaking from a feminist perspective, Braidotti writes, "One cannot deconstruct a subjectivity one has never controlled" (116–17).

Chapter Two: The Televisual Archive and the Nation

1   For an exception to this rule, see Peter Trueman's caustic though rather dated *Smoke and Mirrors: The Inside Story of Television News in Canada*, in which the CBC in particular is given a severe dressing-down.

2   When I tell people I am writing about Canadian television, the most frequent response I get is: "That's going to be a very short book …" Frank Manning addresses the ways in which Canadian popular culture is given short shrift by theorists as well as by the general population. Canadian popular culture is seen as contested—not being Canadian—with ethnic and regional cultures seen as being more authentically national. The more urgent task, within the purview of Canadian nationalism, is to protect these cultures via state apparati. Manning writes, "Paradoxically but perhaps predictably, the unassailable determination to champion Canadian culture has inhibited its study and analysis" (6).

3   This book attempts to question and denaturalize the workings of Canadian television as a surface of emergence for nationalism. The notion of a post-national, therefore, is important, though not central, to this book. For more on Appadurai's notion of the postnational in greater detail, see chapter 4.

4   For more on the relationship between queer and the nation, see Berlant and Freeman.

5   For analysis of earlier Molson Canadian ads, see Keohane.

6   "Sawa" is Arabic for "together."

7   Dwayne Winseck notes that convergence has been part of media since the mid-nineteenth century (795).

8   Winseck notes that these same effects are seen with Canada's public network, CBC, as a result of government cutbacks (799).

9   Global BS Media, a satirical Web project of Vancouver's Guerrilla Media, responds with an article from the "Vancouver Scum" announcing that "the RCMP has formed a new highly trained and top-secret team called the Anti-Embarrassment Special Service (ASS). Included in their arsenal will be weapons of mass embarrassment, including 'high-tech embarrassers such as the wireless joy buzzer and the tele-deprompter which can neutralize a politician's teleprompter and cause painful unscripted silences." (Paulitico Azzkizzer, http://www.globalbs.com/story27.htm; the link is no longer active.)

10 Similarly, Zoe Sofoulis has argued that celebrity is a mode of pleasurable identification that can unify citizens along national lines.

Chapter Three: Whose Child Am I? The Quebec Referendum and Languages of Affect and the Body

1   The 1995 referendum was the latest step in a history of Québécois nationalism that dates back to the origins of a Canadian federation in the mid-nineteenth century. An emerging separatist movement in the 1960s led to the formation of the Parti Québécois, a party pledged to separatism, which came to power in Quebec in 1976. Quebec's first sovereignty referendum was held in 1980. It was unsuccessful. For further analysis of Quebec nationalism, see Keating.

2   Creeber makes some important distinctions between the series (for example, *ER* and *Law and Order*), which is designed to run indefinitely, and the serial, which has a limited number of episodes and a discernible narrative arc. He argues that it is the *serial*, more than the series, that provides a site for somewhat more complex explorations of race and identity

on TV. Examples are the American serials *Roots* (1977) and *Holocaust* (1978). I would argue that these are nominally less official versions of history, but, like the Quebec referendum, their framing within the genre of the serial allows for rich analytical opportunities.

3   Creeber also notes that seriality is so prevalent that television advertising now frequently mimics the serial form (441).

4   For further theorization of the connection between romanticism and nationalism, see Nairn.

5   It has been suggested by Sunera Thobani (informal discussion), former president of the National Action Committee on the Status of Women, and others that francophone feminists actively participated in the obscuring of the race issue in Quebec. For further feminist analysis of the racialized nature of Quebec sovereignty, see Bannerji, *The Dark Side of the Nation*.

6   A Canadian independent film, *Just Watch Me*, tells a story of domestic stress occasioned by the referendum. In it, a real-life couple, an anglo and a francophone based in Quebec, begin to review their options as voting day approaches. They have decided to move if the Yes side wins; they want their children to have easy access to the English side of their family. A heart-wrenching sequence of interviews with each partner, rapidly intercut, reveals the depth of each person's attachment to their part of the country. The Yes vote loses, but the family ends up moving to English Canada anyway, not wanting to live in such a divided environment.

7   This is another intertextual reference, to Hugh MacLennan's 1945 Canadian novel, *Two Solitudes*.

8   Levin also notes that *Viva Valdez*, an American spinoff of *Les Plouffes*, transformed the working-class Quebec City–based Plouffes into a Latino family living in a Los Angeles barrio (136).

9   Such a testimonial is standard for CBC immigrant narratives. As Sedef Arat-Koc has pointed out, gratefulness is usually the only legitimate stance for immigrants ("Tolerated Citizens or Imperial Subjects?").

10   According to J.L. Austin, language is as much a mode of action as it is a mode of information. The meaning of the word is less important than the production of the word. Certain performative utterances, including those of newscasters, do not so much state a fact as perform an action, one that sutures them into normalcy. Hence, one might ask of these newscasters and reporters, What do they mean by their speech? rather than ask, What does this or that word mean? The repetition of certain words or gestures generates performativity: the meeting of certain social conventions, the reproduction of normalcy.

11   For a compelling Foucauldian analysis of the Cartesian subject, see McWhorter.

Chapter Four: Haunted Absences: Reading *Canada: A People's History*

1   Described in library holdings as "a report on multiculturalism in contemporary Canada," this town-hall discussion covered such topics as the history of the federal government policy, arguments from supporters and opponents of multiculturalism, and a profile of a Sikh community in Surrey, B.C.

2   Recently, I saw television footage of a Canadian internment camp that imprisoned Jews during WW II (for alleged security reasons). Overlaid onto it was a soundtrack of men singing "O Canada."

3   Horatio Alger was a nineteenth-century writer of juvenile fiction whose characters suc-
    ceeded on the basis of their individual determination to overcome hardship. Alger's name
    has become a metaphor for the rags-to-riches ascent, American-style.
4   Both accounts, Turk's and Alvin's, were accessed April 8, 2002, on the official website of
    Canada: A People's History, www.cbc.history.ca. The URL has since changed to http://history
    .cbc.ca and the chat feature is no longer available.
5   Warley emphasizes that the First Nations consultants did not have creative control. She
    interviewed several First Nations people who were critical of aspects of the script.
6   *North of Sixty* has had a lively afterlife, with weekly reruns first on CBC and now APTN
    (Aboriginal Peoples' Television Network). The past decade has seen four *North of Sixty*
    made-for-TV movies, which revive the town and its residents in thriller-style dramas.

Chapter Five: An Otherness Barely Touched Upon: A Cooking Show, a Foreigner, a Turnip, and a Fish's Eye

1   I use the terms "transcultural" and "transnational" as distinct but not unrelated. Mignolo
    defines transculturalism thus: "Transculturation subsumes the emphasis placed on bor-
    ders, migrations, plurilanguaging, and multiculturing and the increasing need to con-
    ceptualize transnational and transimperial languages, literacies, and literatures ... allowing
    for the celebration of the 'impure' in the social world from the 'pure' perspectives couched
    in a national language and in 'scientific' epistemology" (220). I use the term "transnational"
    in the sense that it is employed by Appadurai: a world that has been deterritorialized by
    global capitalism (*Modernity at Large*). Transculturalism, I would offer, is the product of
    the ethical, creative, and perhaps even imaginary work required in a transnational world.
2   On the *Loving Spoonfuls* website, Gale's bio includes mention of a major role in a film by
    gay Canadian director John Greyson. In the intertextual realm of television, this associative
    connection becomes an integral part of the way the program is received by audiences.
3   This notion is visible in the film *My Big Fat Greek Wedding*, in which a nondescript white
    suitor is absorbed into the grotesque food-centred doings of his in-laws.
4   By describing this show as a comedy, the producers of *Loving Spoonfuls* make use of tele-
    vision's inherent ability to, as Jane Feuer notes, "recombine across genre lines" (131).
5   For more on camp and television, see Grossberg.
6   In writing about Andy Warhol's shyness and, in effect, about queerness, Sedgwick devel-
    ops the notion of a creatively productive shame: "The dysphoric affect shame functions
    as a nexus of production: production, that is, of meaning, of personal presence, of poli-
    tics, of performative and critical efficacy" ("Queer Performativity" 135).

Chapter Six: National Mania, Collective Melancholia: The Trudeau Funeral

1   The Book of Condolences was accessed online, July 29, 2001, at www.pch.gc.ca/trudeau/
    messages. The link is no longer active.
2   Roland Boer has written about the transference between media figures that occurred at
    Princess Diana's funeral when Elton John sang "Candle in the Wind," a song he had orig-
    inally written for Marilyn Monroe (85). Cohen's and Castro's anomalous presence per-
    formed a similar function at the Trudeau funeral, transferring their larger-than-life
    countercultural presence onto the Trudeau legacy.

3   Peter Trueman writes about colonial tendencies in Canadian television, citing British influences in its early years and American influences thereafter—"the worst features of the BBC plus the weaknesses of the U.S. networks" (16).

4   One year later, on the anniversary of Trudeau's death, several television programs took great pains to erase these challenges to the normal through the excessive use of marriage metaphors. Trudeau was repeatedly referred to as having had a spousal relationship to Canada. Adrienne Clarkson, Canada's then Governor General, said in a CBC interview: "It was an emotional relationship that we had with him. When we wanted to reject him or throw him out of the house it was because we thought he'd misbehaved. But we were always there as long as he was still there" (*Life and Times*, CBC, October 2001).

5   For a more extended analysis of the relationship between media, the erotic, and the haptic, see Marks.

6   The quotation that ends Justin's eulogy is from Robert Frost, who was quoted thirty-seven years earlier at the funeral of President John F. Kennedy. The quoting by Justin marks yet another colonial overlay: for many, including myself, the flag-draped coffin resonated with the first major televisual experience of my generation: the Kennedy assassination and funeral. As an interviewee in the film *Just Watch Me: Trudeau and the 70's Generation* remarked, "Trudeau was our Kennedy that didn't get shot."

7   The Algoma strike is described by Radwanski as "a watershed in Quebec's political history" (64): a struggle between the authoritative, anti-union Duplessis government and an increasingly urbanized and secularized population. Radwanski writes: "The long bitter dispute had served as a rallying point for all progressive elements in the province, simultaneously underlining both the anti-democratic nature of the Duplessis regime and its vulnerability to concerted resistance" (65).

8   The notion of belonging has been reconfigured by Probyn as "belonging, not in some deep authentic way, but belonging in constant movement, modes of belonging as surface shifts" (*Outside Belonging* 19).

Chapter Seven: Homeland (In) Security: Roots and Displacement from New York to Toronto to Salt Lake City

1   The notion of homeland became institutionalized in the US in November 2002 with the formation of the Department of Homeland Security, the largest American federal reorganization in several decades. Immigration would now operate as a security operation, in the same department as the Secret Service and Customs, effectively criminalizing the movement of immigrants. The *National Post* reported that, "All male 'foreign visitors' from a list of 25 mostly Arab and Muslim countries are required to report to authorities for interviews and be photographed and fingerprinted" (Jimenez B1).

2   At the time of writing, this synergy was expanding. In the spring of 2003, the American INS and Canada Immigration held a Border Security Summit, which resulted in, among other things, a safe third-country agreemeent. Under that agreement, most refugee claimants who arrive at the Canadian border after travelling through the United States will be turned back to make claims for asylum under the stricter US system.

3   For further analysis of botanical metaphors with regard to the nation, see Malkki.

4   Many people argue that the Kennedy assassinations were the first such events, but these were recorded on film and later broadcast on television.

5   News announcer Mark Kelley's emotive outpouring is, according to Dumm, not out of line, for, as he writes, "the anchor is able to present herself or himself as a fellow watcher, but one who is a surrogate for the watcher at home, able to ask questions and guide the agenda" (317).

6   The term "preferred reading" derives from Stuart Hall's seminal essay "Encoding/Decoding," in which he identified three ways of decoding media texts: oppositional, negotiated, and preferred (or dominant). Crucial to this formulation is Hall's insistence that, while polysemy creates the possibility of a variety of readings among audience members, the media text is still "structured in dominance." Hall wrote: "Polysemy must not be confused with pluralism.... Any society/culture tends, with varying degrees, to impose its segmentations.... There remains a dominant cultural order, though it is neither univocal nor contested" (134). I find this to be a useful caveat in my own attempts to understand the ways in which mainstream media achieved a kind of monolithic textuality during the events of 9/11.

7   Raymond Williams defines flow as "the replacement of a programme series of timed, sequential units by a flow series of differently related units in which the timing, though real, is undeclared" (*Television* 93). Although he used the term to refer specifically to the structure of television programming, I use it in a much broader sense.

8   Anthony Lane also points out the extent to which people's televised responses to 9/11 came from blockbuster movie scripts like *Independent Day, Die Hard,* and *Armaggedon.* But his citing of the 1998 thriller film *The Siege* most accurately sums up this uncanniness, as when Denzel Washington's character says, "Make no mistake—we will hurt the enemy, we will find the enemy, we will kill the enemy" (79).

9   In a critical article rare for the neo-conservative national Canadian paper *The Globe and Mail,* columnist Russell Smith described the *West Wing* episode as "official art, American-style." He wrote, "The writers of the program may not have to satisfy the demands of a central propaganda committee, but they do have to come up with something that a terrified corporation, the network, would air in a time of greatly heightened sensitivity" (Smith R5).

10   Stanley Cavell, however, cited in Dumm, argues that improvised talk is absolutely characteristic of television and that "the fact that nothing of consequence is said matters little compared to the fact that something is spoken.... Improvisation, no matter how slight, is the sign of life on the television monitor" (311).

Conclusion: Empty Suitcases

1   Ironically, Molson is no longer Canadian-owned. On July 22, 2004, Molson Inc. and the American Adolph Coors Co. announced that they had merged, becoming the Molson Coors Brewing Company.

2   The film *The Corporation* (2003), co-directed by Mark Achbar and Jennifer Abbot, examines the corporation's emergence as a legal "person" and the pathological ramifications thereof.

3   Wagman notes that Molson spent over $1 million in market research to reveal that its target demographic is young men aged eighteen to twenty-four. The study also revealed that this sector showed a significant sense of "national pride" (81).

4   Originally posted on http://www.molson.ca, June 25, 2003. The website address has since changed (to http://www.molsoncanadian.ca) and the bulletin-board feature is no longer available.

Afterword: Fascinating Nationalism: The 2010 Olympics

1 This is contrary to the popular myth (perpetuated by Reifenstahl herself) that the film was commissioned by the International Olympic Committee (Sontag).

2 The film, *Lights Will Guide You Home,* was produced by the Vancouver Olympic Organizing Committee (VANOC) and included twenty-two seconds of *Olympia* footage (Charlie Smith). After complaints by members of the Vancouver Jewish community, the *Olympia* footage was removed.

WORKS CITED

Ahmed, Sara. "Affective Economies." Paper presented at the Transculturalisms Symposium. University of British Columbia, Vancouver, February 2002. 27 June 2004; site access restricted <http://webct.ubc.ca/SCRIPT/Transculturalisms/scripts/serve_home>.

———. "Affective Economies." *Social Text* 79 (22.2) (2004): 117–39.

———. *The Cultural Politics of Emotion.* New York: Routledge, 2004.

———. "The Skin of Community: Affect and Boundary Formation." *Revolt, Affect, Collectivity: The Unstable Boundaries of Kristeva's Polis.* Ed. Tina Chanter and Ewa Plonowska Ziarek. Albany, NY: SUNY Press, 2005.

———. *Strange Encounters: Embodied Others in Post-Coloniality.* New York: Routledge, 2000.

Allen, Robert C. "Talking about Television." *Channels of Discourse: Television and Contemporary Criticism.* Ed. Robert Allen. Chapel Hill, NC: U of North Carolina P, 1987. 1–16.

Allison, Lincoln. "Sport and Nationalism." *Handbook of Sports Studies.* Ed. Jay Coakley and Eric Dunning. London: Sage, 2002. 344–55.

Amery, Jean. *At the Mind's Limits.* Trans. Sidney Rosenfeld and Stella P. Rosenfeld. Bloomington: Indiana UP, 1980.

Anderson, Benedict. *Imagined Communities: Reflections on the Origin and Spread of Nationalism.* London/New York: Verso, 1983.

Ang, Ien. 1985. Watching "Dallas": Soap Opera and the Melodramatic Imagination. London: Methuen, 1985.

Angell, Roger. "Tuesday and After." *The New Yorker* 24 Sept. 2001: 30.

"Another Ice Age begins." *Globe and Mail* [Toronto] 9 Feb. 2002, Sports Special Report: 1.

Appadurai, Arjun. 1996. *Modernity at Large: Cultural Dimensions of Globalization.* Minnesota: Minnesota UP, 1996.

Applegate, Celia. *A Nation of Provincials: The German Idea of Heimat.* Berkeley: U of California P, 1990.

Arat-Koc, Sedef. "Tolerated Citizens or Imperial Subjects? Muslim Canadians and Multicultural Citizenship in Canada, Post 9/11." Paper presented at the annual meeting of the Canadian Sociology and Anthropology Association. Dalhousie University, Halifax, June 2003.

Austin, J.L. 1962. How to Do Things with Words. Cambridge: Harvard UP, 1962.

Bailey, Steve. "Professional Television: Three (Super) Texts and a (Super) Genre." *The VelvetLight Trap* 47 (2001): 45–61.

Baker, Peter. *Deconstruction and the Ethical Turn.* Gainesville: UP of Florida, 1995.

Bakhtin, Mikhail. *Rabelais and His World.* Trans. Helene Iswolsky. Bloomington: Indiana UP, 1968.

Bannerji, Himani. *The Dark Side of the Nation: Essays on Multiculturalism, Nation and Gender.* Toronto: Canadian Scholars' Press, 2000.

———. *Returning the Gaze: Essays on Racism, Feminism and Politics.* Toronto: Sister Vision Press, 1993.

Barker, Chris. *Television, Globalization and Cultural Identities.* Philadelphia: Open UP, 1999.

Barnard, Linda. "Holiday Heritage." *Canadian Living Magazine* 12 Dec. 2001: 195–97.

Barthes, Roland. *Mythologies.* London: Jonathan Cape, 1972.

Baudrillard, Jean. *The Spirit of Terrorism.* New York: Verso, 2002.

Baxter, James, Juliet O'Neill, and Kate Jaimet. "A Time to Say Goodbye: Largest State Funeral in Canadian History Marks a Period of Unprecedented National Mourning." *Vancouver Sun* 4 Oct. 2000: B1.

Beaty, Bart, and Rebecca Sullivan. *Canadian Television Today.* Calgary: U of Calgary P, 2006.

Bennett, Jill. "Art, Affect, and the 'Bad Death': Strategies for Communicating the Sense Memory of Loss." *Signs* 28.1 (2002): 333–52.

Berlant, Lauren. "The Subject of True Feeling: Pain, Privacy and Politics." *Traumatizing Theory: The Cultural Politics of Affect In and Beyond Psychoanalysis.* Ed. Karyn Ball. New York: Other Press, 2007. 305–48.

Berlant, Lauren, and Elizabeth Freeman. "Queer Nationality." *Gendered Agents: Women and Institutional Knowledge.* Ed. Silvestra Mariniello and Paul A. Bové. Durham, NC: Duke UP, 1998. 245–78.

Bhabha, Homi. "Preface: Arrivals and Departures." *Home, Exile, Homeland: Film, Media and the Politics of Place.* Ed. Hamid Naficy. New York: Routledge, 1999. vii–xii.

Bickley, Claire. "A Man Called Horse: North of 60 Just Fine for South of 49 Actor." *Toronto Sun* 9 Nov. 1995: 82.

Bociurkiw, Marusya. "Put on Your Bunny Ears, Take Your TV around the Block: Old and New Discourses of Gender and Nation in Mobile, Digital, and HDTV." *Canadian Journal of Communication* 33 (2008): 537–44.

Bodroghkozy, Aniko. "I … Am … Canadian!" Examining Popular Culture in Canada: Recent Books." *Topia* 5 (2001): 109–18.

Boer, Roland. "Iconic Death and the Question of Civil Religion." *Planet Diana: Cultural Studies and Global Mourning.* Ed. Re: Public. Nepean, Australia: U of Western Sydney, 1997. 81–86.

Boler, Megan. "Disciplined Absences: Cultural Studies and the Missing Discourse of a Feminist Politics of Emotion." *After the Disciplines: The Emergence of Cultural Studies.* Ed. Michael Peters. Westport, CT: Bergin and Garvey, 1999. 157–74.

Bourassa, Alan. "Literature, Language and the Non-Human." *A Shock to Thought: Expression after Deleuze and Guattari.* Ed. Brian Massumi. New York: Routledge, 2002. 60–76.

Braidotti, Rosi. *Nomadic Subjects.* New York: Columbia UP, 1994.

Brand, Dionne. *Thirsty.* Toronto: McClelland & Stewart, 2002.

Brennan, Teresa. *The Transmission of Affect.* Ithaca, NY: Cornell UP, 2004.

Britzman, Deborah. "If the Story Cannot End." *Between Hope and Despair: The Pedagogical Encounter of Historical Remembrance.* Ed. Roger I. Simon, Sharon Rosenberg, and Claudia Eppert. London: Rowman & Littlefield, 2000. 22–47.

Brody, Mary. "Quotidian Warfare." *Signs* 28.1 (2002): 446–47.

Brooks, Peter. *The Melodramatic Imagination: Balzac, Henry James and the Mode of Excess.* New Haven, CT: Yale UP, 1976.

Browne, Nick. "The Political Economy of the Television (Super) Text." *American Television.* Ed. Nick Browne. Langhorne, PA: Harwood Academic Publishers, 1994. 69–80.

Butler, Judith. *Bodies That Matter: On the Discursive Limits of "Sex."* New York: Routledge, 1993.

———. *Gender Trouble.* London: Routledge, 1990.

Canada: A People's History. Official website. Canadian Broadcasting Corporation. 2001. 8 Apr. 2002 <http://history.cbc.ca.>.

Carton, Evan. 2002. "What Feels an American? Evident Selves and Alienable Emotions in the New Man's World." *Boys Don't Cry: Rethinking Narratives of Masculinity and Emotion in the U.S.* Ed. Milette Shamir and Jennifer Travis. New York: Columbia UP, 2002. 112–47.

Caruth, Cathy. *Trauma: Explorations in Memory.* Baltimore: Johns Hopkins UP, 1995.

Caughie, John. "Playing at Being American: Games and Tactics." *Logics of Television.* Ed. Patricia Mellencamp. Bloomington: Indiana UP, 1990. 44–58.

CBC Digital Archives. <http://archives.cbc.ca>.

Chapple, Freda, and Chiel Kattenbelt, eds. *Intermediality in Theatre and Performance.* 2nd ed. Amsterdam, New York: Rodopi, 2006.

Clarke, George Elliott. "White Like Canada." *Transition* 7.1 (1998): 98–109.

Cochrane, Christopher B. "Tuning In, Turning On, and Dropping Out: Canadian Broadcast Regulation on the Front Lines of the Telecommunication Revolution." *Canada: Rupture and Continuity.* Ed. Damien-Claude Belanger and Alistair MacLeod. Montreal: McGill-Queen's UP, 2002. 21–54.

Collins, Richard. *Culture, Communication, and National Identity: The Case of Canadian Television.* Toronto: U of Toronto P, 1990.

Corner, John. *Critical Ideas in Television Studies.* London: Oxford UP, 1999.

Creeber, Glen. "'Taking Our Lives Seriously': Intimacy, Continuity and Memory in the Television Drama Serial." *Media, Culture & Society* 23 (2001): 439–55.

Cvetkovich, Ann. *An Archive of Feelings: Trauma, Sexualities, and Lesbian Public Cultures.* Durham, NC: Duke UP, 2003.

Daniel, E. Valentine. "Suffering Nation and Alienation." *Social Suffering.* Ed. Arthur Kleinman, Veena Das, and Margaret Lock. Berkeley: U of California P, 1997. 309–58.

Dayan, Daniel, and Elihu Katz. "Defining Media Events: High Holidays of Mass Communication." *Television: The Critical View.* Ed. Horace Newcomb. London: Oxford UP, 1994. 352–51.

de Certeau, Michel. *The Practice of Everyday Life.* Trans. Steven Rendell. Berkeley: U of California P, 1984.

Deleuze, Gilles. "Ethology: Spinoza and Us." *Incorporations* (Zone vol. 6). Ed. Jonathan Crary and Sanford Kwinter. Boston: MIT Press, 1992. 625–33.

Deleuze, Gilles, and Félix Guattari. *Anti-Oedipus.* Trans. Robert Hurley, Mark Seem, and Helen R. Lane. Minneapolis: Minnesota UP, 1972.

———. *A Thousand Plateaus: Capitalism and Schizophrenia.* Trans. Brian Massumi. Minneapolis: Minnesota UP, 1980.

Derrida, Jacques. *Archive Fever: A Freudian Impression.* Trans. Eric Prenowitz. Chicago: U of Chicago P, 1996.

———. Spectres of Marx. Trans. Peggy Kamuf. London: Routledge, 1994.

Dick, Lyle. "Representing National History on Television: The Case of Canada: A People's History." *Programming Reality: Perspectives on English-Canadian Television.* Ed. Zoë Druick and Aspa Kotsopoulos. Waterloo, ON: Wilfrid Laurier UP, 2008. 31–50.

Doty, Alexander. *Making Things Perfectly Queer: Interpreting Mass Culture.* Minneapolis: Minnesota UP, 2003.

Druick, Zoë. "Sherene Razack in Conversation with Zoë Druick." Between the Lines. n.d. 15 June 2004 <http://www.btlbooks.com/othertextinfo.php?index=479>.

Druick, Zoë, and Aspa Kotsopoulos. Introduction. *Programming Reality: Perspectives on English-Canadian Television.* Ed. Druick and Kotsopoulos. Waterloo, ON: Wilfrid Laurier UP, 2008. 1–14.

Duara, Prasenjit. "Historicizing National Identity, or Who Imagines What and When." *Becoming National*. Ed. Geoff Eley and Ronald Grigor Suny. London: Oxford UP, 1996. 151–78.

Dumm, Thomas. "Telefear: Watching War News." *The Politics of Everyday Fear*. Ed. Brian Massumi. Minneapolis: U of Minnesota P, 1993. 307–21.

Dyer, Richard. *White*. London: Routledge, 1997.

Eckler, Rebecca. "They Just Can't Get Enough: Never Mind Medals, It's Roots Gear They Really Want." *National Post* [Toronto] 20 Feb. 2002: B6.

Edwardson, Ryan. *Canadian Content: Culture and the Quest for Nationhood*. Toronto: U of Toronto P, 2008.

Eley, Geoff, and Ronald Grigor Suny, eds. *Becoming National: A Reader*. New York: Oxford UP, 1996.

Ellis, John. *Seeing Things: Television in the Age of Uncertainty*. London: I.B. Tauris, 2000.

Elsaesser, Thomas. "Tales of Sound and Fury: Observations on the Family Melodrama." *Movies and Methods*, Vol. II. Ed. Bill Nichols. Berkeley: U of California P, 1985. 165–89.

Feuer, Jane. "Genre Study and Television." *Channels of Discourse*. Ed. Robert C. Allen. Chapel Hill: U North Carolina P, 1987. 113–33.

Fiske, John. *Television Culture*. London: Routledge, 1987.

Flaherty, David H., and Frank E. Manning. *The Beaver Bites Back? American Popular Culture in Canada*. Montreal: McGill-Queen's UP, 1993.

Foucault, Michel. *The Archaeology of Knowledge*. Trans. A.M. Sheridan Smith. 1968. New York: Routledge, 2002.

———. *Discipline and Punish: The Birth of the Prison*. London: Vintage, 1977.

———. *The History of Sexuality: An Introduction*, Vol. 1. New York: Random House, 1978.

———. Introduction. *Anti-Oedipus*. Ed. Gilles Deleuze and Félix Guattari. Trans. Robert Hurley, Mark Seem, and Helen R. Lane. 1972. Minneapolis: Minnesota UP, 1983.

———. "Michel Foucault: An Interview by Stephen Riggins." *Ethics: Subjectivity and Truth*. Ed. Paul Rabinow. New York: New Press, 1984. 122–33.

———. "The Will to Knowledge." Trans. Robert Hurley et al. *Ethics: Subjectivity and Truth*. Ed. Paul Rabinow. New York: New Press, 1984. 11–16.

Francis, Daniel. *The Imaginary Indian*. Vancouver: Arsenal, 1992.

Freud, Sigmund. "Mourning and Melancholia." 1914–1916. *Standard Edition of the Complete Works of Sigmund Freud*, Vol. 14. Trans. James Strachey, 243–58. London: Hogarth, 1957.

Gaillard, Françoise. "Diana, Postmodern Madonna." *After Diana*. Ed. Mandy Merck. London: Verso, 1998. 159–68.

Gallop, Jane. *Anecdotal Theory*. Durham, NC: Duke UP, 2002.

Gellner, Ernest. "Nationalism as a Product of Industrial Society." *The Ethnicity Reader.* Ed. Montserrat Grubenaeau and John Rex. Cambridge: Polity, 1997. 52–68.

Gibbs, Anna. "Contagious Feelings: Pauline Hanson and the Epidemiology of Affect." *Australian Humanities Review* 24 (2001). 22 Mar. 2009 <http://www.australian humanitiesreview.org/archive/Issue-December-2001/gibbs.html>.

———. "Fictocriticism, Affect, Mimesis: Engendering Differences." *Text* 9.1 (2005). 22 Mar. 2009 <http://www.textjournal.com.au/april05/gibbs.htm>.

———. "In Thrall: Affect Contagion and the Bio-Energetics of Media." *M/C Journal* 8.6 (2005). 20 May 2009 <http://journal.media-culture.org.au/0512/10-gibbs.php>.

———. "Mixed Feelings." *Cultural Studies Review* 13.2 (2007): 226–32.

Gilman, Sander. 1987. "Black Bodies, White Bodies: Toward an Iconography of Female Sexuality in Late Nineteenth-Century Art, Medicine, and Literature." *Race, Writing & Difference.* Ed. Henry Gates. Chicago: Chicago UP, 1987. 223–61.

Gilroy, Paul. "One Nation under a Groove: The Cultural Politics of 'Race' and Racism in Britain." *Becoming National.* Ed. Geoff Eley and Ronald Grigor Suny. London: Oxford UP, 1996. 352–69.

Giroux, Henry A. *From Mouse to Mermaid: The Politics of Film, Gender, and Culture.* Bloomington: U of Indiana P, 1995.

Goldman, Anne E. *Take My Word: Autobiographical Innovations of Ethnic American Working Women.* Berkeley: U of California P, 1996.

Goldstein, Richard. "War Horny: Victory Is the Ultimate Viagra." *Village Voice* 15 Apr. 2003. 5 June 2004 <http://www.villagevoice.com/issues/0316/goldstein.php>.

Gomez-Peña, Gullermo. *Warrior for Gringostroika.* St. Paul, MN: Greywolf Press, 1993.

Gregg, Melissa. *Cultural Studies' Affective Voices.* Houndmills: Palgrave Macmillan, 2006.

Griffiths, Linda. "He Could Have Danced All Night." *Globe and Mail* [Toronto] 30 Sept. 2000: R14.

Gripsrud, Jostein. *The Dynasty Years: Hollywood Television and Critical Media Studies.* London: Routledge, 1995.

Grossberg, Lawrence. *We Gotta Get Out of This Place: Popular Conservatism and Postmodern Culture.* New York: Routledge, 1992.

Grusin, Richard. "Affect, Mediality and Abu Ghraib." ENG7007 course webpage. Wayne State University, 29 Oct. 2007. 30 Jan. 2009 <http://eng7007.pbwiki.com/f/GrusinAffectMediality.pdf>.

Guattari, Félix. "Capitalist Systems, Structures and Processes." Trans. Brian Darling. *The Guattari Reader.* Ed. Gary Genosko. Oxford: Blackwell, 1996. 233–47.

Gunew, Sneja. "Introduction: Multicultural Translations of Food, Bodies, Language." *Journal of Intercultural Studies* 21.3 (2000): 227–37.

Guttman, Allen. "Berlin 1936: The Most Controversial Olympics." *National Identity and Global Sports Events.* Ed. Alan Tomlinson and Christopher Young. Albany, NY: SUNY Press, 2006. 65–82.

Hage, Ghassan. "Globalization, Social Belonging and the Political Economy of Hope." Paper presented at the Transculturalisms Symposium. University of British Columbia, Vancouver, February 2002. 27 June 2004; site access restricted <webct.ubc.ca/SCRIPT/Transculturalisms/scripts/serve_home>.

———. *White Nation: Fantasies of White Supremacy in a Multicultural Society.* London: Routledge, 2000.

Hall, Neal. "Metro Vancouver residents remain ambivalent on eve of Olympics: poll." *Vancouver Sun* 11 Feb. 2010. 10 May 2010 <http://www.vancouversun.com/sports/Metro+Vancouver+residents+remain+ambivalent+Olympics+poll/25520 61/story.html>.

Hall, Stuart. "Culture, Community, Nation." *Representing the Nation.* Ed. David Boswell and Jessica Evans. London: Routledge, 1999. 33–44.

———. "Encoding/Decoding." *Culture, Media, Language.* Ed. Stuart Hall et al. London: Hutchinson, 1980. 128–38.

———. "The Whites of Their Eyes: Racist Ideologies and the Media." *Gender, Race and Class in the Media.* Ed. Gail Dines and Jean M. Humez. London: Sage, 1995. 18–22.

Hamilton, Peter. "Representing the Social: France and Frenchness in Post-War Humanist Photography." *Representation: Cultural Representations and Signifying Practices.* Ed. Stuart Hall. London: Sage, 1997. 75–150.

Hart, Linda. *Fatal Women: Lesbian Sexuality and the Mark of Aggression.* Princeton: Princeton UP, 1994.

Hawkins, Gay. "Documentary Affect: Filming Rubbish." *Australian Humanities Review* 27 (2002): n.p. 20 May 2009 <http://www.lib.latrobe.edu.au/AHR/archive/Issue-September-2002/hawkins.html>.

Herman, Judith. *Trauma and Recovery.* New York: Basic Books, 1992.

Hertzberg, Hendrik. "Tuesday and After." *The New Yorker* 24 Sept. 2001: 27.

Hirsch, Marianne, and Valerie Smith. "Feminism and Cultural Memory: An Introduction." *Signs: Journal of Women and Culture in Society* 28.1 (2002): 1–19.

Hobson, Dorothy. *Crossroads: Drama of a Soap Opera.* London: Methuen, 1982.

Hogarth, David. "Reenacting Canada: The Nation-State as an Object of Desire in the Early Years of Canadian Broadcasting." *Programming Reality Perspectives on English-Canadian Television.* Ed. Zoë Druick and Aspa Kotsopoulos. Waterloo, ON: Wilfrid Laurier UP, 2008. 17–30.

Houpt, Simon. "America's Cultural Offensive." *Globe and Mail* [Toronto] 2 Aug. 2001: R1, R7.

Houston, Beverle. "Viewing Television: The Metapsychology of Endless Consumption." *American Television.* Ed. Nick Browne. Langhorne, PA: Harwood Academic, 1994. 81–95.

Hughes, John. *Lines of Flight.* London: Sheffield Press, 1997.

Jimenez, Marina. "America's Refugees." *National Post* [Toronto] 1 Mar. 2003: B1, B4–5.

Kaplan, E. Ann. *Trauma Culture: The Politics of Terror and Loss in Media and Literature.* New Brunswick, NJ: Rutgers UP, 2005.

Keating, Micheal. "Canada and Quebec: Two Nationalisms in the Global Age." *The Ethnicity Reader.* Ed. Montserrat Guibernau and John Rex. Cambridge: Polity, 1997. 170–86.

Kellner, Douglas. *Media Culture.* London: Routledge, 1995.

Kennedy, Rosanne. "Global Mourning, Local Politics." *Planet Diana: Cultural Studies and Global Mourning.* Ed. Re:Public. Nepean, Australia: University of Western Sydney, 1997. 49–53.

Kentner, Peter, and Martin Levin. *TV North: Everything You Wanted to Know about Canadian Television.* Vancouver: Whitecap, 2001.

Keohane, Kieran. *Symptoms of Canada: An Essay on Canadian Identity,* Toronto: U of Toronto P, 1997.

Kotsopoulos, Aspa. "Public Broadcasting/National Television: CBC and Challenges of Historical Miniseries." *Programming Reality: Perspectives on English-Canadian Television.* Ed. Zoë Druick and Aspa Kotsopoulos. Waterloo, ON: Wilfrid Laurier UP, 2008. 149–70.

Kristeva, Julia. *Powers of Horror.* New York: Columbia UP, 1982.

———. *Strangers to Ourselves.* New York: Columbia UP, 1991.

Kristeva, Julia, and Ross Mitchell Guberman. *Julia Kristeva Interviews.* New York: Columbia UP, 1996.

Kroker, Arthur. *Technology and the Canadian Mind.* Toronto: New World Perspectives, 1984.

LaCapra, Frank. *Representing the Holocaust.* Ithaca, NY: Cornell UP, 1994.

———. *Writing History, Writing Trauma.* Baltimore: Johns Hopkins UP, 2001.

Lane, Anthony. "This Is Not a Movie." *The New Yorker* 24 Sept. 2001: 79–80.

Larson, James F., and Nancy K. Rivenburgh. "A Comparitive Analysis of Australian, U.S., and British telecasts of the Seoul Olympic Opening Ceremony." *Journal of Broadcasting and Electronic Media* 35.1 (1991): 75–94.

Leavitt, Sarah A. *From Catharine Beecher to Martha Stewart: A Cultural History of Domestic Advice.* Chapel Hill: U of North Carolina P, 2002.

LeBreton, Gil. "In These Olympics, Canadians Only Paid Attention to Canada." *Fort Worth Star-Telegram* 28 Feb. 2010: 2.

Lionnet, Françoise. *Autobiographical Voices: Race, Gender, Self-Portraiture.* Ithaca, NY: Cornell UP, 1989.

Loving Spoonfuls. Official website. n.d. 20 May 2009 <http://www.lovingspoonfuls.com>.

Lowe, Lisa. *Immigrant Acts: On Asian American Cultural Politics.* Durham, NC: Duke UP, 1996.

Lutz, Tom. "Men's Tears and the Roles of Melodrama." *Boys Don't Cry: Rethinking Narratives of Masculinity and Emotion in the U.S.* Ed. Milette Shamir and Jennifer Travis. New York: Columbia UP, 2002. 34–52.

MacDonald, Bob. "PM's a National Embarrassment." *Toronto Sun* 28 Sept. 2001: 48.

Mackey, Eva. *The House of Difference: Cultural Politics and National Identity in Canada.* Toronto: U of Toronto P, 1999.

MacLennan, Hugh. *Two Solitudes.* Toronto: Macmillan, 1945.

Malkki, Liisa. "National Geographic: The Rooting of Peoples and the Territorialization of National Identity among Scholars and Refugees." *Becoming National.* Ed. Geoff Eley and Ronald Grigor Suny. London: Oxford UP, 1996. 434–53.

Manning, Frank E. "Reversible Resistance: Canadian Popular Culture and the American Other." *The Beaver Bites Back: American Popular Culture in Canada.* Ed. David H. Flaherty and Frank E. Manning. Montreal: McGill-Queen's UP, 1993. 3–28.

Marks, Laura U. *Touch: Sensuous Theory and Multisensory Media.* Minneapolis: U of Minnesota P, 2002.

Marvin, Carolyn, and David W. Ingle. *Blood Sacrifice and the Nation: Totem Rituals and the American Flag.* Cambridge: Cambridge UP, 1999.

Massumi, Brian. "The Autonomy of Affect." *Deleuze: A Critical Reader.* Ed. Paul Patton. Cambridge: Blackwell, 1996. 217–39.

Matheson, Donald. *Media Discourses: Analyzing Media Texts.* Maidenhead, Berkshire: Open UP, 2006.

McCarthy, Anna. *Ambient Television: Visual Culture and Public Space.* Durham, NC: Duke UP, 2003.

McClintock, Anne. *Imperial Leather: Race, Gender and Sexuality in the Colonial Contest.* New York: Routledge, 1995.

McLuhan, Marshall. *Understanding Media: The Extensions of Man.* New York: McGraw-Hill, 1964.

McWhorter, Ladelle. *Bodies and Pleasures: Foucault and the Politics of Sexual Normalization.* Bloomington: Indiana UP, 1999.

Merck, Mandy, Ed. *After Diana: Irreverent Elegies.* New York: Verso, 1998.

Metz, Christian. *The Imaginary Signifier.* Bloomington: Indiana UP, 1975.

Mignolo, Walter. *Local Histories/Global Designs: Coloniality, Subaltern Knowledges, and Border Thinking.* Princeton, NJ: Princeton UP, 2000.

Miki, Roy. Conference discussion. Unpublished. Transculturalisms Symposium. University of British Columbia, 2000. February 2002.

———. "Living in Global Drift: Thinking the Beyond of Identity Politics." Paper presented at the Transculturalisms Symposium. University of British Columbia, Vancouver, February 2002. 27 June 2004; site access restricted <webct.ubc.ca/SCRIPT/Transculturalisms/scripts/serve_home>.

Miller, Mary Jane. *Turn Up the Contrast: CBC Television Drama since 1952.* Vancouver: U of British Columbia P, 1987.

Miller, Nancy K. *Getting Personal: Feminist Occasions and Other Autobiographical Acts*. New York: Routledge, 1991.

Modleski, Tania. "The Rhythms of Reception: Daytime Television and Women's Work." *Regarding Television*. Ed. E. Ann Kaplan. Los Angeles: American Film Institute, 1983. 67–75.

Morley, David. *Home Territories: Media Mobility and Identity*. New York: Routledge, 2000.

Morris, Meaghan. "Banality in Cultural Studies." *Logics of Television: Essays in Cultural Criticism*. Ed. Patricia Mellencamp. Bloomington: Indiana UP, 1990. 14–43.

Morse, Margaret. "An Ontology of Everyday Distraction: The Freeway, the Mall, and Television." *Logics of Television: Essays in Cultural Criticism*. Ed. Patricia Mellencamp. Bloomington: Indiana UP, 1990. 193–221.

Moses, Daniel David, and Terry Goldie. *An Anthology of Canadian Native Literature in English*. Toronto: Oxford UP, 1992.

Moynagh, Maureen. "This History's Only Good for Anger: Gender and Cultural Memory in Beatrice Chancy." *Signs: Journal of Women and Culture in Society* 28.1 (2002): 97–124.

Munt, Sally. *Heroic Desire: Lesbian Identity and Cultural Space*. London: Cassell, 1998.

Nairn, Tom. *Faces of Nationalism: Janus Revisited*. London: Verso, 1997.

Nathanson, Donald L. *Shame and Pride: Affect, Sex, and the Birth of the Self*. New York: W.W. Norton, 1992.

"Native Appropriations." Adrienne K. Blog entry, 18 Feb. 2010. 30 May 2010 <http://nativeappropriations.blogspot.com/2010/02/vancouver-opening -ceremonies-honoring.html>.

Neale, Stephen. *Genre*. London: British Film Institute, 1980.

Negra, Diane. "Ethnic Food Fetishism, Whiteness and Nostalgia in Recent Film and Television." *The Velvet Light Trap* 50 (2002): 62–76.

Neubauer, Deane. "Modern Sport and Olympic Games." *Olympika* 17 (2008): 1–40.

Neveh, Hannah. "Nine Eleven: An Ethics of Proximity." *Signs* 28.1 (2002): 450–52.

Ngai, Sianne. *Ugly Feelings*. Cambridge, MA: Harvard UP, 2005.

Nichols, Bill. 1985. "The Voice of Documentary." *Movies and Methods*, Vol. II. Ed. Bill Nichols. Berkeley: U of California P, 1985. 258–73.

Nickson, Elizabeth. "Every Blade of Grass Is Ours: A Native Warrior Speaks Out." *National Post* [Toronto] 30 Mar. 2002: B2.

Nowell-Smith, Geoffrey. "Minnelli and Melodrama." *Movies and Methods*, Vol. II. Ed. Bill Nichols. Berkeley: U of California P, 1976. 190–94.

Nussbaum, Felicity A. *The Autobiographical Subject*. Baltimore: Johns Hopkins UP, 1989.

Parry, Wayne. "Hundreds of Sept. 11 Detainees Still in N.J. Jails." Associated Press, 9 Mar. 2009. Section: Domestic News. LexisNexis. Web, accessed 20 May 2009.

Pevere, Geoff. *Mondo Canuck: A Canadian Pop Culture Odyssey*. Toronto: Prentice Hall, 1996.

Probyn, Elspeth. *Blush*. Minneapolis: U of Minneapolis P, 2005.

———. *Carnal Appetites: Food, Sex, Identities*. New York: Routledge, 2001.

———. *Outside Belongings*. New York: Routledge, 1996.

———. "Sporting Bodies: Dynamics of Shame and Pride." *Body & Society* 6.1 (2002): 13–28.

Radwanski, George. *Trudeau*. Toronto: Macmillan, 1979.

Radway, Janice. *Reading the Romance: Women, Patriarchy and Popular Culture*. Raleigh: U of North Carolina P, 1984.

Razack, Sherene. *Race, Space and the Law: Unmapping a White Settler Society*. Toronto: Between the Lines, 2002.

Redbird, Duke. "I Am a Canadian." *An Anthology of Canadian Native Literature in English*. Ed. Daniel Moses and Terry Goldie. Toronto: Oxford UP, 1992. 120–21.

Renan, Ernest. "What Is a Nation?" *Becoming National*. Trans. Martin Thom. Ed. Geoff Eley and Ronald Grigor Suny. London: Oxford UP, 1996. 42–55.

Rogoff, Irit. *Terra Infirma*. New York: Routledge, 2000.

Rombauer, Irma S., and Marion Rombauer Becker, eds. Foreword. *Joy of Cooking*. 1931. New York: Plume, 1997.

Rutherford, Paul. *When Television Was Young: Primetime Canada 1952–1967*. Toronto: U of Toronto P, 1990.

Sallot, Jeff. "In Canada, Pain Has No Borders." *Globe and Mail* [Toronto] 15 Sept. 2001: A14.

Sawchuk, Kim. "Wounded States: Sovereignty, Separation and the Quebec Referendum." *When Pain Strikes*. Ed. Bill Burns, Cathy Busby, and Kim Sawchuk. Minneapolis: U of Minnesota P, 1999. 96–115.

A Scattering of Seeds: The Creation of Canada. Official website. White Pine Pictures. n.d. 14 April 2001 <http://www.whitepinepictures.com/seeds>.

Scheff, Thomas J. "Emotions and Identity: A Theory of Ethnic Nationalism." *Social Theory and the Politics of Identity*. Ed. Craig Calhoun. London: Blackwell, 1994. 277–303.

Schulman, Sarah. *Stage Struck: Theatre, AIDS, and the Marketing of Gay America*. Durham, NC: Duke UP, 1998.

Sedgwick, Eve Kosofsky. "Queer Performativity: Warhol's Shyness, Warhol's Whiteness." *Pop Out: Queer Warhol*. Ed. Jennifer Doyle, Jonathan Flatley, and José Esteban Muñoz. Durham, NC: Duke UP, 1995. 134–43.

———. *Touching Feeling: Affect, Pedagogy, Performativity*. Durham, NC: Duke UP, 2003.

Sedgwick, Eve, and Adam Frank. *Shame and Its Sisters: A Silvan Tompkins Reader*. Durham, NC: Duke UP, 1995.

Shaviro, Steven. *The Cinematic Body*. Minneapolis: University of Minnesota Press, 1993.

Shouse, Eric. "Feeling, Emotion, Affect." *M/C Journal: A Journal of Media and Culture* 8.6 (2005): n.p. 20 May 2009 <http://journal.media-culture.org.au/0512/03-shouse.php>.

Silverman, Kaja. *Male Subjectivity at the Margins.* New York: Routledge, 1992.

Silverstone, Roger. *Television and Everyday Life.* New York: Routledge, 1994.

Simon, Roger, Sharon Rosenberg, and Claudia Eppert. *Between Hope and Despair: The Pedagogical Encounter of Historical Remembrance.* London: Rowman & Littlefield, 2000.

Skene, Wayne. *Fade to Black: A Requiem for the CBC.* Vancouver: Douglas & McIntyre, 1993.

Smith, Anne-Marie. *Julia Kristeva: Speaking the Unspeakable.* New York: Pluto Press, 1998.

Smith, Charlie. "VANOC Olympic Torch Video Contains Clip from Nazi Propaganda Film by Leni Riefenstahl," 27 Jan. 2010. 16 May 2010 <http://www.straight.com/article-283576/vancouver/vanoc-olympic-torch-video-contains-clip-nazi-propaganda-film-leni-riefenstahl>.

Smith, Russell. "Welcome to Official Art, American-Style." *Globe and Mail* [Toronto] 13 Oct. 2001: R5.

Smith, Sidonie, and Julia Watson, eds. 1998. *Women, Autobiography, Theory: A Reader.* Madison: U of Wisconsin P, 1998.

Sofoulis, Zoe. 1997. "Icon, Referent, Trajectory, World." *Planet Diana: Cultural Studies and Global Mourning.* Ed. Re:Public. Nepean, Australia: University of Western Sydney, 1997. 13–18.

Sontag, Susan. "Fascinating Fascism." *Under the Sign of Saturn.* New York: Farrar, Straus and Giroux, 1980.

Spitulnik, Debra. "Documenting Radio Culture as Lived Experience: Reception Studies and the Mobile Machine in Zambia." *African Broadcast Cultures: Radio in Transition.* Ed. Richard Fardon and Graham Furniss. Westport, CT: Praeger, 2000. 144–63.

Stam, Robert. "Television News and Its Spectator." *Regarding Television.* Ed. E. Ann Kaplan. Los Angeles: American Film Institute, 1993. 23–43.

Starowicz, Mark. *Making History: The Remarkable Story of Canada: A People's History.* Toronto: McClelland & Stewart, 2004.

Stearns, Peter N. *American Cool: Constructing a Twentieth-Century Emotional Style.* New York: New York UP, 1994.

Strachan, Alex. "Trudeau Mini-Series 'Nation-Building': One-of-a-Kind Production Aims to Reflect Conflicts and Contradictions of Trudeau's Years." *Vancouver Sun* 26 Mar. 2002: A4.

Stevens, Geoffrey. "Bill Overhauls Criminal Code." *Globe and Mail* [Toronto] 22 Dec. 1967, Front section: 1.

Tate, Marsha Ann. *Canadian Television Programming Made for the United States Market: A History with Production and Broadcast Data.* Jefferson, NC: McFarland & Co., 2007.

Tinic, Serra. *On Location: Canada's Television Industry in a Global Market.* Toronto: U of Toronto P, 2005.

Tomkins, Silvan S. *Affect, Imagery, Consciousness.* New York: Springer Publishing, 1962.

Tomlinson, Alan. "Olympic Spectacle: Opening Ceremonies and Some Paradoxes of Globalization." *Media Culture Society* 18 (1996): 583–602

Traganou, Jilly. "National Narratives in the Opening and Closing Ceremonies of the Athens 2004 Olympic Games." *Journal of Sport and Social Issues* 34.2 (2010): 236–51.

Trudeau, Pierre. *Memoirs.* Toronto: McClelland & Stewart, 1993.

Trueman, Peter. *Smoke and Mirrors: The Inside Story of Television News in Canada.* Toronto: McClelland & Stewart, 1980.

Updike, John. "Tuesday and After." *The New Yorker* 24 Sept. 2001: 28–29.

Villarejo, Amy. *Lesbian Rule: Cultural Criticism and the Value of Desire.* Durham, NC: Duke UP, 2003.

Wagman, Ira. "Wheat, Barley, Hops, Citizenship: Molson's 'I Am [Canadian]' Campaign and the Defence of Canadian National Identity through Advertising." *The Velvet Light Trap* 50 (2002): 77–89.

Walcott, Rinaldo, ed. *Rude: Contemporary Black Canadian Cultural Criticism.* Toronto: Insomniac Press, 2000.

Walters, Suzanna. *Material Girls: Making Sense of Feminist Cultural Theory.* Berkeley: U of California P, 1995.

Warhol, Robin. *Having a Good Cry: Effeminate Feelings and Pop-Culture Forms.* Columbus: Ohio State UP, 2003.

Warley, Linda. "The Mountie and the Nurse: Cross-Cultural Relations North of 60." *Painting the Maple: Essays on Race, Gender and the Construction of Canada.* Ed. Veronica Strong-Boag et al. Vancouver: U of British Columbia P, 1998. 173–86.

Watts, Carol. "Unworkable Feeling: Diana, Death and Feminization." *Diana and Democracy.* Ed. Jeremy Gilbert, David Glover, Cora Kaplan, et al. *New Formations.* Vol. 36. London: Lawrence and Wishart, 1999. 34–46.

Wernick, Andrew. *Promotional Culture: Advertising, Ideology, and Symbolic Expression.* Thousand Oaks, CA: Sage Publications, 1991.

Whannel, Garry. *Culture, Politics and Sport.* London: Routledge, 2008.

Williams, Raymond. *Television: Technology and Cultural Form.* London: Fontana, 1974.

———. *The Year 2000.* New York: Pantheon, 1983.

Winseck, Dwayne. "Netscapes of Power: Convergence, Consolidation and Power in the Canadian Mediascape." *Media, Culture & Society* 24 (2002): 795–819.

Wolfreys, Julian. *Deconstruction: Derrida.* London: Macmillan, 1998.

Wood, Helen, and Lisa Taylor. "Feeling Sentimental about Television and Audiences." *Cinema Journal* 47.3 (2008): 144–51.

Woodward, Kathleen. "Global Cooling and Academic Warming: Long Term Shifts in Emotional Weather." *American Literary History* 8.4 (1996): 759–70.

Wray, B.J. "The Elephant, the Mouse, and the Lesbian National Park Rangers." *In a Queer Country: Gay and Lesbian Studies in a Queer Context.* Ed. Terry Goldie. Vancouver: Arsenal, 2001. 160–74.

Wright, Robert. *Virtual Sovereignty: Nationalism, Culture, and the Canadian Question.* Toronto: Canadian Scholars' Press, 2004.

Ziarek, Ewa. "The Uncanny Style of Kristeva's Critique of Nationalism." *Postmodern Culture: An Electronic Journal of Interdisciplinary Criticism* 5.2 (1995): n.p. 20 May 2009 <http://pmc.iath.virginia.edu/text-only/issue.195/ziarek.195>.

Zirin, Dave. "As Olympics Near, People in Vancouver Are Dreading Games," *Sports Illustrated/CNN,* 25 Jan. 2010. 30 May 2010 <http://sportsillustrated.cnn.com/2010/writers/dave_zirin/01/25/vancouver/index.html>.

Žižek, Slavoj. *The Sublime Object of Ideology.* New York: Verso, 1989.

———. *Welcome to the Desert of the Real! Five Essays on September 11 and Related Dates.* New York: Verso, 2002.

FILMOGRAPHY

All in the Family. CBC, Toronto, 1995.

… And the Word Was God. Dir. Ruby Truly. Videorecording. Vancouver, 1987.

Canada: A People's History. CBC, Toronto, 2000–1.

CBC News. CBC, Toronto. Feb. 1995, Sept.–Oct. 1995, 11 Sept. 2001, 10 Oct. 2001, 24 Feb. 2002.

Circus. CTV, Toronto, 1977–84.

The Corporation. Dir. Mark Achbar, Jennifer Abbot. Writ. Joel Bakan. Big Picture Media DVD, 2003.

CTV News. CTV, Toronto. Nov.–Dec. 2001.

The Galloping Gourmet. Writ. and narr. Graham Kerr. CBC, Toronto, 24 Dec. 1970.

General Motors advertisement. Perf. Wayne Gretzky. Dec. 2002.

"Inside Media." *CBC News.* CBC, Toronto, 24 Feb. 2004.

I Want to Know Why. Dir. Dana Claxton. Videorecording, Toronto, 1994.

"Joe Canadian Rant." Molson Canadian advertisement. *I Am Canadian* campaign. Dir. Kevin Donovan. Perf. Jeff Douglas. Bensimon Byrne, 2000.

Just Watch Me: Trudeau and the 70's Generation. Dir. Catherine Annau. National Film Board of Canada, 2000.

Life and Times. CBC, Toronto. Oct. 2001.

Loving Spoonfuls. Women's Television Network. 2000–3.

The Magazine. CBC, Toronto. 1995–96.

Nanook of the North: A Story of Life and Love in the Actual Arctic. Writ./dir./prod. Robert Flaherty, 1922. Criterion Collection DVD, 1999.

The National. Narr. Peter Mansbridge. CBC, Toronto. Feb., Sept.–Nov. 1995.

North of Sixty. CBC, Toronto, 1991–98.

Olympia. Dir. Leni Reifenstahl, Germany, 1938.

Olympic Winter Games coverage. CBC, Toronto, 8–13 Feb 2002.

Olympic Winter Games coverage. CTV. Vancouver, 12–28 Feb. 2010.

"Pierre Trudeau: Just Watch Me." CBC, Ottawa, 13 Oct. 1970. CBC Digital Archives. CBC.ca. 30 Apr. 2010 <http://archives.cbc.ca/war_conflict/civil_unrest/clips/610>.

The Quebec–Canada Complex. Dir. Peter Wintonick and Patricia Vergeylen Tassinari. Canada, 1998.

Remaking Canada. CBC, Toronto, Mar. 1996.

"Round-Table Discussion." *CBC News.* CBC, Toronto, 30 Oct. 1995.

A Scattering of Seeds: The Creation of Canada. Writ./dr. Stavros C. Stavrides. White Pine Pictures DVD, 1998–2002.

"Special Report." *The National.* CBC, Toronto, 16 Sept. 1995.

"Special Report." *CBC News.* CBC, Toronto, 17 Oct. 1995.

"Sunday Report." *CBC News.* CBC, Toronto, Feb. 1995.

Talking to Americans. Writ. and narr. Rick Mercer. CBC, Toronto, 1 Apr. 2001.

This Hour Has 22 Minutes. CBC, Toronto, 1996–2001.

Unspoken Territory. Dir. Marusya Bociurkiw. Canada, 2001.

Who Is a Real Canadian? CBC, Toronto, 1996.

The Women. CBC, Toronto, 1995.

"Yes We Can." Perf. will.i.am. US, 2008.

Books in the Film+Media Studies Series
Published by Wilfrid Laurier University Press

The Young, the Restless, and the Dead: Interviews with Canadian Filmmakers / George Melnyk, editor / 2008 / xiv + 134 pp. / photos /
ISBN 978-1-55458-036-1

Programming Reality: Perspectives on English-Canadian Television / Zoë Druick and Aspa Kotsopoulos, editors / 2008 / x + 344 pp. / photos /
ISBN 978-1-55458-010-1

Harmony and Dissent: Film and Avant-garde Art Movements in the Early Twentieth Century / R. Bruce Elder / 2008 / xxxiv + 482 pp. /
ISBN 978-1-55458-028-6

He Was Some Kind of a Man: Masculinities in the B Western / Roderick McGillis /
2009 / xii + 210 pp. / photos /
ISBN 978-1-55458-059-0

The Radio Eye: Cinema in the North Atlantic, 1958–1988 / Jerry White / 2009 / xvi + 284 pp. / photos /
ISBN 978-1-55458-178-8

The Gendered Screen: Canadian Women Filmmakers / Brenda Austin-Smith and George Melnyk, editors / 2010 / x + 272 pp. /
ISBN 978-1-55458-179-5

Feeling Canadian: Television, Nationalism, and Affect / Marusya Bociurkiw/ 2011 /
viii + 184 pp. /
ISBN 978-1-55458-268-6